M000200060

Modernizing Joan of Arc

Modernizing Joan of Arc

Conceptions, Costumes, and Canonization

ELLEN ECKER DOLGIN

McFarland & Company, Inc., Publishers
Jefferson, North Carolina, and London

Library of Congress Cataloguing-in-Publication Data

Dolgin, Ellen Ecker, 1951–
Modernizing Joan of Arc : conceptions, costumes,
and canonization / Ellen Ecker Dolgin.
p.   cm.
Includes bibliographical references and index.

ISBN 13: 978-0-7864-3120-5
softcover : 50# alkaline paper ∞

1. Joan, of Arc, Saint, 1412–1431— Portraits.   2. Joan, of Arc, Saint,
1412–1431— In literature.   3. Christian women saints— France —
Historiography.   4. France — Historiography.   5. Idols and images—
Costume — France — History.   6. Canonization.   I. Title.
DC104.D65   2008   944'.026092 — dc22   2007042477

British Library cataloguing data are available

©2008 Ellen Ecker Dolgin. All rights reserved

*No part of this book may be reproduced or transmitted in any form
or by any means, electronic or mechanical, including photocopying
or recording, or by any information storage and retrieval system,
without permission in writing from the publisher.*

On the cover: Dante Gabriel Rossetti, *Joan of Arc* (1864).
Watercolor on board, 53.3 × 57.1 cm. Tate Gallery, London.
(Tate, London / Art Resource, New York / ART73276)

Manufactured in the United States of America

McFarland & Company, Inc., Publishers
Box 611, Jefferson, North Carolina 28640
www.mcfarlandpub.com

For Ron,
who recognized my voice,
watched me come to understand it,
and reveled in its growth.
This work is testimony to our
kindred spirits and life together.
In Memoriam.

In an Artist's Studio

Christina Rossetti

One face looks out from all his canvasses,
One selfsame figure sits or walks or leans;
We found her hidden just behind those screens,
That mirror gave back all her loveliness.
 A queen in opal or in ruby dress,
 A nameless girl in freshest summer greens,
 A saint, an angel — every canvass means
The same one meaning, neither more nor less.
He feeds upon her face by day and night.
And she with true kind eyes looks back on him
Fair as the moon and joyful as the light;
 Not wan with waiting, not with sorrow dim;
 Not as she is, but was when hope shone bright;
 Not as she is, but as she fills his dream.

Contents

Acknowledgments

This book has evolved over a period of years, so many people have had a hand in its foundation. I begin with Dominican College of Blauvelt: Christina Pratt and Ann Vavolizza, who spurred me on, and the Arts and Sciences colleagues who offered suggestions and read portions of the proposal and text. For all of my students, particularly those who were part of my Joan of Arc, "Voices of Authority" courses in 2003, 2004, and 2006, my gratitude and applause go to you for your own discoveries, and the inspiration I have taken from these. Special thanks to Tara Rose, my research assistant in libraries, museums, and at the computer for the spring and summer of 2006.

To Kay Fowler of Ramapo College, I give enormous thanks for staunch support at the nascent beginnings of this project. More importantly, my unlimited gratitude goes to you for exhaustive comments and suggestions for each chapter in the manuscript.

To Elizabeth Petroff, thank you for encouraging my different vision.

For artistic suggestions and editorial savvy for the book's basis, my thanks to Kerry Dennehy. For readings and discussions, my thanks to Marilyn Jacobs. And to my former Ramapo College students and friends, thank you for allowing me to talk about this project for years, and for all of your input along the way. I also wish to recognize the friendship and support of Jennefer Mazza and Judith Jeney of Ramapo College.

Thank you to all my contacts at the Metropolitan Museum of Art in New York, Art Resource, NY, University of Pennsylvania, The Library of Congress, and the National Archives for your courtesy and the quality of the images.

To my parents, Esther and Milton Ecker, thanks for the support as well as the invaluable "primary source" material about clothing and popular culture ca. 1930–1950.

To my daughter, Eva, appreciation goes for historical and feminist insight and the kinds of questions that helped to shape the eventual design of the book. To my daughter-in-law, Trella, goes my appreciation for consistent belief in my subject and my progress. My son, Andrew, allowed me to share his photographic and artistic eye. I thank him for the design for where these visual elements should be placed in the text of the manuscript, and for his perceptive questions about the role of the images in my version of the Joan of Arc legacy.

Special thanks to my former student, Michael Sciame, for the especially apt phrasing I've borrowed for the title of chapter 2.

Prologue:
Cut on the Bias

Some years ago, while writing a comparative essay on the treatment of Joan of Arc in Bernard Shaw's *St. Joan* (1923) and Bertolt Brecht's *St. Joan of the Stockyards* (1929), I was struck by each writer's treatment of Joan's acknowledged powers among the people. The dichotomy between those who believed in her heavenly mission absolutely and those who were cynical and convinced that she was diabolically inspired resonated strongly in each play. More modern perspectives about individual powers and responsibilities were even more obvious in Shaw's and Brecht's plays. What had surprised me when I read these plays was their ambiguous presentation of her accomplishments. Joan of Arc had become Saint Joan in 1920, so I expected the representations of her story to be more "finished." Brecht saw the premiere of *St. Joan* in Berlin, and admired Shaw, but created a very different character and context, so I will begin with *St. Joan.*

Shaw's play, which he labeled a "chronicle," surely sounds like it should be a completed history, so bafflement with its open-ended approach would have been understandable. Reviews from 1923/24 reveal a true spectrum of reactions, only one of which matters here. Jeanne Foster, writing in the *Transatlantic Review* of 1924, announces that the play gives us a "Shavian Joan ... a super-flapper, a pert hoyden...."[1] For the moment, just focus on this quote without reference to Shaw's text, and notice the blurring of centuries that it represents. A hoyden, originally a term for a rude, boorish fellow, had transferred its insults to boisterous young women by the 1600s.[2] Flappers could be considered a continuation of hoydens' behavior, since these young women broke all the sacred rules of Victorian propriety regarding appearance and social roles. Since Shaw drew much of Joan's "objectionable" traits and even actual dialogue from the transcripts of the trial, it seemed a very apt twist. Shaw himself probably enjoyed the joke. He claimed not to have looked at any literary representations of Joan before he wrote his own. More to the point, in his 1924 review, Walter Tittle reported what Shaw had told him about his intention to undo the audience's expectation of a saint's portrait. Shaw believed his play did not conform to the tendency to "pamper the public taste for a vision of Joan as a lovely, insipid slip of a girl, divinely guided, but possessed of mental and physical attributes utterly incongruous with and unfitted to her achievements."[3] Shaw's remarks introduced the more modern dichotomy of the images of young women. Brecht, while admiring Shaw's commitment to social issues, believed that true change could never come from the ideology of the past, which is why his Joan figure enjoys only marginal success before her doom.

What was there about this story that transcended time and resisted closure?

One logical place to begin searching for the answer was the coverage of the canonization of Joan of Arc in the *New York Times*. I turned first to an article entitled "From Sorceress to Saint," published on the actual date of the canonization, May 16, 1920. The main premise of the article was that canonization completed Joan of Arc's redressed historical reputation. Yet, the writer of the article seemed untroubled by large chronological gaps in Joan's story. Apparently, in 1920 it seemed sufficient to begin with Joan's downfall. The reporter accurately explained that she was proclaimed a relapsed heretic by the Inquisition and burned in 1431, and then absolved ["rehabilitated"] twenty-five years later. Yet no official process of canonization had begun until the mid-nineteenth century. Declared venerable in 1894, blessed in 1904, and beatified in 1909, Joan was set for canonization in 1931, the 500th anniversary of her burning. In the midst of this historical data, the article casually stated: "The great war may have had something to do with hastening the final date" ("From Sorceress to Saint" 6). What did World War I have to do with determining sainthood for a fifteenth-century individual? Re-reading this article made the underlying issue clearer. There simply had to be strong connections between what Joan had provoked in her confrontation with the power structure and the social context of the nineteenth and early twentieth centuries. While the article had made no mention of any parallels to anything other than World War I, this was enough to alert me to be cognizant of continuing feelings about Joan of Arc. More than actual facts, the association between Joan and the vitality of idealistic causes had obviously never diminished over time.

A similar concept underlies the title of this Prologue. It is a conclusion that I suspected early on, but have only confirmed after tracing the trail of the historical Joan and the history of her subsequent representations in literature, biography, visual art, and film. Each version reflects its own era's perspectives on the nature of hero/ines, especially in connection to gender and social class, as well as iconoclasm. The rise and fall of Joan of Arc touches upon all of these, yet no one version incorporates all of the variables of the original events and personalities. Each is "cut on the bias" of its creator. Moreover, the history of Joan of Arc and the subsequent representations of that story are essentially dramatic, not only in terms of plot, but because there are so many layers of interpretations—and texts—attached to them.[4]

In the *New York Times* article that reported the celebration of Joan's canonization on May 16, 1920, the Archbishop of New York, Patrick J. Hayes, spoke of Joan's consecration at the Statue of Joan, situated at Riverside Drive in Manhattan. That statue had been designed by Anna Vaughn Hyatt in 1915, but, ironically, the speech made no mention of the special achievement of the statue's site. Instead, the Archbishop linked Joan's image solidly to the idealized feminine: "Joan of Arc's benediction will go out, not only here, but all over the world. It is the benediction of womanhood, of maiden-hood, and it means a great deal, for, by her example, Joan of Arc will lead the lives of American women and of others to a still higher plane, both in religion and in patri-otism." Many women had risen to the occasion during World War I, even working in traditionally male jobs to help out. Women and Joan had also been immortalized in patriotic posters and slogans, urging patriotism and faith in traditional activities appro-priate to women's domestic sphere.

I found the sweetness of the Archbishop's depiction of Joan remarkable for two reasons: Joan appeared so consistently noble, as well as a model of the "good girl," while at the same time the speech clearly acknowledged Joan's public functions. By 1920, therefore, the legacy of Joan of Arc had emerged as both worldly and religious. But what had happened to all the rough edges surrounding her actions and demeanor? The article's encapsulization of Joan as unspoiled, demure and prudent bemused me because it seemed a glaring contradiction. If anything, the Joan of Bernard Shaw was more like the wholesome All-American girl—chaste, but spunky—who represented the young women the Archbishop addressed. It was this confusion over the depiction of young women that prodded me to dig deeper. In the early twentieth century, suffrage posters, pins, and even parades invoked Joan's name and style of pageantry. At the time of World War I, her story had been immortalized in the newest art form, cinema. War posters in the United States as well as Great Britain and France called upon her legacy to inspire patriotism. These visual images were by no means unified in their represen-tation of Joan's body or costume — armor with skirts, close-fitting male clothing, short pageboy hairstyles, and long, plaited hair all figured in these depictions. Representa-tions of women in paintings ca. 1840–1920 also showed the extremes of ultra-femi-nine costumes and poses on one hand, and cross-dressed androgynous figures on the other. Thus the issues surrounding women and clothing were even more central to the time than they had been in Joan's own day. Fashion remained more than style — it was emblematic of one's public as well as private convictions.

Clearly, the modern interpretations of Joan of Arc could balance the earthly and supernatural aspects of her life and experience, and go beyond her social status: the central causes of controversy in Joan's own lifetime. Consequently, religious and social hierarchy on the one hand, and the dramatic change in the status of the individual that had evolved since Joan's time, had both simplified and complicated her story and its ramifications.

There is no doubt that the public role played by Joan of Arc was explainable as more than God's will: Joan embodied for her advocates traditional female virtues—and vulnerability. I no longer wondered how the archbishop's words could really apply to Joan of Arc, and the canonization documents link Joan concretely to the Church Triumphant, while, at the same time, castigating the Church Militant of the fifteenth century for its shameful treatment of Joan of Arc. But I kept scrolling down the microfilm of the 1920 *New York Times* archive; the name Hays jumped out at me again.

American World War I poster: *Woman Your Country Needs You: State & National Councils of Defense* (1918). This remarkable image reflects the seriousness of the wartime effort as well as the power of women's archetypal roles and powers, as demonstrated in paintings and *tableaux vivants,* and also shows the passing of these to a young girl who looks about as old as Joan was when she first heard her Voices at age thirteen *(Library of Congress).*

What I didn't notice at first was the different spelling of the name, but I did catch the drift of the headline: "Suffragists Jeer at Chairman Hays." This May 19 article was obviously about the push toward ratification of the nineteenth amendment. The dates of the two events seemed merely coincidental, but my curiosity urged me on. This Hays was the Republican National Chairman and he was trying to deal with what we would now call the *uppity women* in his audience. Apparently, the women were impatient and refused to be "ladylike" in their manner, tone of voice, or message.

Suffice it to say that *they* behaved like the Joan I had read about. A steadfast and stalwart young woman, Joan had saved France by being someone who did not hesitate to say and do what she felt was right. The treatment by Chairman Hays of the suffrage supporters, spurred by their disruption of the session, was altogether too reminiscent of the judges who were prompted to condemn Joan, at least partly because she stood her ground and refused to bow to their earthly authority. Here's a sample from the *New York Times Article:* after constant interruption, Congressman Hays admonished the group, avowing that "this kind of conduct on the part of women makes it hard to get Republican Legislatures to ratify the amendment." At this point I could not help but hear the fifteenth-century military and church leaders' wish that Joan would either *shut up* or *go home.* The tone and content of this report brought me back immediately to the Brecht text, *St. Joan of the Stockyards.*

Brecht's portrayal focused more on issues of Marxist concerns than the history of Joan of Arc, but revealed gender issues as well. Set in the twentieth-century Chicago stockyards, this play demonstrated how and why Joan's world view no longer applied to modern times. Joan Dark's work as the leader of the Black Straw Hats failed for this reason. Costume again came to the fore; in Brecht's case, the corollary was not hard to figure out: suffragists wore either black or white hats in their marches. As the suffrage movement became more radical, Joan's style of pageantry became a visible part of these events. Often a woman led the parade, on horseback, carrying a standard. The "Votes for Women" poster campaign had used similar images, and, brilliantly, had incorporated the "best parts" of the cult of domesticity as well: the vote would make women more effective mothers.[5] Virginia Woolf had pinpointed this very same suffrage symbol in her work, *A Room of One's Own,* which was written the same year as Brecht's play. In this text, Woolf reflected on the *querrelles des femmes* and the "Woman Question" by selecting key historical as well as literary texts that reveal the way women have been perceived by men since the time of Shakespeare. By the closing chapter, she concludes:

> No age can ever have been so stridently sex-conscious as our own.... The Suffrage campaign was no doubt to blame … it must have made them lay an emphasis upon their own sex and its characteristics which they would not have troubled to think about had they not been challenged. And when one is challenged, even by a few women in black bonnets, one retaliates, if one has never been challenged before, rather excessively.[6]

Woolf's use of black bonnets is especially intriguing. Bonnets were not twentieth-century attire; they were considered too old-fashioned. Precisely. Woolf's suggestion of the far-reaching impact of the suffrage cause was unmistakable. It was her generation who had to go beyond the cult of domesticity in order to embrace their new-found potential, yet the earlier generation had begun the fight. The purpose of her speech/extended essay was to illuminate what had gone wrong in the past between the sexes, and what could be done to alter it. Woolf's audience, college women, had to fight for themselves individually and collectively in order to change society as a whole. I realized at that moment that much more than coincidence was at work. Both Shaw and Brecht were right. Shaw felt that Joan represented the outstanding individual: one who saw past the specifics of era, but who was always condemned by society as a result. Brecht felt that looking towards the past for guidance was no longer viable, since more had changed than stayed the same by the 1920s. Perhaps that is why both plays had "condensed" Joan's martyrdom and canonization scenes in order to show us that stasis as well as evolution are our modern legacies ... and our challenge.

Introduction:
The Pattern in Pieces

The mere mention of Joan of Arc connects to mythologized associations as well as historical events. While Joan is one of the most studied and widely represented individuals in western culture, the amount of actual knowledge people have about Joan or her accomplishments varies just as widely. For some reason, however, even vague details foster interest in the story, even hundreds of years later. It is certainly true that both the historical figure of Joan and its legacy are inherently dramatic in structure as well as content. Hers is a story of the fight against all odds to overturn oppression. A popular scenario goes along these lines: a young girl from the countryside appears abruptly, dressed like a man, and saves France by rallying the troops in battle. She is known as the "Maid of Orléans," to commemorate the battleground of the victory of the French over the English; legend has it that Joan's influence and prominent position at the head of the troops revived the spirit of the French. Sometime later, Joan burns at the stake for her political daring and her individualized religious convictions, yet is considered a hero and a saint by those who feel her actions were noble.

Clearly, it is not so much the story of an actual person that ignites our imaginations. We are intrigued by the *image* of such a person. We are further both fascinated and bewildered by an individual who was "nobody from nowhere" and who could, simultaneously, be a hero/ine and a bane to society. Joan of Arc was recognized by her followers, as well as her enemies, as one whose actions were to change history. Consequently, even in her own time, controversy regarding her role arose, and the casting of Joan as icon began. Since then, Joan has been coded as religious mystic, rebellious girl, national hero[ine], "unnatural" transvestite, woman warrior, and martyr. Joan's "crime" defied easy classification. Because her actions rallied a weary and jaded people, her significance could not be denied. Therefore, she has been both ridiculed and admired, honored and betrayed, burned and, finally, sainted. Most of what follows here revolves around the shift from the praise/blame criteria for viewing Joan to the recognition that her actions were admirable, albeit for differing reasons. Recognizing the complexity of the ideology that produced and condemned Joan allows us to determine the fullest measure of her place in the popular imagination.

The vantage point of this study was born with the notion of coupling the representations with particular social concerns that correlate with Joan's story. More

Eugene Delacroix (1798–1863), *Liberty Leading the People* (1830). Painted between the French Revolution and the beginning of Joan of Arc's process of canonization, Delacroix's archetypal female figure captures the Revolutionary Spirit, and portrays a large, powerful, and inspired woman. This "Marianne" figure, like Joan of Arc, represents the virtue of French women *(courtesy Erich Lessing/Art Resource, New York; Louvre, Paris)*.

specifically, one overriding issue extends from the fifteenth century onward: the irritating, inappropriate public woman. Retelling a story gives people the sense that they must discover the connections between modern lives and those of the fifteenth century. Viewed from this perspective, the appeal of Joan's story lies squarely in its sociopolitical and archetypal aspects. This same predisposition led later artists to translate Joan's spirituality and its accompanying steadfastness into general (secular) stabilizing virtues, ones that continue that part of Joan's mission that transcends her own time and place: the struggle of an individual wholly committed to a valued ideal. Joan of Arc as a determined leader has inspired many to emulate her, in style as well as substance. No time seemed as well matched to Joan as the late nineteenth and early twentieth centuries, when Joan became a suffragette, a New Woman, and an obedient daughter of faith and traditional authority. It was this era that completed the task of transfiguring "The Maid of Orléans" into St. Joan. The Church alone granted the sanctity, but the social upheaval regarding appropriate gender roles and widening economic and educational opportunities for women and working classes were important factors in the re-interpretation of Joan's history as well as legacy. The pageantry that dominated fifteenth-century history was given new form and context by the suffrage campaigns and the stage and screen actresses who portrayed both traditional and "new" women.

The amount of material describing Joan of Arc and her exploits is staggering.[1] There are, however, some portions of the story that comprise the essence of her legendary life. She was born on or about January 6, 1412, in the village of Domrémy in the province of Lorraine. Her father, Jacques Darc, was in a position of some importance as a representative of his community to Robert de Beaudricourt, the captain then assigned to this area. Joan (Jeanne), along with her siblings, helped on the farm, but Joan preferred to help her mother with the inside work, especially spinning. Although known to be loving and kind, she also was considered rather serious and solitary. Her compassion and ready tears showed her sweetness. While generally obedient, she possessed an innate need to think things out for herself and never demurred in speaking her mind. The combination of directness and simplicity in Joan was noted by those who knew her in childhood, as well as those who would see the determined individual in battle.

When the Voices came to her around the age of 13-14, Joan became dreamier, less conscientious about her work. She did, however, keep the Voices and the accompanying dreams/visions a secret, partly to shield her family from the terror of the saints' messages, and partly to avoid direct confrontation. Joan's innate humility is emphasized by her reluctance to obey the commands of the Voices. Just as most of us would, Joan felt unworthy of the task, so she procrastinated; this caused her not only to wrestle with her own decision, but also to endure her parents' disapproval for her altered attitude.

As the demands for action intensified, Joan began to utter an intention to go outside her family to be with the army. Her father threatened her, going so far as to say he would drown her because, naturally, he assumed she meant to go as a camp follower. Joan's compulsion to stand her ground and speak passionately and bluntly obviously came from her father. Her mother's concerns for her daughter's safety and normalcy — the desire for Joan to marry — connect to Joan's earth-bound and practical nature.

It is important to note the hardships suffered by the people of Joan's region in her youth; by July 1428, they were forced to flee to Neufchateau because of the never-ending war. It is clear that the time spent in Neufchateau strengthened her resolve; maybe it was a simple case of seeing a larger world, albeit in the company of her family, which helped Joan to grasp the immense need of the people. The pathos of their situation aroused her compassion, and almost every account of the historical Joan includes her proclivity to tears over the afflictions of others. Joan's indignity over the abuses from the English (godons) and her lack of patience with leaders who did not feel similarly is readily understandable.

By the time she and her family went to Neufchateau, she had listened to the Voices for approximately four years and had begun to gather the courage and determination to do their bidding. It is reasonable to assume that this concrete representation of the cause the Voices had asked her to serve became more real and more urgent. Her decision to go forward shortly afterwards is far less hasty and outrageous in this context; her ability to persuade her uncle to help her get to Vaucouleurs is the first indication of the kind of strength and charisma that were to become emblematic of Joan of Arc in the chronicles of the fifteenth century.

The meetings with Robert de Beaudricourt and the ensuing journey to Chinon are resplendent with the adventurous spirit of medieval romance. As the captain assigned to this part of Lorraine, de Beaudricourt knew many people, including Jacques Darc. In de Beaudricourt's opinion, Darc was a bit of a troublemaker, so his daughter was easy to dismiss as an annoyance. The first two visits yielded no results, but the third time Joan showed the persistence that was to become a trademark, and her self-assurance nonplussed him. He agreed to help her, providing Joan with armor, horses, and an escort. When she and her small party completed the arduous and dangerous ride to Chinon, where the Dauphin and his court were housed, a soldier spoke rather obscenely regarding Joan's costume and presence. She warned him not to speak this way because he was close to death. He drowned moments later. Thus her reputation for supernatural powers was born. Coupled with the well-known prophecy that a virgin from Lorraine would emerge as France's saviour, the mixed blessing of notoriety began. When she recognized the Dauphin unaided, despite his hiding among the courtiers, it was considered a sign that she could work miracles. The next one was causing the wind to change on the banks of the Loire, which allowed the Siege of Orléans to begin. This miracle occurred within moments of Joan's meeting the commander of the French army, Dunois (also known as the Bastard). He was the first person to perceive Joan as a legitimate individual, recognizing both the power as well as the limitations of this girl.

Recognition of Joan as extraordinary is not difficult; pinpointing just where and when she went beyond the parameters of her gender and social class is the point to focus on. Noblewomen had been in charge of estates and defense of their borders throughout the Middle Ages, but Joan had not been privy to that world, so her ability to assess situations on the spot and direct others must have been startling. On the other hand, her seemingly innate abilities in managerial and military matters can also be seen as clear reflection of her divine guidance, as well as the power of the Prophecy of Merlin in the popular imagination. Dunois was apparently able to perceive these merits at once. Acknowledging her role as symbolic more than strategic, the general was also impressed by the following she had so quickly attained, and the charisma that beguiled more and more soldiers to join her and give up their swearing and licentious behavior.

Despite the magnitude of her role, Joan of Arc was already part of an established tradition regarding an occasional woman's role in battle; she was not the first "martial maid" in myth, history or literature, nor was she the only woman who took hold of a precarious situation for the sake of her people. Deborah Fraioli points to several in her article "The Literary Image of Joan of Arc: Prior Influences."

Fraioli argues that the use of biblical role models was a usual methodology in Joan's time, in both ecclesiastical and secular treatises. These references aimed to establish authority for a story in an era that used literature as rhetoric: that is, to arouse people to necessary action. Esther, Judith, and Deborah are the Old Testament figures who served this purpose for Joan's contemporary apologists.[2] Another genre was important at the time: patriotic literature. Although Fraioli recognizes that the concept was "ill-defined" in the fifteenth century, concern for the future of France as a country predominated, even in pieces in circulation before Joan left her home in Domrémy in 1429. Moreover, the patriotic literature revolved around prophecies, so once the word spread that the "Maid of Lorraine" of Merlin's prophecy had emerged, the reactions recorded "ring unmistakably with the sound of awe and wonder."[3] The writings also contained "overtones of a still broader mission awaiting Joan after her initial objectives were met. Some ascribed to her a role in the Last Days, and she herself at times hinted at an all-encompassing Christian mission."[4] Fraioli emphasizes that the historical chronicles written in this same era did not use this same tradition; these unadorned encapsulizations of events, therefore, lend us less clarity since they included scanty interpretive remarks about the accomplishments of Joan of Arc.

When the Siege of Orléans turned the tide of the Hundred Years War in 1429, Joan's role became known throughout Europe; thus, her renown and notoriety came about simultaneously, depending on what side of the conflict the writers were on. Throughout her brief rise to fame, and subsequent downfall, Joan was apparently aware that she herself was composing her story as she lived it. After the Battle of Orléans, Joan was known as The Maid, a name she had given herself. Joan added to the legend by making each public occasion an open spectacle for the people who witnessed the events, appearing always in soldier's garb, with her standard and sword with her. On the other hand, Joan was equally steadfast in her religious zeal, fasting regularly and praying publicly and privately, consistently explaining her actions as obedience to the commands of her Voices. With a unique combination of cheekiness and *naiveté*, Joan confronted the *status quo* to accomplish her aims. Along the way, Joan defied convention both openly and obliviously. Distinctions of gender, social class, and hierarchical power were treated as trivialities by her, as was the notion that ordinary people were supposed to speak to God through their parish priests.

Just as timing of the canonization of Joan seems cemented to its era, so too was the literary assessment of her actions at Orléans. The first representation of Joan in literature came from Christine de Pizan, a writer whose earlier works about the moral roles of women had also played a key role in the epistolary gender war known as the *querelles des femmes*. The poem about Joan was written shortly after Charles VII's coronation in July 1429. It first praises the king and then reminds him to give proper thanks to Joan. Then de Pizan represents the medieval tradition of praising contemporaries on the basis of biblical characters. For women, the most prominent were Deborah, Judith, and Esther, about whom de Pizan writes: "…Worthy ladies, through whom God restored his people which was so oppressed, and I also learned about many others who were brave, but there was none through whom he has performed a greater miracle than through the Maid" (verse 28). In addition to these, however, de Pizan's poem also compares Joan to Moses, saying that he "…led his people out of Egypt, without tiring of it. In the same way you have led us from evil, elected Maid!" (verse 23). Joan "undid the rope that held France tightly bound" (verse 21) and de Pizan concludes that Joan was "Born at a propitious hour … ordained by God, in whom the Holy Spirit … poured His great grace and never refused any of your requests, how can we ever reward you?" (verse 22).[5]

Ruefully, this ebullient praise wore thin within a year. By that time, Joan had lost sight of her humility towards those in authority. Captured in 1430, she was sold to the English for 12,000 pounds. Many charges were proposed for her Trial of Condemnation in 1431; however, the one that was repeated most often was her cross-dressing, and the links between this breach and heresy.[6] Joan shrugged off these breaches in the face of her higher mission. She accepted without question that adherence to God's mandate necessitated breaking the rules of dress and social propriety, and was bewildered when those above her did not share her understanding.[7] To both the English and the French, therefore, Joan of Arc could be perceived as a dangerous infidel. Conversely, there is no question that Joan's charisma captivated royalty as well as common soldiers, on both sides. Opinions divided regarding the source of her inspiration. Was she divine or diabolical? Was she a sorceress or a saint? Most importantly for a young woman's status, was she a virgin or a whore? These dichotomies are rooted not only in medieval misogyny, but also in the medieval coding of witchcraft and mystics. A virgin was thought to be closer to innocence and to the Virgin Mary's state of grace.[8]

Worldly criteria were also at work. Joan of Arc not only wore men's garments, but she sported a made-to-measure set of armor that was beyond the reach of her social class as well as her gender. As biographer Vita Sackville-West points out in her 1936 work, *St. Joan of Arc*, Joan not only used pageantry to great effect but also loved finery, and this enjoyment unwittingly facilitated her capture at the battlefield of Compiègne in 1430. Joan was easy to spot that day because of the white and gold apparel given to her by the grateful Duke of Orléans. Both of these anecdotes illustrate another important phenomenon: the blending and/or blurring of gender distinctions and roles via clothing as well as action. Joan understood that such breaches of custom were connected to the mission she believed her Voices commanded her to fulfill, and to prevent soldiers who slept on the ground next to her from carnal desires. Yet Joan's judges at the Trial of Condemnation in 1431 were relentless in their charges and questions about Joan's transvestism, and her persistence in wearing male attire off as well as on the battlefield. Their questioning centered on why Joan would not return to woman's dress when she was not at combat, and used her refusal to deny her access to confession and communion. Because transvestism was specifically forbidden in the Book of Deuteronomy, the link between Joan's costume and a denunciation of her mission of faith was hardly a leap for those who lost power as a result of her actions.

Since Joan lived in the post–Sumptuary Laws era, there was considerable sensitivity to the loss of class markers in the fifteenth century; the power structure chafed against the notion of people's dress being a means of upward mobility. Joan herself understood that clothing and accessories were both empowering and symbolic, even her use of the standard that featured both France's official symbol, the *fleur-de-lys*, and Mother Mary. In the Chronicles that were written about this key battle by an international group of writers, Joan was either loved or despised for her appearance and participation in the male domain of war and its accompanying pageantry. An extraordinary letter written by Henry VI encapsulates the reasons why Joan of Arc was insufferable for the English, and touches on these very points. The king addresses the prelates of the Church, nobility, and "loyal cities of our realm in France":

> Reverend Father in God,
>   It is sufficiently well-known, reports are scattered in every direction, that a woman who had herself called Joan the Maid, an erring prophetess dressed like a man these two years or more, a state of affairs contrary to divine law and to the condition of the female sex, an abomination to God, while arrayed in this fashion was brought to our foremost enemy [Charles VII]. To him and his adherents—churchmen, nobles, and the people — she gave to understand (and she did this often) that she was sent by God. Through such deceits and by the guarantee of assured future victories she beguiled and deluded many. She diverted the minds of men and women from the way of truth. She led them to a belief in fables and falsehoods. This is not all. She put on armor like a Knight or Equerry and designed a banner and what is more outrageous, through excessive pride and presumption she made the demand to have and to display the truly noble and surpassing Royal Arms of France.[9]

Yet it is also abundantly clear from the records that the English even more than the French recognized Joan's influence and its likely posterity — before the burning. Because such deaths were public spectacle, the crowd saw her saintly behavior, particularly when Joan did not allow a soldier to offer her a cross because the flames might have engulfed him as well. Perhaps a chief puzzlement of the aftermath was the immediacy of their regret, supposedly begun when the Executioner reported that Joan's heart would neither drown nor burn, belying two widely acknowledged tests of diabolical influence. Why then did the rectification take nearly five centuries when the questioning of the validity of their actions began immediately? This unresolved question contains the core of continued interest in Joan's story, particularly for post-canonization writers who see the perpetuity of the attitudes that condemned her. Even the canonization process itself was spurred, in part, by political and religious self-interest. Because Joan had come to symbolize both iconoclasm and the sanctity of church and state, each faction benefited from the change in Joan's official status.

It is supremely ironic that the two pieces of Joan's story that are most familiar are likewise a study in contradiction. The image of "The Maid" raising the Siege of Orléans (alongside Dunois) can be seen as a mirror image to the girl dragged through the marketplace in a cart and then tied to the stake to be burned as a heretic. When one considers that these two events were a mere two years apart, amazement and curiosity arise simultaneously. These reactions intensify when one learns that Joan became a living legend throughout Europe immediately after the Battle of Orléans in April 1429[10] and was already a figure of enormous controversy by the time of the capture at Compiègne in March 1430. After her initial tasks had been fulfilled — success at Orléans and the crowning of the Dauphin — one more remained: recapturing Paris. Joan's impatience caused her to be impudent and careless, resulting in the damaging of her reputation among the authorities. Dunois stayed loyal despite his frustrations with her. While some continued to laud her and believe in the wisdom of her leadership, others began to think that she had gone too far and needed to acquiesce to the professional judgment of those in power.

Even those who believed her to be saintly rued her confrontational style. The chief puzzlement, therefore, was her gender; how dare an illiterate peasant girl interfere with military operations and their political ramifications? How dare she wear male apparel, let alone garments which the prevailing sumptuary laws relegated to a higher social class than hers? The secondary issue thus became social class; Joan's ordinariness could not be reconciled easily in the authorities' minds with her extraordinary achievements and iconoclastic attitudes. While many of these men believed in her innocence, their belief in patriarchal ideology was obviously stronger. Her demise became expedient for the English and their Burgundian allies because she embarrassed them in battle. Moreover, their common belief in Providential history dictated their assumption that her inspiration had to be diabolical.

During her time of imprisonment and trial in Rouen she was admired by the common people and spurned by the authorities. No wonder her burning on May 30, 1431, was a public spectacle of such magnitude. More appalling was the attitude of the French clergy, who condemned her for not adhering to their institution's powers. The theologians of the University of Paris, then under English rule, aligned themselves with the French Church, specifically the self-serving bishop of Beauvais, Pierre Cauchon, who had mercenary as well as egotistical motives for going against the Maid of Orléans. Even Dunois, the Bastard and commander of the French troops, could no longer support Joan when she refused to find a reasonable position within the power structure. Worst of all, Charles VII, whose crown had been put in place by Joan at Reims in July 1429, turned his back and allowed her to become a victim of the Inquisition.

Joan was imprisoned by the English and guarded by men; a key controversy revolved around whether or not she was harassed sexually and, more importantly, whether or not this factor was responsible for Joan's persistence in wearing men's apparel. After months of tedious questioning, Joan recanted. She agreed to wear a woman's garment and believed she would return home. Back in prison, she had her real test of faith. She left her cell to relieve herself; when she came back, only her male garments were there. Once she had those on again, the authorities perceived this action to be that of a relapsed heretic. Joan then returned to her original position that her Voices were right. Immediately afterwards, Joan of Arc was burned.

It was not until twenty-five years had passed that Charles was willing to clear Joan's name. In 1456 a Rehabilitation Trial was undertaken, ostensibly at the urging of Joan's mother,[11] but actually at the prompting of Charles VII. Though overtly dedicated to clearing Joan's name and overturning the verdict of 1431, this trial was really aimed at removing the blemish of Charles' coronation. As in the original circumstances, Joan's fate was secondary to the political priorities of an essentially patriarchal power structure. Paradoxically, more information about Joan's early life was solicited in the second trial than had been in the first. Neither trial, however, represents fairness. The original trial, in its zeal to be rid of a dangerous and annoying iconoclast, relied upon circumstantial evidence and was motivated by expediency; the later trial, in its desire to illuminate the evils of a power structure no longer functioning, went out of its way to show Joan as a victim.[12]

Quite simply, an examination of the conditions which surrounded Joan's story shows that it predicts contemporary feminist concerns by hundreds of years. Specifically, Joan's confrontation with the fifteenth-century power structure was construed as outrageous because she was a young girl from an undistinguished family, and an individual who dared presume that the mission she received from her Voices was reason enough to go beyond the parameters of her gender and social class. Despite the complexities of medieval ideology, especially those which inform the religious/mystical issue of the possibility and/or validity of Joan's Voices, the story of Joan's rise and fall transcends them.

The records of the treatment Joan received while imprisoned, and the unjust punishment meted out by the Inquisition which tried her, indicate that it was Joan's assumption of power across class lines that most baffled and enraged her judges. Coupled with the financial strain of the waning Hundred Years War, these emotionally based condemnations of Joan found another layer of justification: expediency. Circumventing the unification of the French people was beneficial to the French/Burgundian clergy who were supported by English monies and to the English power structure, who were humiliated by the victories attributed to Joan's leadership. The Dauphin Joan crowned, Charles VII, was no hero; he barely accepted the responsibility of his role, and remained under the control of advisers long after Joan was killed. England's king, Henry VI, was eight years old at the time of Joan's capture at Compiègne in 1430. Both regions were ruled by self-serving ministers who were loath to relinquish their power.

The transcripts of Joan of Arc's Trial of Condemnation of 1431, presumed "lost" for centuries, resurfaced in the 1790s, when a French scholar discovered them in a library.[13] Western Europe was once again at a crossroads, mirroring the anxieties of the fifteenth century. It is no coincidence that the era that reconfigured "The Maid of Orléans" into "St. Joan" (ca. 1790–1920) was the same time span that grappled exhaustively with the specific dilemmas that Joan's history and legend identify as well as complicate: criteria for authority, validation of the individual, and the rise to power of the middle and working classes. However, perceiving an instantaneous shift in the public imagination's image of Joan in this later period is a dangerous assumption, one that overlooks the very relevance of Joan for this more modern time: her legacy remained controversial.

From the late eighteenth century to the time of the canonization of Joan of Arc after World War I, the power structure still chafed at the idea that ordinary women of their own time could rise to such heights. Gender bending around public, political life became represented by articles of women's clothing. In the eighteenth century, it was the petticoat. "Petticoat government" was the coded reference to all manifestations of women ruling men, and when Mary Wollstonecraft suggested that she was the first of a new genus in *Vindication of the Rights of Woman* (1792), one of her detractors, Horace Walpole, labeled her a "hyena in petticoats." Ironically, Wollstonecraft focused squarely on a critique of women who cared more about their petticoats than their character.[14] By the 1790s, there were distinct parameters regarding the rights as well as responsibilities of women, both privately and publicly. Wollstonecraft's call for female education did not run contrary to prevailing opinion; once feminine liberty became linked to more public roles, the split in thinking emerged. Neither Wollstonecraft nor her followers advocated for woman suffrage, so Walpole's remark should be viewed in light of the social behavior associated with Wollstonecraft: her sexual freedom.[15] Robert Southey wrote an epic about Joan in 1796, one which characterized her as a representative of "the people." Southey's colleague, Samuel Taylor Coleridge, read this work and rebuked Southey (in a marginal note) for turning Joan into a "Tom Payne [sic] in petticoats." Since Southey alluded to Joan of Arc in a poem about Wollstonecraft, the parallels are more than likely. More to the point, Wollstonecraft's *Vindication* ... supported Tom Payne, which again is doubly interesting because Coleridge himself believed that "a great mind must be androgynous."[16]

Women's struggle for change intensified in France and England beginning in the late eighteenth century. The social crises of Joan's own time peaked when the American and French revolutions validated individual participation in and shaping of public as well as private life. In a realm at once private and semi-public, literary circles and salons among the upper classes in France and England were run by women known as bluestockings. French women like Mme. de Staël and her following boldly confronted their diminished status, and wielded political influence in the *salon*. Meeting to debate the issues of the day in private homes, men accepted women not only as hostesses, but as participants in the conversation. It was unfortunate as well as ironic that these intellectual and influential women lost considerable ground after the Revolution failed, when salons were condemned as aristocratic.

Eighteenth-century women picked up the threads of de Pizan's arguments and expanded them to their own era. Thus the literary *querelle des femmes* of de Pizan's era was revitalized in essays and poems by both men and women. While the earlier writers had focused on woman's character and innate abilities, those of the republican era implied more direct action. These epistolary debates revealed more confrontational attempts by women to gain equality in public as well as private aspects of their lives. Not surprisingly, retaliation came from the patriarchal power structure, relying once again on women's costume as metaphorical, but also visual, symbols in political cartoons. The use of "petticoat" to designate female influence of an offensive sort, either within a home or as infiltration of political activity, was widespread in England and the American colonies at this time. By the eighteenth century, gender was becoming more codified in writing and on stage, focusing particularly on the meaning of "woman." Through reading the debates of the time, it becomes clear that gender was recognized as a social construction. Women who appeared onstage in theaters were deemed whores by some elements of society for parading themselves in costumes in a public space.[17] Likewise, in her assumed role as leader of the French army, Joan of Arc had been labeled a whore by the English army because she dictated letters that offered them the possibility of withdrawing with honor. Although she acted in strict accordance with medieval rules of engagement, her gender, age, and social class precluded serious attention to Joan's actions.[18]

Interlaced political topics became embodied by actresses, especially because legitimate theatrical productions in eighteenth-century England and France featured "breeches" roles, and the repertoire went beyond the plays of Shakespeare. An unusual example is Hannah More's 1777 tragedy, *Percy*. This early work of More's shows that her more famous conservative stance regarding male and female spheres was not yet formed. Moreover, the success of this work was, according to Dror Wohrman, occasion for the renowned David Garrick to write a prologue to the play, one "dedicated to singing the praises of crossing gender boundaries."[19]

Garrick's prologue asserted that women could do things comparably to men, including: mounting high horses, making long speeches, and "with dignity, some wear the breeches;/ And why not wear 'em?— We shall have our votes,/ While some of t'other sex wear petticoats./ Did not a *Lady Knight*, late *Chevalier*,/ A brave, smart soldier to your eyes appear?/ Hey! presto! pass! his *sword* becomes a *fan*,/ A comely *woman* rising from the *man*."[20] Garrick's allusions to popular theatrical conventions of the day foreground the semiotic meaning of costume and prop, as well as plot elements here.

Such embodiments of female power to speak, act, and even write the plays illustrate the point that gender roles were uncomfortably fluid by the 1770s. Yet, as the practice continued, coupled with the contexts of burgeoning nationalism and the rise of the common people, Joan of Arc became a national/international cultural hero/ine. Regardless of the ideological position favored by interpreters of Joan's story or their audiences, the familiarity and importance attached to these contemporary contexts narrowed the gap between the praise of her religious virtues and the condemnation of actions that went beyond the parameters of women's supposed roles. The variables then became the definitions of hero, heroine, and honor, in terms of the newly defined designations of gender. Vern and Bonnie Bullough remind us that eighteenth-century thought may have given rise to socially proscribed notions of gender, but these applied only to the reexamination of woman's role; man's status remained the constant factor which "assured them of continued dominance and influence."[21]

Fundamental changes in the perceptions of acceptable gendered behavior that emerged by the time of the American and French revolutions would evolve throughout the nineteenth century. The continuous struggle over these same issues allowed for the turnaround in the universal image of Joan of Arc. By this time in history, there could be a ready acceptance of Joan as a remarkable individual, a young woman whose courage and loyalty could and should be admired. Joan's cross-dressing apparently could be comfortably explained because the logic of her costume was clear to them, as long as the exceptional woman was clearly, safely in the past. Further, even before the trial documents' return to the public imagination, some notions about Joan of Arc were crystal clear. Thomas Paine, in *The American Crisis* (1776), makes use of her legacy in a most valuable context. As Joan had done by impassioned speech, Paine is urging full commitment from "the people." In the "times that try men's souls," he refers to the "summer soldier and the sunshine patriot" as those who will "shrink" from fulfilling this obligation, but "he that stands it *now*, deserves the love and thanks of man and woman ... [and] the harder the conflict, the more glorious the triumph."[22] Joan's ability to arouse and maintain the morale of the soldiers in similar circumstances is at the heart of her appeal. Paine later focuses on the panic that can go through a country, paralyzing the people. It is at this juncture that he turns to Joan. Although he believes it was the fourteenth century, the rest of his remarks are apt:

> the whole English army, after ravaging the kingdom of France, was driven back like men petrified with fear; and this brave exploit was performed by a few broken forces collected and headed by a woman, Joan of Arc. Would that heaven might inspire some Jersey maid to spirit up her countrymen, and save her fair fellow sufferers from ravage and ravishment![23]

Paine was exceptionally liberated in his views, however. For most men, only limited admiration was possible. The exchanges of John and Abigail Adams on the subject of women's possible role/voice in the new country her husband was helping to design are still exceptional, but they are far more representative. Abigail strongly urged her husband to make the new government truly revolutionary by enfranchising women:

> I desire you would Remember the Ladies, and be more generous and favourable to them than your ancestors. Do not put such unlimited power into the hands of Husbands. Remember all Men would be tyrants if they could. If perticular care and attention is not paid to the Laidies we are determined to foment a Rebelion, and will not hold ourselves bound by any Laws in which we have no voice, or Representation.... That your Sex are Naturally Tyrannical is a Truth so thoroughly established as to admit of no dispute, but such of you as wish to be happy willingly give up the harsh title of Master for the more tender and endearing one of Friend.[24]

John's response is remarkable for the conscious split he specifies between his private and public reactions:

> As to your extraordinary Code of Laws, I cannot but laugh. We have been told that our Struggle has loosened the bands of Government every where ... [but] Depend upon it, We know better than to repeal our Masculine systems. Although they are in full Force, you know they are little more than Theory.... We have only the Name of Masters, and rather than give up this, which would compleatly subject Us to the Despotism of the Petticoat, I hope General Washington, and all our brave Heroes would fight[25] *[italics added]*.

As Elizabeth Fox-Genovese emphasizes in her 1987 essay about the intellectual history of European women, the mid-eighteenth century marked the end of blatant misogyny; it persisted, but "...lost official standing and retreated into indirection. The prevailing images of shrew, harlot and Amazon gave way to the image of the romantic heroine and loving mother."[26] John Adams again provides a penetrating glimpse at the way a powerful, yet privately egalitarian, man looked at women's particular gifts. This time he explains his position in a letter to Mercy Otis Warren, an American activist and friend to both Adamses: "The ladies I think are the greatest Politicians that I have the Honour to be acquainted with, not only because they act upon the Sublimest of all the Principles of Policy, viz., that Honesty is the best Policy, but because they consider Questions more cooly than those who are heated with Party Zeal and inflamed with the bitter Contentions of active public Life...."[27]

Therefore, despite the substantial revisions in the framework of power structures since the fifteenth century, neither monarchical nor republican ideologies of the eighteenth century were ready to brook gender equality in their present reality. These questions would escalate to critical heights when the Woman Question emerged; on the one hand was a movement that demanded suffrage, property rights, and economic as well as educational opportunities, and on the other stood the resistance to extensive reform. The softening (aka "feminizing") of Joan during the era of the New Woman is clear evidence for Fox-Genovese's claim of misogyny as indirection; both sides capitalized on what the Victorians valorized as "earnestness" and could use aspects of Joan's personality and accomplishments as key elements of their own agenda.

Analyses of biographies, literary depictions, and visual representations of Joan and women of the nineteenth and twentieth centuries in chapter 2 will indicate that the cultural shifts did not subsume the earlier categories; rather, the clear-cut boundaries were merely blurred. This phenomenon partially can explain why the movement to alter the ecclesiastical status of Joan appears to be ideally suited to the nineteenth century. Joan of Arc was already an icon, and her story incorporated a number of acceptable representations of woman's virtue — in both directions. Women were seen as the cement of middle- to upper-class society via their role in the private sphere of family life; why should we wonder that authority figures believed that such exemplary women needed male protection rather than legal, social, or political rights? The emblem for both the clash between these two ideologies and the need for each side to connect to large segments of the population continued to center on the female body: women's costume changes and choices, specifically the sporadic movement known as dress reform in the 1850s and the more far-reaching controversy over corsets and divided skirts that dominated the era of the New Woman, from the 1880s through the 1920s.

During the nineteenth century, the notion of what would be labeled "feminism" by the early twentieth century became more widespread, and thus the "antidote" appeared: the cult of domesticity. Rather than focusing on sexy temptresses, mother-figures were the central concern. Women were considered innately superior morally, as long as they were "unspoiled" by classical liberal arts educations, did not read too many novels, and confined their energy to home. Advocates for woman suffrage would capitalize on this ideological trump card, using it as a frame of reference in written and visual materials. In similar fashion, social and religious conservatives would surround Joan's character and accomplishments with verbal and visual elements of duty, purity, and subservience to higher authority. Thus, the long-established dichotomy surrounding the figure of Joan of Arc, as either diabolical heretic or devout mouthpiece of God, gave way to a more complex, if more unified, point of view: Joan became a heroi/ine of "the people." These theatrical components were more than metaphorical, as women participated in private *tableaux vivants*: women impersonated abstractions like "liberty," but also created versions of famous women's history. The coronation of France's Charles VII by Joan of Arc was a favorite theme. Suffrage parades would use the same technique by the 1910s in both Great Britain and the United States.

By the time the official process of canonization began in 1869, a fascinating double vision of Joan of Arc had emerged. On the one hand, she was a precursor to feminism. Yet on the other, she was an obedient daughter to those in authority: a young woman totally in keeping with the cult of domesticity. In light of biographical sketches it was clear that the enormous split between the point of view that venerated Joan of Arc and that which condemned her centered on whether or not to accept a young girl from humble origins as God's choice for a messenger and savior of the French cause. But in addition to the traditional uses of Joan, her image was also appropriated by dominant social causes of the nineteenth century: workers' rights and women's rights. Conversely, traditional femininity saw Joan as a model. These social touchstones connect directly to the evolution of Joan's image. The rise of nationalism, revolution, and the struggle for the rights of the working class and of women accompany every shift in the perception of Joan's role, as it moved from dangerous virago to heroic martyr to liberated woman.

Public figures of women, both literal and metaphorical, became parallels to images and representations of Joan on both sides of the Atlantic by the early twentieth century. Interestingly, women appeared in either traditional feminine guise or androgynously. Visual images of Joan long had reflected eras' representations of women and political figures. According to *Joan of Arc: Her Story* (1998), there was a firmly established tripartite division of representations: virago, martyr, and visionary. Since there had never been an official portrait of Joan of Arc, these depictions had been products of imaginations all along. With this in mind, the variations in her costume, length of hair, and facial expression are essential to discerning the ideological stances behind the works.[28] Prominent images of women in newer, more popular, media expanded the import of her story in these more modern times. All were assessing a cultural *icon*, a figure who becomes a series of representations.

By the 1890s, prominent actresses, especially Sarah Bernhardt, showed that women could be artists and entrepreneurs, and maintain private as well as public lives. Best known at present for her melodramatic acting style, Bernhardt's role as a cultural icon should not be underestimated. Classically trained, Bernhardt turned to melodrama because she could be more instrumental in productions of these plays, and because she must have seen that these were the pulse of the time. Although she lived until 1923 and even made films, hers was a nineteenth-century approach to performance, and that included the continued interest in "breeches roles." These were her favorite roles for many years, despite the link between Bernhardt and her portrayal of Dumas' Camille, for which she died beautifully and differently each night. Bernhardt could use gender, and was aware of its power, just as Joan of Arc had been.[29] Suffragettes took their cue, so to speak, from such women of the theater and the era's love affair with technology and spectacle, drawing attention to themselves as public women. Mass production of posters, ready-to-wear fashions, and films established an international popular culture based on image.

Stage dramas, as well as banners, pins, and pageantry symbols for social causes, particularly woman suffrage, bore the unmistakable imprint of the legend surrounding Joan of Arc. Visual representations of women and Joan herself were used selectively to spark recognition of historical precedent on the one hand and inspire actions that were future-oriented on the other. More significant than anything else in consolidating the importance of Joan of Arc in the public imagination, however, was her persistent use as a wartime symbol. Her canonization process began just prior to the Franco–Prussian War, the first in which both sides claimed her. France's humiliation in that war gave rise to even more need for Joan's story, which was captured in a stunning painting by Jules Bastien-Lepage in 1879. This depiction of Joan encapsulates her earthly and spiritual inspiration and strength simultaneously.[30] World War I, however, was the apparent watershed. Battles were fought on the same ground as those in the Hundred Years War. Entire frameworks of the socio-political order were likewise challenged. Popular songs hailed Joan of Arc and so did government efforts in Britain and the United States to raise money for the troops.[31] Women were part of the war effort, and shown with banners and swords. They also dressed the part in skirt suits, man-tailored shirts, and even ties.[32] As my prologue points out, even Joan's canonization was changed from its originally scheduled date of 1931 to 1920 because of the role Joan's image played in World War I.

While the medieval/early modern power structures labeled Joan's public accomplishments as unnatural, outrageous, and even heretical, contemporary theorists are less concerned with adjudicating them than they are with perceiving Joan's public actions through the lenses of gender construction and performativity. So despite the parallels between Joan's breaches of custom and the early feminists' "acting out," the idea of women in trousers remained a hot topic. Anne Hollander's study on the evolution of the suit for men, and then women, provides a succinct explanation of why:

> Trousers for respectable women were publicly unacceptable ... and they were not generally worn even as underwear until well on in the nineteenth century ... only acceptably brought out on the surface with the bicycling costumes of the 1890s, and only finally confirmed in the later twentieth century with the gradual adoption of pants as normal public garments for women.[33]

Despite the lampooning anti-suffrage visual images in magazines and newspapers pre–World War I, average women did not begin to "wear the pants" until the World War II era. In the "correction" to women's across-the-board public roles after the war, trousers became weekend wear, and girls could not wear pants to school until the 1970s.

Vern and Bonnie Bullough cite anthropologist Anne Bolin's assertion that an understanding of gender involves awareness of the distinction between status and role;[34] Joan of Arc's mission, accomplishments, and eventual demise foreground this very difference because Joan refused to be bound by the social codes she knew she was up against. Even the name the Voices told her to give herself, "La Pucelle" (The Maid) underscores the importance of both her status and her role, whether these are considered in light of Joan's presumption of public power or as fulfillment of the Prophecy of Merlin that stated that France would be ruined by a woman and saved by a virgin from Lorraine.

Once these connections are examined side by side, an important notion emerges— the modern and medieval contexts reflect and illuminate each other. A sampling of the canonization documents clearly illustrates the pervading concept of "true womanhood," an ideal with four interlaced components: "piety, purity, domesticity, and submissiveness."[35] According to Virginia Frohlick's unpublished novel, *The Lost Chronicles, The Story of Joan of Arc* (1997), the bishop of Orléans, Dupanloup, along with eleven other French bishops, petitioned Rome in 1869 to begin the process of canonization. Dupanloup put the case succinctly: "Not only Orléans and France but also the whole world venerate God's actions through Joan of Arc, the piety and enthusiasm of this young girl, her purity and selflessness with which she always carried out the will of God..." (quoted by Frohlick).[36]

This double vision of the historical Joan's public image and that of the modern public woman becomes more powerful when placed within Judith Butler's definition of gender as a "persistent impersonation that passes as the real."[37] By presupposing recognizable semiotic signs that individuals are supposed to acknowledge, particularly those surrounding discourses and costume, Butler's work is more interested in the effects of these institutionalized "norms" than in searching for origins of gender. Her performative theory locates gender acts that "disrupt the categories of the body, sex, gender, and sexuality." Butler further notes that her purpose is to "trace the way in which gender fables establish and circulate the misnomer of natural facts."[38]

Reflecting on the connections as well as the contrasts in these contemporary representations of women's public roles, the rationale for twentieth-century writers' depicting Joan of Arc as more than a protagonist/hero/ine makes sense. Her story had long been mythologized in the public imagination of France and had become more international in its importance during the canonization period. The language of the official pronouncement of canonization of 1920 was strikingly similar. Part I of the document[39] characterizes Joan of Arc as "the bravest maiden within the recollection of men and the most innocent."

The chapters that follow examine the ways in which representations of the historical Joan, the evolution of proletarian causes, and the Woman Question intersect. Chapter 1 concentrates on assessments of the historical Joan, with particular emphasis on the notions of gender and authority in the fifteenth century, and the trials of Joan. Then the discussion turns to the canonization era in chapter 2, including the biographies that appeared after the Trial Transcripts were found and the push to redress Joan's official status became a *cause célèbre*. Cultural and historical events and trends are the heart of the chapter, especially representations of women onstage and as fashion plates. The dialogic relationship between clothing and women's roles and images is further explored through close readings of key literary texts. Chapters 3 and 4 expand the analysis of the canonization era, by focusing upon dress reform, visual images in fine art, graphics, and the first feature film about Joan of Arc in 1915. The performativity of woman suffrage parades in the 1910s, and the work of influential actresses for social issues, is likewise central to this discussion.

Chapter 5 provides the "bridge" between the canonization era and the post-canonization images of Joan as illustrated by Bernard Shaw. The analysis of his *St. Joan* (1923) looks at his representation of Joan in the context of two of his "unwomanly women" plays: *Major Barbara* (1905) and *Pygmalion* (1913): works that intersect labor issues and the woman question. Brecht's portrayals of Joan ca. 1929–1945 follow in chapter 6. Brecht uses Joan to illustrate the futility of models from the past, as their world view was too removed from the present moment. Brechtian theatre encompassed film techniques as well as the cabaret that dominated Germany in the 1920s. Two important films, Fritz Lang's Metropolis (1927) and Carl Dreyer's *The Passion of Joan of Arc* (1928) exemplify the continuation in the social vs. spiritual uses of Joan through that period. While Brecht and Lang use film to underscore the increasingly alienated and fragmented world that impinges on human dignity, Dreyer, conversely, uses the modern technology of film to create a timeless look at suffering and strength of faith and character. In the Epilogue, the focus shifts to the World War II era, as well as its aftermath in the 1950s. During this time, Joan retains prominence for conservative and radical perspectives. The study moves from one war and upheaval to the next, tracing the formation of modern women's roles, backlashes against feminism, and the shift from fixity to fluidity regarding private as well as public life.

As a segue from modernity to the chapter on the historical Joan, some remarks from Vita Sackville-West are particularly apt. In her post-canonization biography, *St. Joan of Arc* (1936), she zeros in on the complex social and psychological aspects of Joan's moment in history, through her role at Orléans:

> She arrived at what is now called the psychological moment.... The particular inspiration which she brought to them at Orléans ... reflects, as a sort of symbol, the general inspiration which she brought to the whole of France after nearly a hundred years of war.... [Yet] her exploit there has been much exaggerated, and Orléans is for ever historically associated with her name. History does always, for some odd reason, give rise to such disproportionate associations; on examination, they seldom prove to be wholly justified; on examination, one usually finds that they stand as the symbol of a wider truth.[40]

"A wider truth" is precisely my aim in this book: the interplay between the historical documentation about Joan of Arc and the popular cultural images this material has inspired. Taken together, these reveal our complex reaction to individuals who not only change history, but also alter our sense of what history should teach us.

1

All Dressed Up and Nowhere to Go: The Historical Joan

If the ambiguities surrounding the story of Joan of Arc are the source of fascination for twenty-first-century readers, then it is equally important to note that these very "gray areas" were the causes for Joan's "problem" status in her own time. The outline of Joan's biography provided in the Introduction highlights the factors that could account for the fairy-tale qualities, both good and evil, which surrounded her rise and fall. From the outset, chroniclers from various countries included her exploits in their interpretations of fifteenth-century events. Their vantage points on Joan depended on their view of the Hundred Years War with England, as well as their attitude towards the more modern concepts Joan represented, especially regarding women of action, and their need to dress/pose as men. In an era which accepted duality, logic dictated an either/or approach to any given set of circumstances. There was no official place for a persona as complex as Joan's: chaste and devout, willful and presumptuous. Her mixture of virtues and vices, both religious and secular, defied comprehension as well as codes of acceptability. Herein lies the focus of this chapter: how do the historical "facts" and their interpretations combine to form the image of Joan of Arc as an historical figure? It is only when this question is answered that the concept of an evolution in her literary and cultural significance comes to light.

That Joan of Arc was an irritant to the patriarchal structure must be accepted, not only as historically documented, but also as inevitable. Her appearance in the public eye, an illiterate "peasant girl" dressed as a soldier, came at a particularly sensitive time for the Church and its authority, which only compounded the problem. Ironically, the self-serving actions of several prominent men of the cloth only exacerbated the conflict.[1] Further, the contradictions inherent in her character bordered on the then-prevalent belief in the ability of the devil to assume an appearance of good and thereby mislead an ignorant soul.

The contemporary cultural historian, Marina Warner, claims that this concept accounted for the propensity for lay people as well as clergy to mistrust anything but the most orthodox of positions. Stories were circulated that the devil was so cunning that he could reveal himself in the guise of a person's beloved, a well-known saint, even Christ himself. Warner characterizes the attempt by this society to "pinpoint the nature and the place of evil, to find the person embodying it … [as] like trapping mercury, for

Jean Auguste Dominique Ingres (1780–1867), *Joan of Arc at the Coronation of Charles VII* (1854). Ingres' portrait of Joan of Arc is markedly different from his usual depictions of women in their gorgeous gowns, but it does represent his trademark: idealization of the figure. Here Joan is clearly the dominant figure, both because of her stance and because of the heraldic features of her costume. Although she has a skirt, her imposing figure wears armor, but her face is transfixed, with a halo discernible above her head. Her hair is long, but pulled back to draw even more attention to her rapt expression *(courtesy Erich Lessing/Art Resource, New York; Louvre, Paris)*.

what seemed evil slipped away from the analyst's finger and thumb with maddening agility."[2] As proof was so amorphous, medieval judges tended to go after smaller crimes and assume their role as inevitable links to the larger ones. In Joan's case, this explains the emphasis on minor links to sorcery (i.e. telepathic knowledge) which could be interpreted as "heresy."

Susan Schibanoff's analysis of Joan's transvestism as her undoing extends the parameters of this argument by incorporating internal and external factors. When Joan in essence tore up her recantation by resuming male dress, her enemies had what they needed. No matter that her woman's dress had been stolen that morning: her passionate statement that her Voices were right and the Church Militant authorities wrong sealed her doom inexorably. Schibanoff states that on the date of her "relapsed heresy" Joan's transvestism "became synchronized with her invisible idolatry, her visions." Throughout the trial the costume had introduced concretely her inner, and suspect, revelations.[3]

Several of these salient points converge when one considers the nature and function of Joan's "Voices." While steadfast in her claim that white light accompanied her saints' visits, Joan's explanation of their instructions and attitudes were very much in human terms. The presence of white light correlated to the acceptable aura of angels,[4] but the more earth-bound descriptions linked more readily to medieval romance than to its theological contexts: thus the consternation of the judges. Joan identified the Archangel Michael as her chief source of comfort; he was far less direct than the female saints in his commandments to Joan. But Michael was the "emblem of French resistance" during the Hundred Years War.[5] More to the point, the other two Voices were St. Margaret and St. Catherine of Alexandria, whose cults were then prominent, especially for the young women. Consciously or unconsciously, this factor may have swayed the authorities towards the diabolical explanation.

As her more modern judges at the time of the canonization process would say, Joan could have been suffering from "delusions of grandeur" by professing visitations from two saints who had defied convention and also encouraged the widening of women's sphere. According to Warner, St. Catherine had tackled the political and clerical authorities of her own time intellectually on behalf of her people when she had pleaded on behalf of early Christians like herself. St. Margaret had cross-dressed to avoid marriage and had jumped from a high building to maintain her chastity; Joan mirrored each of these actions. Like Joan, Catherine and Margaret were tortured. Proto-feminist aspects in combination with the rebellious ones in these saints' stories paired unmistakably with several of the charges brought against Joan, particularly those that pinpointed her transvestism as emblematic of her disregard of dogma.

There was also no way for her judges at the Trial of Condemnation to rule that Joan's was "holy transvestism." A designation begun by St. Thomas Aquinas, it held that women who "passed" as men for safety or spiritual sake were not considered an affront to established ideology. Those who cross-dressed but did not conceal their visible female anatomy displayed behavior considered anathema.[6] Schibanoff cogently identifies the underlying issue as gender ambiguity. The outrage was not over Joan of Arc, "or what her gender was, but what gender itself was, specifically the male gender—what constituted it, what menaced it, what preserved it, and what relationship it bore to biological sex ... what was 'at stake' was not merely God, king, and nation but the traditional constituent of all three, manhood."[7]

The twelve charges that were brought against Joan of Arc in 1431 centered around three major points: diabolical influences, blasphemy/irreverence, and unorthodox representation of religious devotion. Charge I observed that Joan's "manner and person" revealed diabolical influences—her presumptuous speech and male dress. Charges II & III dealt with Joan's interpretation of angels. The former declared that the king's "sign" to receive Joan as messenger (the crown she later used at Reims) was "contrary and derogatory" to angels and their dignity; the latter stated that her means of recognizing her saints was "insufficient" for divine inspiration: again, her earth-bound descriptions were mistrusted. Joan's prescience was interpreted as either superstitious or vain boasting in Charge IV. The charges which supported the idea that Joan was a blasphemer and heretic concentrated on her outrageous pride and confidence, as well as on her effrontery to standards of feminine behavior. Joan's refusal to submit to sumptuary laws, the Church Militant, and her parents' wishes were proof enough for her judges: cross-dressing, charge V; using "Jhesu Maria" on her standard, charge VI; and leaving home without sanction, charge VII. The remaining charges revolved around issues of adherence to the dogma of the Church Militant, the institution of the Catholic Church on earth.[8]

Joan's claim that St. Margaret and St. Catherine spoke to her in French because they were on that side was felt to be "contrary to the spirit and commandment to love our neighbors," charge X; her very commandments from her Voices violated principles of womanly behavior and adherence to Catholic teachings about the role of priests in communication with God and his messengers, charge XI. The astonishing jump from the tower at Beaulieu was seen as either a possible suicide attempt or a presumptuous assumption of forgiveness, charge VIII.[9] Charge XI also centered on Joan's claims to bodily embrace with her Voices.

During the questioning, several of these issues arose again and again; the relentless pursuit of different answers was a tactic which bore little fruit, as Joan would refuse to divulge certain information, saying that her Voices had not given her permission to do so. She also reminded them that they could not understand certain things: a double insult to be sure. Nonetheless, she persisted, calling often for the records to be brought from Poitiers,[10] and finally asked to be brought before the pope regarding the issue of Church Triumphant versus Church Militant. Her requests were denied. The issue of her transvestism was brought up on many different sessions of the Trial and was linked to her putative desire to be a man (which she claimed to have answered elsewhere) and her denial of access to Mass. If she could not dress "appropriately," she could not be worthy to attend church.

Conversely, if she returned to woman's dress, these learned authority figures believed they could control Joan of Arc. Karen Sullivan's study of the perspective of Joan's judges focuses on the form and mindset of the interrogators and emphasizes the distinction between the Church's perspective and popular culture's assessment of Joan. For most people, Joan's overt spiritual devotion and her heroism on behalf of her people was sufficient evidence of her divine inspiration. But for the clerics, that was not enough. They needed to understand Joan's inner experiences, and then see if those dovetailed with established ecclesiastical criteria. Joan's refusal to answer, or answer thoroughly enough, was especially irritating to a group of men whose own training had emphasized this very precision.[11]

The interest in clothing as coding even extended to the saints. When asked about how they appeared to her, Joan was required to describe their headwear and the cloth of their garments (Fourth Session 27 February).[12] In this same day's testimony, Joan was asked if God "ordered" her male attire. Her reply to this question is of interest not only for its content but also for its simplicity, directness, and confidence in her mission: 'the dress is a small, nay the least thing. Nor did [I] put on man's dress by the advice of any man whatsoever.... Everything I have done is at God's command; and if He had ordered me to assume a different habit, I should have done it, because it would have been His command.'[13]

In medieval times, however, clothing for women could not be viewed in Joan's terms, at least not to the orthodox mind. As Howard Bloch points out in his essay "Medieval Misogyny," clothing was intimately connected to the essence of misogyny: woman is inferior, ornamental, artificial, while man is superior, substantial, the participant in events. Bloch argues that this mindset was responsible for the predominance of the Fall in medieval doctrine. Thus woman as seductress became the key image, and clothing a key weapon in her design to undermine man's morality. Early medieval writers like Tertullian are often seen as repelled by the flesh; Bloch's position is that the draping of the body was the anathema because to decorate the body was done to show oneself to advantage, an act of pride. He sums up the link between these attitudes and clothing very neatly: "This is why Tertullian is able to move so quickly and naturally from the idea of dress to a whole range of seemingly unapparent associations—e.g., between transvestism and the monstrous; or between the toga and lust, adultery."[14] Even more essential to our understanding of the judgment of Joan in this area is Bloch's insight that clothes are "secondary, collateral, supplemental. Dress is unnatural since, like all artifice, it seeks to add to, to perfect, the body of nature or God's creation."[15] Therefore, from the judges' viewpoint, directives regarding clothing could not be conceived as divinely inspired; conversely, the judges' concern with clothing likewise represented secular rather than religious concerns.

The linking of Joan's costume choices to the spirit and vocabulary of the mercan-

tile mindset once again defers the religious context to the social one: the class struggle. Warner contends that the role Joan has played in history has been fluid because
she personifies "certain causes with a consoling lack of ambiguity."[16] Joan explained
her mystical experiences in concrete, sensory detail, and the iconography of biblical
legends when she chose to answer the questions posed to her. Because the limitations
of any individual's interpretation lead inevitably to misinterpretation, Joan's image was
destined to remain ambiguous in scholarly estimation until the modern era. Sullivan
cautions us not to fall into the trap of reading Joan's testimony as the pathway to her
inner thoughts, as has been the response of so many since the transcripts were published in the mid-nineteenth century. Sullivan extends her point when she draws a parallel to modern interrogations, in which equipment is turned on and off, and
microphones placed at the discrimination of court officials. Conversely, Sullivan
reminds us that Joan's interrogators "opened up the space within which Joan was
allowed to speak, and it was they who furnished the elements with which she was
allowed to express herself.... Though in a historical sense Joan may have spoken ...
the production of the minutes reflects a collaboration between the speaker and her
scribes."[17]

Joan's contemporary chroniclers were either Burgundian (pro-English) or Arma-
gnac (pro-French). Both Burgundian and Argmagnacian writers focus on her remarkable accomplishments; it is the source of them that leads each side in a different
direction. Each side assumes that a young girl could never just happen to possess such
abilities, courage, and effectiveness. Further, a person of peasant (or at best lower-
middle-class) stock could not become a leader of such magnitude. These original
chronicles, most notably by the Burgundian Monstrelet and later the English Caxton,
focused almost entirely on her rise to power, her successes, her failures, and her demise.
Their synopses were then adopted/adapted by the later English chroniclers, Halle and
Holinshed, and used as source material for Shakespeare's Pucelle in *1 Henry VI.*

While we as moderns are prone to skepticism, as readers of the chronicles we cannot fail to be impressed most strongly by the firmness of the reporters' beliefs. Whether
participants in or interpreters of the action, there is clarity of vision. The clouding began
later and stemmed from the contradictions between versions. One of the earliest examples of this true dichotomy surrounding Joan can be seen in the sixteenth-century
Chronicles of England, Scotland, and Ireland by Raphael Holinshed. When he reported
her "shamefullie reiecting her sex abominablie in acts and apparell to haue counter-
feit mankind, and then all damnablie faithlesse, to be a pernicious instrument to hos-
tilitie and bloudshed in diuelish witchcraft and sorcerie" he fully understood, even
commended, Cauchon and her sentencing. When she abjured, his tone mollifies, laud-
ing Joan for seizing the opportunity to return to the bosom of the Church. Her recantation sent Holinshed back to the strong language of disparagement: "she fullie afore
possest of the feend, not able to hold hir in anie towardnesse of grace, falling streight
waie into hir former abominations ... stake not (though the shift were shamefull) to

confesse hir selfe a strumpet." At this point, he included the story reported by the English chronicler, Caxton, that Joan claimed to be pregnant in order to avoid burning. Holinshed believed whole-heartedly that the appearance of piety surrounding the Maid was the work of the devil: "satan ... can change himselfe into an angell of light, the deeplier to deceiue." Halle's assessment was far simpler: "She was no good woman; she was no sainct."[18]

In relation to the position of Charles, however, Holinshed provided a more complex picture. He recognized the shadow of witchcraft and sorcery surrounding not only his crowning, but also his "dignitie abroad foulie spotted.... Which maladie he full sorilie salued (like one that to kill the strong sent of onions would cheaw a cloue of garlike)." With no trouble at all, Holinshed reported "a quite contrarie sentence" with all blemishes removed from Joan and Charles in his description of the Trial of Rehabilitation. What disturbed Holinshed were the versions of the story which did not account for "hir heinous enormities, or else any difference betweene one stirred up by mercie diuine ... and a damnable sorcerer suborned by satan." And yet, his final remark to his reader is to "judge as ye list."[19] In précis form, Holinshed's turning of the question to his reader foreshadows the message of the post-canonization playwrights who represent Joan of Arc's legacy in the twentieth century. Warner's argument on the same point highlights Joan's uniqueness as a woman of her time. Warner contends that Joan became prominent "because she belongs to the sphere of action, while so many feminine figures or models are assigned and confined to the sphere of contemplation."[20]

Another layer of signification and dilemma derived from the very virtues she so visibly represented; in Warner's words, "in an age of chivalry she assumed its most successful guise." Assumption and guise are the key words here because, as Warner neatly encapsulates, in the fifteenth century, "clothes were capital."[21] Vita Sackville-West, in her influential 1936 biography *St. Joan of Arc*, posits the notion that Joan's role was personal, internal, not really related to what she wore or her official status. Because she recognized right away that the troops were dissolute and disillusioned, Joan "conducted herself from the first in her usual high-handed manner.... She interfered with them.... She had them all under her control."[22]

Daniel Rankin and Claire Quintal present an annotated translation of the first biography of Joan, a chronicle written by a Burgundian friar of Joan's own time. While this account praised Joan's achievements and acknowledged her power, the implications are clear that hers was a bewitching power, and was the source of the Dauphin's strength:

> With the Maid in arms and always near [to help] him ... the Dauphin of Viennois acquired new courage.... She did astonishing feats of arms with her bodily strength. She handled the thrust of a lance with great vigor.... Hearsay had it that whenever she appeared before a fortress the people within ... became, all of then, mute and feeble and had no power to defend themselves against her, so they gave up at once.[23]

Later in the chronicle, the friar notes that Joan's capture was a "great joy" to the

Duke of Burgundy and his followers because they "held her in suspicion." For others, "because their hopes were in her ... [it] was a great sorrow." But for everyone, the capture was a major event, and "was noised about excitedly everywhere." Regarding her abjuration, this chronicler credits the "noble sermon preached to her on the subject of her conduct ... delivered in the presence of the Regent of France [Bedford] and of several high princes and prelates" with granting Joan her life. The central issue that altered Joan's fate was her return to male attire. As the first biographer said: "when she realized she was to be obliged to dress as women do, she remembered her past and said she preferred to die as she had lived."[24]

In actuality, Joan was horrified by the "merciful" life imprisonment sentence. She had believed that recanting would have earned her a return to the world at large. Furthermore, the reason for Joan's reappearance in male attire, while not universally confirmed, seems more related to the behavior of her English male guards than to any desire to avoid her proper role. One version of this claims that the guards removed her female garb from her cell when Joan went out to relieve herself and the male garments she had discarded were left in their place. Regardless of what she wore, the key concern ought to have been the causes of both the recantation and its subsequent denial. Was it the costume rather than principle that spurred the final judgment against her? Or, conversely, was the costume used as an expedient to guarantee the English determination to burn her and rid themselves of the embarrassment Joan had caused them?

Both Anatole France and Andrew Lang, whose canonization-era biographies are analyzed further in chapter 2, make constant references to Joan's attire during the trial, reminding their readers that Joan's appearance hardened her judges against her. Many of the young priests had never before seen a woman's hair until Joan was brought into court in "a page's black suit, an outrage to the chaste eyes of the learned."[25] Anatole France adds the psychological dimension here: "We marvel at the profound meditations into which the Maid's doublet and hose plunged these clerics. They contemplated them with gloomy terror and in light of the precepts of Deuteronomy."[26]

As a modern reader weaves these strands of evidence together, it becomes increasingly clear that so much of Joan's history is embedded in ambiguities and double-edged swords. A telling illustration of how scrupulously Joan was observed both during her career and after her capture are the many reports of her amenorrhea. This had weighty religious significance because it was associated with Eve's state before the corruption of sexual knowledge and also because fifteenth-century scholars associated amenorrhea with outstanding strength.[27] Warner and Vita Sackville-West connect this state to her likely anorexia; Joan was known to eat only a few hunks of bread soaked in wine as an entire day's nutrition. This abstemiousness can also be viewed in religious terms: she was continuously fasting.

On the same theme, Joan's female body, the issue of virginity must be recalled. In one view, this state was believed to be protection from the devil, in another, proof of her presumption, since she believed that her Voices had promised her paradise if she remained chaste. In the secular context, Joan's virginity and place of origin were both integral factors in the prophecy (based on Merlin and Bede) that a maid from Lorraine would save France. The merging of religion, mysticism, and legend here is unmistakable and supersedes the possibility of ever determining "the truth" about these issues. More important is the placement of Joan's life and time in the framework of women mystics and virgin saints, particularly those who were incorporated into the Church in the thirteenth century. Because of that era's heretical cults, women mystics had gained prominence. Even though these women were clearly pious, their behavior likewise contradicted medieval codes for the good woman. Elizabeth Petroff explains this as a paradox between women's supposed proprieties and the criteria for sanctity. Not only did saints have to possess moral goodness, but they also had to take responsible actions for themselves and others. Petroff lauds the Church's decision to accept these mystics and their cults rather than spurn them, since they had already become saints in the public imagination. She further notes that two centuries later, the social and ecclesiastical climates would have decided the opposite.[28]

Petroff also emphasizes the necessity of appeasing male ecclesiastics, particularly if the women's own actions had superseded the men's. In this way the other controversy could be averted: the recognition of women's "natural" inclination for mystical inspiration and the "suspicion that it was impossible effectively to repress female power."[29] Unfortunately, Joan of Arc never learned this lesson, which accounts for the extremity of clerics' negative response to her. What Joan did pick up from her knowledge of women saints was the special province of the virgin mystic. These women enjoyed more public freedom than any other women in the Middle Ages. Yet, dangers came with this privilege, particularly sexual harassment. Both of Joan's female saints were tortured, but escaped rape. As a result, they escaped traditional sex roles, "moving into a new kind of freedom of action that is neither passive nor aggressive, female nor male. This new transformative vision allows them to act in totally unconventional ways when the situation seems to demand it — the woman saint may act as either a man or a woman, or as both or as neither [and this] is clearly revealed in the legend of Joan of Arc."[30]

However limited his acknowledgement of Joan's military powers might have been, Anatole France recognized the fusion of her belief in her Voices, and her association of male attire and a fulfilled mission. Because her return to male clothing was part of her repentance of the lies (abjuration) told to save her life, France grants Joan a conscious decision here. The clothes were a signal for her death, but this does not surprise France, who asserts that Joan's "steadfast belief in her deliverance [was] fearless simplicity; whence came her confidence in her Voices if not from her own heart?"[31] He embellishes the praise further when he claimed: "against the courage of this child, all the reasons and all the eloquence of the world would have availed nothing."[32]

Equally insightful is Sackville-West's assessment of the attitudes and actions of the English towards Joan. When Joan wrote to Bedford *pro forma* at Orléans, it should not be even noteworthy that he dismissed the message as "the most outrageous piece of impertinence. As, indeed, it was." Sackville-West comments further that the English are not "imaginative" except in poetry, and "rely on strength, a rule that works ninety-nine times out of a hundred. Jeanne was the hundredth time."[33] Their mistake was far graver, though. For all their threats to capture and burn her from the outset, the English really did nothing, though they had the opportunity. Sackville-West uses these observations as fertile ground for her feminist stand: "Was it because, in their English arrogance and stupidity, they did not take her seriously?" In answering her own question, Sackville-West concludes: "She was good enough to burn, but not good enough to bother much about."[34] She also acknowledges the French response, that Joan had "terrorized" them, had almost cast a spell upon them, thus underscoring the misogynistic viewpoint underneath the surface.[35]

She might give credence to the English belief in the sorcery related to Joan, but Sackville-West scrupulously rejects the magical elements throughout the book. She cites Joan's disregard of her supposed "powers" as well as the witnesses at the Rehabilitation Trial as evidence that Joan was more of a realist than a mystic. This connects to her portrayal of Joan as an honest, bold individual. Even at the Trial, Sackville-West emphasizes:

> although frequently shrewd in her replies, [she] was never so cautious as to grow sly ... [rather] she was forthright and sincere, even rash, giving the impression that she had nothing to hide, except, indeed, when she replied that her voices would not allow her to answer.... Nor was she ever intimidated to the extent of trying to placate her judges by untruths; indeed, she frequently answered their questions in a fashion better calculated to annoy than to placate.[36]

Going beyond the glorification of Joan and her martyrdom is how one discovers the sordid sub-text of the trial. A prime example was when an official, Maitre Andre Marguerite, stated it was important to learn why Joan resumed male attire; the men-at-arms called him a traitor and he retreated. Obviously, he recognized the hopelessness of going against the tide. Cauchon was equally swift in handing Joan over to the secular arm. Not only was this immoral, but illegal, as Inquisition "form" was ignored; it was the usual custom to take the condemned heretic to the town council for sentencing.[37]

The shrewdness of Joan's enemies should not be underestimated. Lang reminds us, with the help of the seventeenth-century historian George Mackenzie, that even "wealth, rank and gallant military service could not save an accused heretic, even among his own people."[38] Conversely, what Joan's enemies could not predict was her behavior on the day she died. It was only after the Rehabilitation Trial verdict that the incidents surrounding Joan's tragic end could be connected to those usually narrated about "the martyrdom of virgins ... the dove taking flight from the stake ... the name of Jesus written in letters of flame ... the heart intact in the ashes."[39] These wonders found their way into later legends, later versions of Joan's story. The political overtones of the proceedings themselves, especially Cauchon's actions, implied an even broader, deeper, context. Inquisition practices were disregarded, blatantly. The later scholar Regine Pernoud, in *Joan of Arc by Herself and Her Witnesses* (1966), encapsulates these neatly:

> Throughout the whole course of the trial Joan was held in a civil prison, looked after by English gaolers and kept in irons. This was in flagrant disregard of the rule of Inquisitorial tribunals by which she had a right to be held in the archbishopric prison and guarded by women. Another irregularity: Joan had no advocate ... anyone who tried to encourage or advise her, did so at his risk and peril.[40]

Pernoud points out that Cauchon rescinded his promise to take Joan away from the English, when he commanded the guards to: "Take her to where you found her." Pernoud cements her condemnation of Cauchon and the others when she states that Joan was a political prisoner, "whose enemies contrived to get her dealt with as a heretic in order to destroy the prestige which her personal saintliness and her extraordinary exploits had made for her."[41] This prestige became the essence of the legends that had begun to circulate since the Siege of Orléans in 1429. An even more serious charge came from the trial notary, Guillaume Manchon, at the Rehabilitation proceedings. It was his assertion that Joan's testimony was interrupted often, and much had been omitted from the records: "her excuses and what might serve to acquit her ... were, then, recorded as she gave them, then collated and examined by the judges and assessors who sought for weak points in her answers which might give them a basis for further questioning."[42] Therefore, the modern interpretations that point out that Joan's trial did not follow the conventions of heresy trials obviously stand on solid grounds.

In depicting the plight of Joan during her imprisonment, Sackville-West observes that no notes existed regarding the care of Joan's clothes at this time. After her attempted escape from Beaurevoir, Joan was taken to Arras; once again she refused to adopt feminine attire. But here Sackville-West turns our attention inward: "Her small human problems suggest themselves inevitably to our curiosity. How did she manage to cut her hair?... All we can imagine for certain is that she must have arrived at Arras looking very shabby, very forlorn, and very young."[43] There is a world of difference between this individualized portrait and Michelet's larger-than-life representation of Joan as waif/heroine/martyr. Whereas Michelet, France, and Lang forge a symbolic suffering in Joan, Sackville-West prefers a more reserved, yet more penetrating, representation of Joan's doom. She simply states: "Trapped, friendless, she had nothing left to rely on but her courage and her wits. Neither failed her, but she knew very well that fate had closed around her as surely as the walls of her cell." Despite her condemnation of the reprehensible behavior and attitudes of Joan's judges, Sackville-West expresses surprise that "they troubled to give her a trial at all."[44] What is said here, albeit obliquely, is that her enemies did not treat Joan as "only a woman."

The care taken to interpret the foundations of Joan's moral character, filial responsibilities, and social interactions during the Trial of Rehabilitation matched that which had been expended to presume her flawed nature at the Trial of Condemnation. It is grimly ironic that witnesses on behalf of Joan could have been so plentiful twenty-five years after her death. Once again, the external political expediencies were foremost in the plans of those who produced this re-working of evidence and judgment. It was comparatively easy to shift the blame of Joan's injustice to the Church of her time since several key players, including Bishop Pierre Cauchon, were already dead.

Witnesses were asked a series of twelve questions about Joan's early life, strikingly parallel to the twelve charges originally pressed against her. These questions revolved around her moral and religious education, familial responsibilities/obedience, the reputation of her parents and their social standing,

Dante Gabriel Rossetti (1828–1882), *Joan of Arc Kissing the Sword of Deliverance* (1863). Rossetti captures three salient aspects of Joan and her legend in this painter's bust: her reverence, her androgyny, and her medieval garments. Yet her hair is long and flowing, even if it is off her face, while, at the same time, her hands and Adam's apple are quite masculine in shape and size *(courtesy of Réunion des Musées Nationaux/Art Resource, New York; Musée d'Art Moderne, Strasbourg)*.

her activities as a child and youth (age seven and upwards), including the infamous "Fairy Tree." The emergence of the idyllic and charismatic peasant girl permeates the testimony of witnesses, including her godfather, Jean Moreau, and her best friend, Hauviette. The phrase that can stand as a motif for Joan's image at this second trial is Hauviette's, who characterized Joan as "good, simple, sweet." Moreau's description is fuller, emphasizing Joan's individual traits as at once distinctive and at the same time appropriate for her way of life.[45]

The Vicar of Domrémy heard her confession two or three times when Joan was at Vaucouleurs and witnessed her departure, with her entourage, for Chinon to meet the Dauphin. He reported: "I can conscientiously say that she seemed to me a good girl, who showed every sign of being a good Catholic and a perfect Christian. She went to church gladly." Joan's pleasure in attending church was matched by the frequency of her attendance and adherence to other practices, such as confession and fasting. These qualities were used by the friendly witnesses to corroborate their belief that Joan never went to the Fairy Tree alone or with any intention to conjure evil spirits; they stressed the innocence of the activity there as well as its being always a group activity.[46]

Subtler but no less salient issues were Joan's behavior and whereabouts at Neufchateau; Hauviette and others stressed the constant companionship of Joan and her parents for the duration of their stay. This evidence was critical to maintaining the purity of Joan's sexual image, since the soldiery had driven them from Domrémy and it would have been relatively easy for Joan to then commence a life as a camp follower. Testimony from a Doctor of Theology from Poitiers offered crucial impressions regarding the examinations that had approved her mission. One would expect a glowing report of her piety above all else, yet it is Joan's confidence, forthrightness, and quickness that inform his remarks:

> When we arrived we put various questions to Joan and, among other things … asked her why she had come, saying that the king was most anxious to know what had impelled her to come to him. And she answered, boldly, that when she was watching the cattle her voice had spoken to her, saying that God had great pity for the people of France, and that Joan must go to France. On hearing this she had begun to weep…. I said to her: "God cannot wish us to believe in you unless he sends us a sign, to show that we should believe in you. We cannot advise the King to entrust you with soldiers … on your bare assertion." She answered: "I have not come to Poitiers to make signs. But lead me to Orléans, and I will show you the signs I was sent to make."[47,48]

Dean Seguin also recalled her prophesying that the English would be defeated at Orléans, the king would be anointed at Reims, the city of Paris would return to the king's rule, and the Duke of Orléans would return from England. "I have seen all this come true," he told the judges at the Rehabilitation Trial. Because the last two of these prophesied events occurred after Joan's burning, the aura of magic lingered around her name and legend, whether for good or ill.

The actual decision to begin a canonization process for Joan of Arc would not be taken until 1869, but the popular imagination considered her as saintly long before any official designation. During the canonization process, both of these factors played a role. The first Promoter of the Faith, aka Devil's Advocate, emphasized that Joan's case was both outstanding and difficult because of the need to distinguish between her heroism and sanctity: "No age has been silent about Joan's *political* virtues, joined certainly to piety and religion, indeed also to a prophetic spirit. But it is only in our times that one has begun to think about her possession of true and heroic virtues befitting to saints."[49] Several men played this role, and all grappled with the dilemma of Joan's earthbound frame of reference regarding her Voices as well as her actions. Saints had often become involved in social and political issues, so why was Joan's activity so different for them? Her lack of regard for gender constraints was naturally a sticking point. Another criterion they struggled with was Joan's fear and "hysteria" about torture; she seemed to lack the transcendent attitude of other saints. In other words, the feminine as well as masculine aspects of Joan's attitudes were hard for them to reconcile. The Pope overruled each of them in turn over these criteria.[50]

The interpreters of Joan's life and times which follow her canonization in 1920 no longer share the mission of redressing the wrongs of history; rather, their historiographical interest is in determining the connections between our lives and those of our fifteenth-century counterparts. Most apparent is the parallel between the ideological struggle surrounding the Hundred Years War and World War I and its aftermath. Both eras share the struggle between old and new forms of thinking, with the ambivalence and jadedness that predictably accompany times of transition.

While much of Sackville-West's attitude and selection of details followed patterns from the canonization-era biographers urging Joan's official sanctity, this later writer seems to have less interest in pinning down one "correct" image. Sackville-West exceeds these works' portraits of Joan because hers concentrates on Joan's life as a young woman, not only as a hero/ine of history. In grappling with the issue of Joan's love of finery, Sackville-West is succinct. The tone is almost droll when Sackville-West remarks: "For all her privately religious integrity, she had no inclination in favor of the hair shirt.... The woman in Jeanne made the most of the chance provided by her sudden emergence from obscurity into a public personage."[51]

The savvy she attributes to Joan here, using the trappings of fame to her personal advantage, was and is particularly significant in light of two factors: the newly enfranchised young women of England, and Vita Sackville-West's own experience with fame and notoriety. It was 1928 when women under thirty were finally granted the vote in England, the same year that Sackville-West's intimate friend, Virginia Woolf, produced *Orlando*. Though termed a biography by Woolf, it is actually a novel of fantasy. Its protagonist lives for several centuries, first as a man and then as a woman. Woolf dedicated the book to "V. Sackville-West" and presumably based its androgynous, transvestite character on Vita.

The link to Woolf's novel rests not only on its hero/ine, but also to the similar treatment of history that is an inherent characteristic of this novel, and Virginia Woolf's writings in general. Even in terms of style there is a clear dialogic between the two women's voices: both treat their subjects from the inside looking out, focusing on specific detail and situation to explore abstract concepts and the nature of human experience. A vivid example from Woolf is the explanation of Orlando's psychological response to the overnight "sex change" that one would expect to be a trauma: "Orlando had become a woman. The change of sex, though it altered their future, did nothing whatever to alter their identity.... The change seemed to have been accomplished painlessly and completely and in such a way that Orlando herself showed no surprise."[52]

The blatant inattention to physical appearance by Orlando expresses the feminist message to focus on the inner, rather than the outer, self. Sackville-West echoes it when she cites Joan's famous answer from the Trial regarding her refusal to return to women's clothes: 'It is true that at Arras and Beaurevoir I was admonished to adopt feminine clothes; I refused, and still refuse. As for other avocations of women, there are plenty of other women to perform them.'[53] The unromanticized answer by Joan is matched by Sackville-West's explanation of both why and how Joan was a cross-dresser: "the practical inconvenience of belonging to the wrong sex must be faced and overcome; and Jeanne, with her usual common sense, took the obvious step of turning herself into the least outward semblance of a woman possible…. However she managed it, it was done."[54] Sackville-West dismisses the idea that Joan could have been pretty since none of her witnesses mention the fact, one of "outstanding importance, especially to Latin minds, in the case of a woman." Instead, Sackville-West urges her readers to think of Joan "prosaically, sensibly, logically … well-made: strong, healthy, plain, sturdy."[55] The perspective of New Woman, the generation that would see the canonization of Joan of Arc, is encoded in every word here.

One salient distinction between Woolf's Orlando and St. Joan according to Sackville-West must be incorporated into this examination: Orlando was an androgyne, while Joan was a transvestite. Marjorie Garber, in her contemporary study *Vested Interests* (1992), cites the twentieth-century German sexologist, Magnus Hirschfeld, to distinguish between these two concepts. Androgynes concern themselves with "*physical* marks of gender" while transvestites focus on "*psychical* or psychological gender signs, like dress and names."[56] While both of these terms have been applied to the historical Joan, these definitions clearly label her as transvestite. If the clothes Joan chose were male, the name her saints instructed her to use definitely cast her as a "good girl." Garber's framework of the early twentieth-century cultural *milieu* makes the establishment of various gender identifications more than recognizable; Garber's perspective on clothes and other semiotic gender codes illustrates the continuum along which Joan of Arc belongs as well as her twentieth-century counterparts. The generation of Vita Sackville-West pushed themselves and those around them to accept individual as well as group identifications that illuminated the sweeping social changes of their time.

Sackville-West emphasizes that "all evidence points to her having been a serious and aloof little girl … considered rather a prig by the other children."[57] In her public appearances, Joan was known to have "wept copiously at every possible opportunity" which Sackville-West noted as particularly curious, "a queer mixture of feminine and masculine attributes as ever relentlessly assaulted the enemy and then must cry on seeing him hurt."[58]

This last point alludes to the contrast between the mythology of battle's glory and its grim reality, a concept even more dominant in post–World War I thinking. In describing the psychological context of the Siege of Orléans, Sackville-West admonishes the reader to remember that in that time, "the personal element was much more dominant for each man concerned. He was in no danger of being suddenly blown to bits by an unseen gun a couple of miles away. He could dodge the stone; if he was very quick, he could even dodge the arrow."[59] Sackville-West's vivid depiction of the hand-to-hand, sweat-to-sweat style of medieval combat set up her real point here:

> When we remember this, it becomes easier to understand the astonishing effect of Jeanne's presence upon the French troops. Her position as a leader was a unique one. She was not a professional soldier; she was not really a soldier at all; she was not even a man. She was ignorant of war. She was a girl dressed up. But she believed, and she made others willing to believe, that she was the mouthpiece of God.[60]

Woolf gives this same sort of latitude to her character, Orlando, at different historical time periods. While often remarking that little if anything had changed in the English environment, at other places in the novel the character sees the progression and/or deterioration of human history. The "sex change" occurs in the eighteenth century, in the time of Swift and Pope and on the eve of Wollstonecraft; one consequence for Woolf's character is the loss of formerly inherited property. Other reflections by Orlando, however, are more like Sackville-West's inner observations. The importance of family life and the expansion of the British Empire in the nineteenth century are observed as a "dampness" within and without the houses, causing "swelling"; the average woman "married at nineteen and had fifteen or eighteen children by the time she was thirty."[61]

Woolf's ingenious melding of individual and cultural realities connotes the same kind of private/public speculation that Sackville-West evoked. When she describes Joan's relationship to women when not in battle, Sackville-West contributes a perspective her male counterparts did not include: our "unconscious habit of regarding Jeanne's life as led entirely in the company of men."[62] She continues:

> We have really grown so well accustomed to the rattle of armour that the rustle of a skirt comes as something of a surprise.... Jeanne, most wisely, had always been careful to safeguard her reputation by sleeping with women under a roof when not sleeping under the stars with men ... [yet] she lived the life of a man so naturally that we cease to be conscious of her sex one way or another.[63]

The parallel between this assessment of her readers and Woolf's in *Orlando* is unmistakable. The other common viewpoint, the personalization of history, also characterizes Sackville-West's narrative. Writing almost fifty years later, Marina Warner recognizes the sexual politics that Sackville-West implied, but emphasizes the psychological stress on both sides. Warner disavows the "cheeky" image of Joan so popular with the dramatists of this study and contends that exhaustion was Joan's primary condition during the trial, which led ultimately to her confusion. Joan's inability to understand the full context of the questions and her enemies' motivations made Joan more desperate and frustrated than angry.[64] Warner seems to contradict her own argument here, but it is fair to say that either desperation or anger can produce the dynamic that permeated that trial. More to the point, the judges were also thrown off balance by Joan's unnerving combination of "heresy and chastity," accompanied by her "intransigent conviction of her personal truth." As a result, Warner goes on, Joan "destroyed her enemies' equilibrium."[65]

The ambivalence of these positions corresponds to those of the literary artists who took up her story, from the Renaissance to the early nineteenth century. In these influential interpretations of Joan of Arc, diverse texts represent her as an "historical" figure, but also as a paradigm of a young woman who dared to defy patriarchal codes. The first major literary work was Shakespeare's *1 Henry VI* (1592), in which Joan's character is known as The Pucelle. Shakespeare embellished what he found in the Burgundian-based chronicles of Halle and Holinshed, and thereby emphasized the unnaturalness and danger of this woman warrior turned sorceress and heretic. His Pucelle (The Maid) reconfirms the Burgundian position that Joan was powerful but diabolical. To his credit, however, Shakespeare took Joan's power seriously, and showed how much negative influence she had on the English military establishment, whose humiliating defeat at Orléans was blamed squarely on Joan and her unnatural, witch-like powers.

Shakespeare's image of Joan went largely without rivalry for centuries. In the 1750s Voltaire, using the same name for his character as well as the title of the piece, penned a mock-epic about Joan and the courtiers around her. It reflected the Rehabilitation image of purity and charisma, but minimized Joan's military accomplishments more than Shakespeare had. More interesting to Voltaire was the ridicule of the power structure that produced and then condemned Joan. Voltaire was relentless regarding the spiritual/mystical issues, and the overt sexuality he inferred was present in her relationships with powerful men. Keeping her virginity for a year was her most important accomplishment, according to the opening section of the poem. Voltaire's satire might have been aimed at the speciousness he found in religion as well as the portrayals of Joan of Arc he felt were saccharine, but the sexual innuendos found their way into many visual representations of Joan and "lovers."

Robert Southey and Friedrich Schiller responded with indignation to Voltaire's portrayal, which they read as an affront to Joan's spirituality and uniqueness. Though working in different genres, Southey in epic poetry, and Schiller in verse drama, both of these Romantic figures aimed at creating a heroic image in and for Joan. Southey's Joan is much more feminist than Schiller's, possibly owing to Southey's friendship with and admiration for Mary Wollstonecraft. Schiller's version became far more well-known and influential, however. Schiller's Joan (Johanna) contains the essence of spiritual goodness and heroism, but is dependent on her male "protectors" (Schiller's term). Schiller's aim was to place Joan's legend within the parameters of classical tragedy. Joan's *hubris* was certainly apparent, as was her downfall. Yet Schiller felt it necessary to include a love interest, so that her virginity was at risk — and her powers depended upon that. Taken together, Southey's natural hero/ine and Schiller's feminized good girl pay homage to the ideology of the eighteenth-century French philosopher and writer Jean Jacques Rousseau regarding idealized country folk as well as women's roles and capabilities. Although both Southey and Schiller felt passionate about the nobility of Joan of Arc and wanted her position redressed, neither had the full history available, so their works are truly visions of a heroine's character out of context.

Schiller's own idealism and lofty style became paradigmatic; Verdi and Tchaikovsky adapted his storyline in opera, the play was produced internationally into the twentieth century, and Cecil B. DeMille's World War I–era film *Joan the Woman* used Schiller's plot of Joan falling in love with an English soldier. In the attempt to incorporate the legend of Joan into modern times, it would take more than a push to rectify the official position of the historical figure. What would prove problematic and difficult would be the construction of a frame of reference to fully recognize the reality of an outstanding young woman without social pedigree, and grant her public as well as private credit.

2

Divine Threads:
The Canonization Era in Context

On May 16, 1920, the world formally acknowledged Joan of Arc as "Saint Joan," thereby bringing official closure to the controversy that had surrounded her death and its ramifications for nearly five centuries. Over the centuries, Joan of Arc had gained unquestioned renown, and the number of those who felt her actions more inappropriate than heroic slowly dwindled. Yet, no official action occurred from the time of her Rehabilitation Trial in 1456 until the 1840s. But why then? What were the underlying factors that were so decisive for cementing the cultural significance of Joan? Such questions would have made sense to Joan herself, who understood enough about the importance of timing to present herself to French leaders when morale was at its lowest. While the celebrity of Joan of Arc had been a constant cultural factor since the Siege of Orléans in 1429, it was this later time that would turn her treatment by the power structure into a *cause célèbre*. In the 1840s, the transcripts of the trial of Joan of Arc were published in modern French, which gave a detailed context to the myth of Joan. The retelling of her story often reappeared when social and moral questions took on crisis proportions, particularly when questions about the status of women intersected issues of political authority. If the late eighteenth century had seen the re-emergence of the *querelles des femmes* and reshaped it to suit the revolutionary shift in political structure, the issues expanded throughout the nineteenth century and spilled into the twentieth.

As the notion of gender as social construction became clearer, the worry over blurred distinctions between masculine and feminine identities deepened. Thus a nineteenth-century version of the medieval Eve/Mary dichotomy emerged, known as the "Woman Question." The radical redefinitions of individuals and the glorification of the common people were twin principles introduced by the Enlightenment and heralded by Romantic writers, philosophers, and visual artists. As Virginia Woolf cogently phrased it in *A Room of One's Own*, something remarkable happened towards the end of the eighteenth century. She said if she were "rewriting history," she would "describe [it] more fully and think [it] of greater importance than the Crusades or the Wars of the Roses. The middle-class woman began to write." Woolf was not focusing here on an aesthetic shift, although that could not be denied, but rather, on the women's recognition that they could do more than meet privately and share their thoughts on reading materials: they could write material and that effort would "put money in their purses."[1] The counterpart of women participating in the world at large was the notion of separate "spheres," a notion built upon Renaissance notions of male supremacy, and reinforced by Enlightenment conceptions of society. Women's proper sphere was the home and private life, while men were destined to grapple with the public realms of society. Woolf's remarks reflected the results of the struggle between the two sides, since she wrote these words in 1929. Her specific references to medieval conflicts also show us the borders for the changes, with Joan of Arc's achievement squarely ensconced in the framework.

Jules Bastien-Lepage, *Joan of Arc* (1879). Painted to inspire faith and confidence in the French people after their humiliation in the Franco-Prussian War, Bastien-Lepage's Joan is an extraordinarily detailed glimpse of Joan hearing her Voices while still in Domrémy. Like Delacroix's "Liberty," she is a very large figure, and her hands show her connection to the land as well as to the people of France. Her immovable features and startlingly blue eyes are often said to pierce through to the soul of those who look upon her. This painting embodies the canonization era's devotion and fascination with Joan. Amazingly, this very French painting has been housed at the Metropolitan Museum in New York since the 1880s (*Metropolitan Museum of Art, New York*).

Throughout the nineteenth century and into the early twentieth, the character as well as behavior of women was a constant topic of conversation and writing. A designation from the French Revolution was woman as 'deity of the domestic temple.' A seemingly unrelated development, the establishment of the Immaculate Conception as an article of faith in 1854, singled out Mary as the only human being to be born free of original sin. Stephane Michaud argues that these two phenomena "moved the Church closer to the secular state." He points to works of art that had appeared in the intervening years that collapsed the distance between the two sectors, such as the engravings that portrayed the goddess Reason as a Madonna.[2] Ironically, the same era would see declarations of women's unsuitability for learning on one hand, and the kind of celebration of her capabilities on the other. The most intense concentration of energy on the Woman Question came between 1880 and 1920, with the New Woman appearing by the mid–1890s. Throughout the decades that wrestled with the issues, however, there seemed to be a "kind of force that vanquished ideology and removed woman from the realm of fact. Although contemporaries forthrightly insisted that it was Nature, we cannot take them at their word. No, it was the force of the *image*. The women in these representations are *imaginary*. For the nineteenth century, woman was an idol."[3]

The Old Latin transcripts of the original Trial of Condemnation were uncovered in the late eighteenth century, first by Clement de L'Averdy, who published his study in 1791, and then by Jules Quicherat, who published his five-volume edition from 1841 to 1849.[4] The clash between established authority and emerging factions that characterized Joan's own time was repeated in the ideological struggles of nineteenth-century Europe, with one reversal: the connotation of nationalism. What had been new thinking in the fifteenth century had become the establishment. Therefore, Joan as icon could be attached to either side of the more modern struggle. This new dimension to Joan's story began when the Revolution rescinded the tax exemption for Domrémy (Joan's birthplace), a bequest to Joan from Charles VII. Conversely, in 1803, in promotion of his own image and a "desire to reconcile himself with the Church," Napoleon Bonaparte designated Joan as a national symbol. This action "led to a restoration of her cult, firmly expressed in nationalist terms" and the renewal of the May 8 feast at Orléans.[5]

In an era that raised new questions about the role of the individual in society, Joan's story rang true and a secular movement to redress the historical wrongs began. Despite the fragmentation regarding women's struggles, the crisis of the times once again sparked interest in Joan of Arc as the symbol of the French people. According to Henri Guillemin, French longing for *revanche* (revenge) after the Franco-Prussian War produced a proliferation of statues as well as the 1884 announcement of a national holiday on May 8, the anniversary of the Battle of Orléans.[6] At the same time, the disgrace of the Franco-Prussian War rekindled interest in Joan, especially because she was from Lorraine, the province that would have been lost to the invading Prussians.

Although both sides had claimed Joan as their symbol in that war, France's defeat reinforced Joan's role as saviour to the common people. Her dual role in World War I, described by Regine Pernoud as "the angel of comfort to the dying" or the "general who led her troops to victory,"[7] mirrors the twin images of women and the ongoing questions of their social status. The archetypal issues and open-ended questions inherent in Joan's rise and fall have encouraged perpetual fascination, inspiring writers and artists of various historical periods to present their interpretations. Diverse as these resulting images are, there exists a clear evolution, one that traces the paths of gender construction and class struggles from the early modern period to the twentieth century. Even the *New York Times* of 1920 perceived this, entitling its feature article about Joan's canonization: "From Sorceress to Saint: Final Canonization of Joan of Arc Has Worked This Change in Her Official Ecclesiastical Status." The headline acknowledged the fluidity of these contradictory designations about public women as well as Joan herself.

Worry over anti-clericalism simultaneously convinced the Church to consider Joan of Arc for canonization. Formal panegyrics were sent to the pope in 1869, which started the process. The disgrace of their defeat in the Franco-Prussian War and the recognition that their ruler had neglected the needs of the people led the French to establish the Third Republic. However, contrary to its title, it was a government comprised mainly of royalists. Ironically, this was the result of the fear of republicanism among the French populace, especially within the peasant class. The Paris republicans rebelled against the conservative make-up of the government and broke off. The worst fighting in French history ensued, and the republicans acquiesced. Therefore "the Third Republic was born in an atmosphere of class hate and social terror."[8] In the midst of all of this social upheaval, the Church conducted its inquiries. Joan was declared venerable in 1894, and beatified in 1909, at which time 1931, the five hundredth anniversary of her burning, was set for her canonization.

The pope who received the first panegyrics to request canonization for Joan of Arc was Pius IX. In 1846 he had been known as the "liberal pope," but the revolution of 1848 had changed his position dramatically. Pius' reforming minister was assassinated, and the pope himself had fled Rome. The intervention of French troops restored his position in 1849; the troops remained as protectors until the outbreak of the Franco-Prussian War. Obviously, there was mutual interest between Pius and the French, but no decision was reached at that point. What matters is that the breach between the Catholic Church and liberalism that had started with the French Revolution widened after 1848.[9]

The year 1870 was a turning point in church/state relations. When the French troops left for the war, Italy seized control of Rome and removed the pope's temporal powers.[10] In turn, the Church held a Vatican Council and established the now familiar concept of "papal infallibility." The actions of both sides indicate clearly why the official view of Joan became increasingly conservative between the time of the panegyrics (1869) and the declaration of her venerability (1904). Thus a contradiction arose between the ideology of the literary apologists for Joan as heroine and political visionary, and the Church's representation of Joan as a virgin martyr, thereby removing the process of canonization from the liberal spirit that engendered it in the first place. One essence of Joan's appeal, her pure and original approach to life, was compromised once again, as great care was taken by the Church to present Joan's story within acceptable notions of a young lady's reputation. The softening of Joan's notorious blunt tongue and impatience served as a requisite wrap; the layers of sentimentality served the same purpose as a velvet cape did to hide a nineteenth-century lady's bare shoulders from public view. Joan's confrontation with the power structure, considered outrageous behavior in her lifetime, was transformed into pious zeal: presumption became ingenuousness. Interestingly, the Church's representation of Joan clearly placed her on the conservative side of the nineteenth-century gender war: the "woman question." Focus on Joan's feminine virtues softened the rougher edges of Joan's career, aligning her within the guidelines of woman's proper "sphere."

By the time panegyrics were sent to the pope in 1869 to begin the canonization process for Joan of Arc, women crusading for suffrage and temperance, and against slavery and slave-like working conditions in factories, were lampooned in magazines as would-be men, abandoning crying infants to helpless fathers wearing aprons, while they were dressed in menswear-inspired skirt suits, with starched collars.[11] Joan, a military leader and notorious public figure in her own time, was recast in secular as well as religious formats as an acceptable model of young womanhood, and thus the "Maid of Orléans" became the chaste, obedient devotee of higher powers. Joan's outrageous worldly behavior, the confrontations with the power structure, and steadfast belief in her own authority that caused her downfall, were encased in sentimentalized frameworks. The contradiction is transparent to us, but was it to them? If an illiterate adolescent could save France in the fifteenth century, why were her nineteenth-century counterparts portrayed as women who no longer recognized their true and sacred duties?

Carol Mattingly, in the introduction to her study of women's dress and rhetorical style, emphasizes that individual women were not usually the threat: it was the collective effort that engendered the flurry of headlines insulting the participants in women's conventions in language that referenced articles of women's clothing. Mattingly cites examples such as these from the mid-nineteenth century: 'Insurrection of Petticoats,' 'Women's Scramble for the Breeches,' 'Corset-Strings and Suffrage,' and 'A Bustline Army of Crusaders.'[12] Such synecdochic designations reduced women's goals, but likewise revealed the gender blurring which it was feared women's public roles would promote. In no way do these headlines announce concern over the causes themselves. Joan of Arc understood that she had to dress according to the function she was commanded to perform by her Voices, as her trial testimony confirmed. When questioned for months about why she persisted in wearing male garments, she finally called her mode of dress "a small thing:" Joan saw what her accusers would not.

In light of the abovementioned factors, it clearly was the nineteenth century that seems destined to reconsider the status of Joan of Arc. Interlaced social struggles over gender construction and roles, governmental design, religion, and the demands of a rising proletariat intersected the variables surrounding Joan of Arc's career, and her mistreatment. The Romantics had seen her as a child-like wonder, but one of nature. Once the historical data was disseminated, the push toward canonization intensified and Joan was idealized further. Her assertive manner and military acumen became overshadowed by emphasis on her victimization, spiritual devotion, and more feminine virtues.

Jean Jacques Rousseau had written two prominent works in the 1760s, *The Social Contract* and *Emile*, from which the basis for the above casting of Joan derived. In each, he emphasized the primacy of "natural" tendencies for men and women. The relevant concept from *The Social Contract* was Rousseau's assertion that the "oldest form of society — and the only natural one — is the family."[13] *Emile* posited that public domains were for men, while women should concentrate on pleasing men and influencing them in private: "In the union of the sexes, each alike contributes to the common end but not in the same way. [This] may be observed in the moral relations.... The one should be active and strong, the other passive and weak. It is necessary that the one have the power and the will; it is enough that the other should offer little resistance." If such sentiments seemed to be the basis of the family structure to Rousseau, he obviously felt patriarchy was as natural as it was essential, according to the following remarks:

> Men and women are made for each other, but their mutual dependence is not equal. Man is dependent on woman through his desires; woman is dependent on man through her desires and also through her needs. He could do without her better than she can do without him. For women to have what is necessary to them; for them to fulfill their role we must provide for them, we must want to provide for them, we must believe them to be worthy of it.[14]

Rousseau went on to say that women relied on their "charms," men on their powers of reason. He scolded the idleness of women, which even his opponents would applaud. It was Rousseau's pairing of feminine wiles and power in personal relationships that confounded his detractors. How could such a position be consistent with his belief that women were innately superior morally? Mary Wollstonecraft's *The Vindication of the Rights of Woman* (1792) confirmed the assault on women's frivolity, but argued squarely against Rousseau's premises for its foundation. In this work, which was written as a corollary to *The Rights of Man*, Wollstonecraft was responding to the then-ongoing "feminization" of culture, particularly middle-class culture, which made propriety a central concern, not merely related to matters of etiquette. There had been two perspectives of "woman" offered in the seventeenth and early eighteenth centuries:

woman as a courtly, showy presence, and woman as a domestic paragon of virtue. The one influential writer to combine factors from each was Jean Jacques Rousseau. The ideal woman for him was docile and virtuous, and a moral inspiration to her acknowledged superior, the man in her life. Rousseau thus undermined the vanity of the courtly mistress.

To rebut the model of the morally reprehensible, decorous female, Wollstonecraft argued for sufficient education and physical exercise to give women challenge and discipline.[15] Like other women writers that preceded and followed her, Wollstonecraft urged the designation of virtue regardless of gender. According to Gary Kelly's study of Wollstonecraft, *Revolutionary Feminism*, the designation of gender roles and privileges that followed from Rousseau was part of the establishment of the middle class as a dominant force in popular culture. As Kelly phrases it: "Whereas man thinks, reasons and abstracts, woman feels, sympathizes, and puts into practice." A key distinction would be the "putting into practice" aspect, as this could be read both as private and public. If women were credited with action following feeling/instinct, then their actions could be enabling the men in their lives, or establishing socially conscious institutions that were wider in scope. Capitalizing on the desire for individuals to act as citizens rather than subjects of a monarch, Wollstonecraft posited that women's first two duties were "to themselves as rational creatures" and then as citizens/mothers. She bemoaned the social system that barred them from participation, accusing it of turning women into "mere dolls. Or should they turn to something more important than merely fitting drapery upon a smooth block ... they have it not in their power to take the field and march and counter-march like soldiers, or wrangle in the senate to keep their faculties from rusting."[16]

Such an argument was reminiscent of Joan of Arc's sudden appearance during the Hundred Years War, as well as her tactics during her career. In the weeks before the Siege of Orléans, Joan dictated letters to the English king and his regents, offering them an honorable peace, but only if they gave in to her commands. In the excerpt that follows, Joan presumes power of gender and class lines, and, more to the point here, acts in ways appropriate to both masculine and feminine behavior: "Surrender to the Maid, who is sent here by God, King of Heaven, the keys to all the good towns you have taken and violated in France. She is come from God to uphold the blood royal. She is ready to make peace with you if you will do justice, relinquishing France and paying for what you have withheld."[17] In this terse paragraph, Joan of Arc displayed a true melding of gendered persuasive strategies, and was obviously cognizant of the brazenness her mission demanded.

Joan of Arc had acted in both of these ways, albeit in a style that came off as more abrasive. She had the instinctive ability to rally support among the faithful, but an equally impressive way of alienating those in opposition. There must have been something eerily familiar then to a power structure confronted with women demanding a greater share of public roles, whether approached in acceptable manner — solicitous—

or by more masculine self-assertion. In a similar vein, the intrinsic part of the arguments set forth by Wollstonecraft and her followers logically focused on behavior and traits, rather than biology.[18]

After the publication of the trial transcripts by Quicherat, a steady flow of histories and biographies urged the formal redressing of Joan's official status; many of these works cast Joan in an heroic, martyr role. The first of these biographies, Jules Michelet's *Joan of Arc* (1847), recognized the inherent drama in the situation surrounding Joan's career, and used it to underscore public indignation. His portrait of Joan argued for action to redress Joan's compromised historical status, but depicted an outstanding individual who was, nevertheless, a child of the countryside and of humble origin. Michelet acknowledged Joan's accomplishments, but laid more heavy emphasis on the emotional heartstrings attached to the unfolding of her life story. In literature as well as the plastic arts of the nineteenth century, Joan of Arc was similarly transformed into a sentimentalized heroine, as were other women subjects who were, in turn, objectified as weak and/or charming figures.

The correlation between exceptionality and heroism informed their individual representations of Joan as a model young woman. As cultural products of their own time, portions of the works reflected either the misogynistic or paternalistic attitudes towards their subject. Joan's well-known explanation that the Voices first "terrified" her because she felt unworthy and unprepared to fulfill their commands would appeal to the construction of Joan as a sentimental heroine: a virtuous but helpless young woman in need of male guidance and protection. The following statement illustrates both realistic and social consciousness on her part: "I told them I was a poor girl who knew nothing of riding and warfare."[19] Once Joan recognized that she was not solely acting on her own, her words conveyed the faith and strength that would both make and break her: "But since God had commanded me to go, I must do it. And since God had commanded it, had I a hundred fathers and a hundred mothers, and had I been a king's daughter, I would have gone. It pleased God thus to act through a simple maid in order to turn back the King's enemies."[20] In these few sentences, Joan reconfirmed her trust in God and the higher order of rules that faith represented. Simultaneously, her dismissal of long-established practices of parent/child relations emerged. The last sentence anticipated the retort, and also confirmed the closeness between the King's authority and its divine origin.

One issue repeatedly emphasized by her nineteenth-century biographers was Joan's recantation at the Trial of Condemnation, 1431. Writers offered diverse explanations of the lapse in faith that led Joan to disavow her Voices to save her own life. Biographers assumed that her regret and subsequent introspection might also have given Joan a more in-depth understanding of the duplicity of her judges, which, in turn, gave her the courage to face the fire. Michelet's version of this characterized the conviction of Joan as a "relapsed heretic" for her return to male clothing as outrageous because the guards had stolen her dress. The true character of Joan was noted by all when "clothed in woman's garb ... put on a cart" she was dragged to the stake. At the same time, he represented a Romantic penchant for the long-suffering heroine of sentimental fiction and melodrama by focusing on the especially large pyre. Michelet recognized the drama within the historical fact. The large pyre made her death slow and painful, designed to please the crowd and, more importantly, to "expose at last some flaw ... wrench from her some cries that might be given out as recantation ... barely articulate words that could be so twisted ... a craven prayer ... as one would expect from a woman demented with terror."[21] Michelet emphasized that Joan retained her dignity and piety, concerning herself with the safety of her well-wishers, asking only for a cross. Those closest to the fire heard only murmuring of Jesus' name. Michelet's story blended melodramatic and gothic elements with documented details: a multifaceted appeal for mid-nineteenth-century readers in particular.

Another aspect of Joan's testimony regarding her Voices that was especially difficult for her judges to reconcile was their concrete representation. She claimed: "I saw them with my bodily eyes as well as I see you."[22] Michelet perceived the need for Joan's patriarchal authorities to seek answers that conformed to their notions. As modern interpreters, we are likely to perceive this answer as evidence for her sound mind, but her contemporary analysts were disturbed over the atypical nature of Joan's "mystical" experience.[23] However, they, too, were struck by her consistent and vivid replies. The issue of her state of mind was clearly in the minds of the University of Paris doctors, since they used it as one of two criteria for her punishment: the other stipulation was her remaining obdurate by refusing to bend to the authority of the Church Militant.[24] Joan's common sense was more than the scholarly logicians who judged her could bear. They were "all the more cruel because they could not despise her as a mere lunatic, because, more than once, she invoked a higher reason which silenced their reasoning."[25]

Ultimately, great effort was made to appeal to Joan's faith and its accompanying obedience. Finally, a combination of physical illness and mental exhaustion caused her to give in, to abjure. Joan was told on May 23 that she must confess or face the fire. A sermon was preached to her in the public square, urging her to return to the bosom of the Church and save her life. What Joan did not understand was that she would be imprisoned for life; what she could not know was that Cauchon's promise to release her from the English would be broken. What the authorities could not predict was the reaction of the crowd when Joan abjured. As Michelet put it: "it was not only the common soldiery, the English *mob* that evinced thirst for blood. Substantial people, men of high station, the lords, were as savage as the rabble." Stones had been hurled at the cardinal and the doctors from the university. England's representative, Warwick, recognized: "Ill fares the King in all this: the woman is not to be burnt."[26]

Jules Quicherat's five-volume translation of the trial records offered crucial evidence for the push toward her canonization; they also put forward a much more positive image of Joan's personal power. According to James Darmesteter, a French historian viewing English attitudes in 1896, Quicherat was the man who: "best served

Joan of Arc ... [he] showed how, far from being a simple enthusiast in the hands of political wire-pullers, Joan knew how to assert herself and dominate, aye transform, her environment."[27]

Jacques Barzun's analysis of Michelet stressed the fusion of revolutionary and conservative perspectives: an ongoing trend in Michelet's time. Barzun claimed it's not surprising that both permeated Michelet's biography of Joan of Arc. For the people, however, the effect of Napoleon's actions went beyond the regime, as Michelet's impassioned, documented portrait of Joan crystallized.[28] The Romantic historians were not as blatantly one-sided in their view of history as the early chroniclers were, but neither were they as concerned with accuracy as their twentieth-century counterparts would be. Therefore, reading Michelet requires an understanding of history's new role in the nineteenth century. Ideologically, according to Jacques Barzun, its "aim was rather to heal the wounds inflicted by decades of social turmoil and achieve a reconciliation of all parties in support of the new national state."[29]

Barzun's assessment provides an impressive encapsulization of Michelet's probable purpose, but Darmesteter provided another important angle: the fixity versus fluidity of gender politics. In his statement about Quicherat, the gendered descriptions are an obvious reference to the "New Woman" of the 1890s. If Joan was not "simple," aka childlike and naïve, and she could "dominate," "assert," and "transform," rather than manipulate, cajole, or influence, Darmesteter seemed to show that even in 1896 a Joan figure could be problematic; conversely, what the new women of the 1890s were capable of had been in the public realm far earlier.

Even if the suffrage and labor leaders were labeled "unnatural," as their Renaissance foremothers had been, that was evidence of the fixity of the ideological aspects their actions touched. In *The Subjection of Women*, Mill argued this very point, focusing on his own time's leftover mentality regarding women: "The social subordination of women [is] an isolated fact in modern social institutions; a solitary breach of what has become their fundamental law; a single relic of an old world of thought." Without pinpointing the relic precisely, Mill went on to intimate the prevalent perspective from the late Renaissance through the Enlightenment: "It will not do ... to assert ... that the experience of mankind has pronounced in favour of the existing system. Experience cannot possibly have decided between two courses, so long as there has only been experience of one. If it be said that the doctrine of the equality of the sexes rests only on theory, it must be remembered that the contrary doctrine also has only theory to rest upon."[30]

Barzun stressed the fusion of revolutionary and conservative "agendas" that informed its purpose. The first feature of Michelet's work to earmark its uniqueness was its presentation of Joan as a member of a family. Again, Barzun provided the context: "To a generation raised on Jean Jacques Rousseau, the importance of childhood and family was axiomatic."[31] Within this framework, it is easy to appreciate Michelet's enraptured depiction of Joan learning her religion by her mother's side; he contends that Joan's religion came to her: "not as a lesson or a ceremony, but in the folk-like and naive form of a lovely tale told of an evening, like the simple faith of a mother. That which we thus receive with our blood and our milk is a living thing is life itself."[32]

It is therefore very plausible that Joan "absorbed" the actions of the women saviours in the Old Testament (Deborah, Judith) and the prophesy of Merlin, that a Virgin from Joan's very region would save the kingdom that Charles VII's "unnatural" mother from Bavaria had given away to the English in the Treaty of Troyes, 1420.[33] Not only is it logical to presume that a child's imagination would be incapable of distinguishing between the two examples, but it is also imperative to note that Michelet's assessment belied his belief in Rousseau's prescription for limited education for girls.[34] Conversely, Michelet applauded her folk wisdom, explaining that the countryside she grew up in "offered another kind of poetry, fierce, atrocious, and, alas! All too real: the poetry of war!"[35]

The region of Joan's birth (between Lorraine and Champagne) likewise accounted for several salient traits in Joan, and this helps us to understand Michelet's position on "the people." To his mind, the proletariat was not considered; rather, his focus was on "the solid peasantry and ... the artisans of pre-industrial France."[36] In Michelet's explanation, Lorrainers were "brave ... born fighters, but they are inclined to be wily and crafty" while folk of Champagne lack asperity; they are gentle, "a blend of simplicity, good sense, and shrewdness." It was the combination of these qualities, especially her common sense, that gave Joan her "eminent originality" because young women having visions or even bearing arms were, according to Michelet, "known occurrences."[37]

This perspective marked the beginning of representing Joan as a heroine of the people because of her similarity to them. To Michelet, Joan clearly was stouthearted. A good indication was the way he described her determination to obey her voices; she gathered her courage, and told those close to her: "I alone can bring succor, though I should prefer to stay at home by my mother's side, and spin; for this is not my work; but go I must, and accomplish it, for such is the will of my Lord."[38,39]

Michelet's insight also encompassed the dubiousness of Joan's "inappropriate" image as a female warrior. Therefore, the description of Joan's male attire emphasizes the practicalities of the clothing as well as a rationale for her persistently wearing it. "Tight-fitting, strongly fastened," these garments would be her "best protection."[40] If Michelet's terms alluded to chastity, I believe this was quite intentional because he reminds his readers that Joan's virgin state, and its connection to divine inspiration, was consistently a key factor. Further, since it was widely accepted that the devil couldn't compact with a virgin, her desire to keep herself "asexual" should have been automatically understood. Michelet's tone regarding this was one of perplexity, as friends and foes alike found her transvestism a "cause of scandal ... after her capture, these worthy dames [guards] entreated her to dress as a well-behaved girl should."[41] If her own gender could not rise above convention in this, how could her male judges? As a result:

"science, driven into a corner, unwilling or unable to pass upon the delicate distinction between holy and satanic inspirations, referred a matter of the soul to a test of the flesh, made this grave spiritual problem depend on the mystery of a woman's body."[42]

In light of the way Michelet viewed women, the assessment cited above takes on even deeper meaning. The way Jacques Barzun explains it: "Man owes the original gift of material life to woman, to nature, but woman and nature are dependent on man ... for rebirth to the life of the spirit ... [their] evolution is from mother to daughter, from mistress to ward."[43] Such an attitude clearly informs Michelet's perception of Joan as a superior individual, close to what he considered an ideal woman: one who was "almost a man."[44] Yet for all his fervor about Joan's virtues, Michelet was a shrewd judge of the effects of the glory upon her, declaring that her rise to prominence and power led inevitably to the alteration of her "heroic simplicity ... loss of integrity.... One cannot become rich, honored, the equal of lords and princes, all of a sudden, without having to pay the price."[45] Interestingly, here Joan's gender is not part of the frame of reference; for this instance, corruption by power can happen to anyone, but especially an individual not born to privilege.

Later in the book, Michelet stirred the emotions of his readers in true Romantic style, by concentrating on Joan's ordeal after her triumphs—when she was captured in Compiègne. He argued that it was: "essential ... without it her image would never have been cast in the public, historic imagination.... She had to undergo that suffering. Without the ordeal and the purification of her last moments, dubious shadows would have remained in the radiance of that holy figure; she would not have stood in the memory of men as THE MAID OF ORLÉANS."[46] Despite its historical inaccuracy then, Friedrich Schiller's play of the same title from 1801 captured this same essential point. In creating his Joan, Schiller was convinced that the missing piece of the story as he had heard it was classical tragedy's structure and premise, so he invented this context. Joan's *perpeteia*, however, was not caused by love of power, but love of a man, an English soldier. She thereby betrayed her promise to remain pure and was killed in battle. Schiller's play was written in staunch opposition to Voltaire's mock epic of 1762, which downplayed Joan's power as well as her spiritual heroism. By elevating the story, however, Schiller diluted the character, as his Joan was infused with the paternalistic attitudes towards women that remained popular in his own time, and even in the twentieth century.[47]

An English writer who at once appreciated the aura surrounding Joan as well as her material accomplishments was Thomas DeQuincey. Acquainted with William Wordsworth and Samuel Taylor Coleridge, DeQuincey knew Robert Southey's epic poem about Joan of Arc written in 1796, and may also have heard about Coleridge's and/or Charles Lamb's responses to that work. DeQuincey's insightful essay "Joan of Arc" first appeared in 1849. But DeQuincey's response was directed towards Michelet's portrait. DeQuincey viewed Joan's situation as part of a vaster historical continuum than did Michelet. DeQuincey evinces a preternatural awareness of Joan's eventual canonization, in a single sentence: "When the thunders of universal France, as even yet may happen, shall proclaim the grandeur of the poor shepherd girl that gave up all for her country, thy ear, young shepherd girl, will have been deaf for five centuries."[48] He went on to speculate as to why the mid-nineteenth century was the appropriate time to rekindle interest in the fate of Joan. "Might it not have been left till the spring of 1947, or, perhaps, left till called for? Yes, but it *is* called for, and clamorously."[49] DeQuincey elaborated by emphasizing the traits of Joan's so "fitting" to his own time: her "natural piety" and her daring to confront authorities whose agenda was not in the best interest of the people. While Southey and Schiller wrote during the aftermath of the French Revolution, DeQuincey's argument followed the revolutions of 1848, giving him the added perspective of the cyclical nature of political situations in Western Europe.

In other places in his essay, however, DeQuincey's focus shifted to examination of the details of Joan's life at home,[50] her father and his autocracy, and the treatment of women in "chivalrous France not very long before the French Revolution: 'A peasant was ploughing; and the team that drew his plough was a donkey and a woman.'"[51] Such an image was ample evidence for DeQuincey to conclude this to be Joan's reason for emphasizing her spinning! That Joan was a victim of this peasant culture was important to him, and he criticizes Michelet for going along with Joan's friend Hauviette's perspective on this. This connection is important to support the idea that Joan's time was a part of a movement towards change that was still ongoing in 1849. What is questionable was DeQuincey's transference of his own political acumen to Joan. He claimed that she recognized the problems of her own age as "one section in a vast mysterious drama, unweaving through a century back, and drawing nearer continually to some dreadful crisis."[52] The rest of his argument blended additional praise for her intellect and the idealized, Romantic image of Joan as a people's heroine: "Oh child of France! shepherdess, peasant girl! trodden under foot by all around thee, how I honour thy flashing intellect, quick as God's lightning, and true as God's lightning to its mark, that ran before France and laggard Europe by many a century, confounding the malice of the ensnarer, and making dumb the oracles of falsehood!"[53]

In a parallel time frame to the newer representations of Joan of Arc, women began to organize, pushing for legal status, educational and employment opportunities, and suffrage. Over the next several decades, the women's movement developed a myriad of strategies, from the most radical to the more traditional approaches to a similar end: parity with men. A crucial component of these was the use of woman's sphere as more than a starting point; it became the given around which to build their bridges.

In France, the best-known woman writer at the time of Michelet's biography was George Sand. She is an important benchmark here because of her ideological stance, and because she was both admired and reviled for her lifestyle as well as her work, just as Wollstonecraft had been. Each of these women had escaped an abusive relationship, and lived and loved more freely than most women dared. So their personal choices opened the door to scathing critiques of their lives in the disguise of their literary premises.

In the case of Wollstonecraft, the most pointed attack came from the Reverend Richard Polwhele. As Allison Sulloway notes, his lengthy and scrupulously footnoted essay, "The Unsex'd Females," classified any women writers who wrote on behalf of women's education or parity with men as "Wollstonecraftian" because they "dared to vindicate *The Rights of womankind*." He gloated over Wollstonecraft's love affairs, her marriage to Godwin late in her pregnancy, and, above all, her agonizing death in childbirth as "Providential ... [so] that the effect of an irreligious conduct, might be manifest to the world."[54] Sand's conduct was even more shocking than Wollstonecraft's, however, on three levels: her novels establishing women's right to full and independent lives, even in the bedroom, her own multiple love affairs, and her cross-dressing.

As with Joan of Arc, Sand's costume choice came from necessity rather than principle, at least at the outset. Once she left her husband, Sand found work writing reviews of plays and art. The pay was scant, and she had to buy her own tickets. Worse still, a lady was expected to sit in the boxes, and so the tickets cost more than her remuneration. Fortunately, a friend suggested that she attend performances in men's apparel to save money. Unfortunately, there was already a "whiff of androgyny" attached to her name, which "became stronger as she appeared dressed in men's clothes elsewhere also. She paid little attention to it, finding that this style of dress made her ... free as a bird. 'Lounging, cigar in mouth,' as one journal put it, she was able to ... pass as unnoticed as any young male journalist."[55] Although Sand continued to live life in both masculine and feminine guise, her behavior certainly upset social standards and directly confronted the images of public women.

Proto-feminist though she was, George Sand backed away from immediate roles for women in government, but for very different reasons. Offered a post in 1848, she turned it down because she felt it was premature: the structure of society had to change internally (privately) before such work would truly matter. Sand's primary cause was the refocusing of the family structure, and the subsequent undoing of Rousseau's "natural" paradigm described above. Turning the tables back on the Central Committee, Sand wrote on the subject of the emancipation of women, claiming that it could be "immediately brought about to the extent that our present state of morals allows. It would consist simply in giving back to the woman all the civil rights which marriage alone takes from her, and which she may preserve only by remaining unmarried."[56] It was the moral center of her argument.

Sand closed her letter of refusal for the political post with this recommendation: "So, civil equality, equality in marriage, equality in the family, this is what you can and what you must seek and demand...."[57] Sand incorporated her own theories into her last published work, the novella *Marianne*. Written in 1876, but set fifty years earlier, it illustrated the attitudes of various social classes regarding love, marriage, and friendship. Despite her name, the title character did not represent French womanhood, as the allegorical "Marianne" had since the French Revolution.[58] Rather, Sand presented her as someone fortunate enough to have an independent income and a mind that longed for knowledge, reminiscent of Sand herself. More importantly, Sand implied that the symbol of womanhood, whether that be Marianne or Jeanne d'Arc, should be reconfigured if society were to progress.

One of England's most popular poets, Elizabeth Barrett Browning, wrote elegiac sonnets to George Sand and satirized domesticity in her semi-autobiographical "Aurora Leigh" around the same time that Michelet's biography appeared. Barrett Browning lauded Sand as a "large-brained woman and large-hearted man,/ Self-called George Sand" whom the poet considered "True genius, but true woman! dost deny/ The woman's nature with a manly scorn,/ And break away the gauds and armlets worn/ By weaker women in captivity?"[59] Clearly, Barrett Browning was reconsidering woman's nature here, and did so in depth in the longer poem. In Book I of "Aurora Leigh," Aurora chafed at the confinement mentioned in the poems to Sand. Her aunt made sure that she concentrated on appropriate activities for a woman of the upper class: "I read a score of books on womanhood/ To prove, if women do not think at all,/ They may teach thinking.../ Their right of comprehending husband's talk/ When not too deep, and even of answering/ ...As long as they never say 'no' when the world says 'ay,'/ For that is fatal.— Their angelic reach/ Of virtue, chiefly used to sit and darn."[60] "Aurora Leigh" clearly took a stance against restrictions on women's intellect and also took on Coventry Patmore's 1854 poem "The Angel in the House," an extensive panegyric to the dutiful woman described in the books Aurora Leigh loathed. Ironically, Patmore's title became a shorthand for the paternalistic attitudes toward women that were at the heart of the "woman question."

England's monarch Victoria ascended the throne in 1837, when she was only seventeen, and would rule until 1901. Yet it was more as a social than as a political influence that Victoria reigned. No friend to the women's rights movement, Victoria believed in and embodied Patmore's ideal woman. She was both a persona and a woman, and Victoria apparently had no trouble with her identification as the middle-class-mother queen. She took her domestic duties very seriously, and raised nine children. Although later generations would label Victoria/ Victorian as prudish, prudence was equally the guiding spirit of the age. As the editors of the *Norton Anthology of English Literature* express it: "Victoria encouraged her own identification with the qualities she admired: earnestness, moral responsibility, domestic propriety."[61] By the time of her reign, the English monarch had far less direct influence than in the time of Elizabeth I. For Victoria, women could accomplish a great deal from their secondary position because at home they were the guiding force.

Queen Victoria's favorite poet was Alfred, Lord Tennyson, and he was equally favored in popular opinion.[62] A poet of wide scope, his perspective on women was startlingly consistent. Like Patmore, he believed in patriarchal society, but also seemed convinced, like the medieval characters he brought to life, in the ability of women to ennoble men. He also had no trouble portraying women as seeking death or being appreciated as beautiful when dead. "The Lady of Shalott" (1832/1842) provides a clear example. In Part I, the Lady in the poem lives in a "silent isle" that "imbowers" her (lines 17–18). In familiar female imagery, the Lady waves from the window. Part II informs us that she is under a "curse" if she looks toward Camelot. So she weaves and checks her work in a mirror, from which "Shadows of the world appear" (line 48). As the Lady observes young people in pairs on their way to Camelot, she says to herself "I am half sick of shadows" (line 71). The tragic turn comes in Part III when she catches a glimpse of Lancelot and is immediately smitten. After years of restraint, she abandons her work at the loom and looks down to Camelot. Immediately, the mirror cracks and she knows the curse is upon her. Finally, in Part IV, she faces her doom. As if in a trance, she goes to her boat, "Lying, robed in snowy white/ That loosely flew to left and right" (lines 136–7), and sings as she floats in the stream, and dies shortly thereafter. Her boat arrives in Camelot, whereupon the knights cross themselves in fear, but Lancelot "mused a little space;/ He said, 'She has a lovely face;/ God in his mercy lend her grace,/ The Lady of Shalott.'"[63]

Tennyson's trademark melancholy and idealization of the past are present here, but can these obscure the image of the imprisoned woman, lovely after death — or perhaps lovely *only* after death? Ambiguity, intended or otherwise, permeates the poems of the era and reflects the desire to literally put women on shelves (or in coffins) or in frames — to be admired as objects and repressed as vital individuals. The first half of the poem evokes the pathos of Lady Shalott's situation, and her unspoken longing. Images of silence and enclosure, on the other hand, present a clear picture of doom from the outset. The long-suffering victim of a curse she does not know the cause of fulfills it at last, but Tennyson never discloses whether or not her few moments of rapture seemed worth the cost to her. Read as a proper Victorian woman, Lady Shalott epitomizes the passivity and acceptance that was considered woman's lot. If Tennyson saw women as innately noble, she fits the bill. From a more modern feminist stance, however, Tennyson presented the Victorian reading public with a static picture. While reminiscent of Rapunzel or Snow White, the magic of love did not solve all in this tale.

An even clearer inversion of fairy tale elements was Tennyson's long poem with songs, "The Princess" (1839/1847). In style and structure, it resembles a medieval romance, but clearly represented his own era's struggle over gender roles. In Canto I, a curse on the prince's family set up fine dramatic foreshadowing: a sorcerer had foretold, on his deathbed, that the family would be unable to know "shadow from substance." Rather than a world of magic, however, the poem traced the issues of masculine vs. feminine domains that were at the heart of the woman question. Princess Ida has forsworn marriage and founded a university for women only, despite the fact that she had been betrothed, as an infant, to a prince. In Canto II, Tennyson revealed more of the arguments of his generation about gender, including the notion that the larger size of heads in men also extended to their brains. Tennyson does all this to "prove" that women could not achieve what men could, but with a twist. Women's achievements and potential were not discounted: "the brain was like the hand, and grew/ With using.... But women ripen'd earlier, and her life/ Was longer/ and albeit their glorious names/ Were fewer, scatter'd stars," women had their ancestors of achievement in diverse arts: government, Queen Elizabeth, war, "The peasant Joan and others," and grace, "Sappho and others vied with any man."[64] The public platforms on both sides of the Atlantic would soon showcase women who satirized as well as challenged this supposedly accepted notion.

Princess Ida's "affianced" had long dreamed of marrying Ida and had a picture near his bed, an unusual factor for the hero and not the heroine, and determined to win her over. He and two companions dressed as women to gain entrance, an instance of transvestism that reverses the stories of medieval women saints who wore monks' cloaks to enter monasteries. When a battle ensued, the prince's father invaded to rescue his son (another interesting twist) and to force Ida to marry him: return from inversion. Since patriarchy has to win, the university became a hospital, since these were controlled by men and only recently had allowed women to train as nurses. Ida relented. The hospital is anachronistic for fairy tale settings, but most appropriate at the outset of Florence Nightingale's career.[65] The final vision of the prince, however, is a vision of a future where men and women could be interdependent. It is in song form, entitled "The Woman's Cause Is Man's," and recognizes that if patriarchal constraints squelch rather than truly support women, all is lost. By no means advocacy of emancipation, it offers a model for a mutually beneficial plan to retain the *status quo*:

> We two will serve them both in aiding her —/ Will clear away the parasitic forms/ That seem to keep her up but drag her down —/ Will leave her space to burgeon out of all/ Within her — let her make herself her own/ To give or keep, to live and learn and be/ All that not harms distinctive womanhood./ For woman is not Undevelopt man,/ But diverse: could we make her as the man,/ Sweet Love were slain:/ His dearest bond is this,/ Not like to like, but like in difference./ Yet in the long years liker must they grow;/ The man be more of woman, she of man" [lines 252–264].[66]

In Victorian England, one woman's attitudes, achievements, and image stood out and were appreciated by soldiers, ordinary people, men of power, and the queen herself: she was Florence Nightingale. Granddaughter of Wollstonecraftian proto-feminists, Florence was raised to be a socialite, despite her father's encouragement of her passion for knowledge. As Princess Ida had done, Miss Nightingale refused marriage, and abhorred the supposedly appropriate activities for women. As the "spheres" dictated, Florence Nightingale wanted to serve others, but not on the fringes of philanthropy. Outraged by the enormous divide between rich and poor in her own neighborhood, Florence organized classes for the female mill workers who lived near her family estate in the Midlands. In these women, she perceived the character traits so prized by the rising tide of feminism in her time: "strength, self-respect, and independence, qualities singularly lacking in most women of her own class."[67]

Nightingale's refusal to marry was more than just disappointing to her family; like families in Jane Austen's novels, hers was bound by entailment, but Florence would not and could not do her duty in that fashion: she felt too strongly that she was bound to do something far more useful for the world. She wrote that since the age of six she had longed for a "necessary occupation, something to fill and employ all my faculties.... The first thought I can remember, and the last, was nursing work."[68] When she was thirty-one, her family ceased to pressure her, and Florence Nightingale became the superintendent of a charitable nursing home. A year later, the Crimean War began, and Nightingale would be given the opportunity to go there because of her connections with those in positions of power, particularly Sidney Herbert, with whom she would have a devoted friendship for many years. The timing was perfect, as Lytton Strachey put it: "For years, Miss Nightingale had been getting ready; at last she was prepared — experienced, free, mature, yet still young ... desirous to serve, accustomed to command." As she got ready to leave, she asked what supplies would be needed; though reassured that all was in order, Nightingale trusted her own instincts and brought money raised from private sources and other provisions, and so the legend around her began almost immediately upon her arrival at the hospital. Florence Nightingale saw conditions that were so deleterious to the men's recovery that she spent weeks getting the place fit for the sick to be in. She sent lengthy dispatches to Sidney Herbert, who began to work on the situation on the home front. The military blunder immortalized by Tennyson in "The Charge of the Light Brigade" (1854), which cost the lives of three-quarters of the six hundred horsemen engaged in a miscalculated skirmish, made it clear that this war was disastrous in many ways. Nightingale had to fight for every improvement through layers of bureaucracy that did not recognize her official capacity because of her gender. Like Joan of Arc, Nightingale never backed down. Strachey commended her for what she accomplished, giving credit to her gender-bending style:

> It was not by gentle sweetness and womanly self-abnegation that she had brought order out of chaos in the Scutatri Hospitals, that, from her own resources, she had clothed the British Army, that she had spread her dominion over the serried and reluctant powers of the official world; it was by strict method, by stern discipline, but rigid attention to detail, by ceaseless labour, by the fixed determination of an indomitable will. Beneath her cool and calm demeanour lurked fierce and passionate fires ... she struck the casual observer simply as the pattern of a perfect lady; but the keener eye perceived something more than that.... As for her voice, it was true of it, even more than of her countenance, that [it] had clear tones [that] were in no need of emphasis.... And they were spoken quietly....[69]

It was the soldiers who saw Florence Nightingale as a ministering angel, "The Lady With the Lamp," who checked on them during the night, and who fostered self-respect and discipline in them. Her actions here were reminiscent of Joan's among the soldiers of the Hundred Years War. Each of these women was a commander of sorts, who believed passionately in what she was doing, and rallying others to find their higher purposes. The royal couple had paid attention, setting Nightingale up as an emissary between the throne and the troops, and sending Florence Nightingale a note and a gift upon her return to England. The brooch, designed by the Prince Consort, "bore a St. George's cross in red enamel, and the Royal cypher surmounted by diamonds." The inscription read "Blessed are the Merciful." Queen Victoria invited her to meet the royal couple, stating that it would be "a very great satisfaction to me to make the acquaintance of one who has set so bright an example to our sex."[70] The meeting proved to the royal couple, particularly the queen, that Florence Nightingale had performed her duties with aplomb, and when the nurse told them of the wretched state of military hospitals, Victoria exclaimed, "Such a *head*. I wish we had her at the War Office."[71]

What remains a mystery is why Victoria chose not to place Nightingale in the War Office, but what is very clear was both the depth and breadth the queen saw in woman's duties, defined as a "sphere" in 1839 by Sarah Stickney Ellis. Ellis' most famous concept, "disinterested kindness," incorporated several aspects of the ideal Victorian woman, from the standpoint of patriarchal society. Despite her own public voice through writing, Ellis urged the women of England to recognize and glorify their domestic responsibilities. There was no doubt in Ellis' mind or thinking that women could compete with men; rather, they had innate moral sensibilities that remained more intact than men's if women did not participate in the "tainted" world of commerce and government. As industrialization permeated more and more of western culture, its ethical paradoxes spilled over into all aspects of life. How could people consider themselves faithful to religious teachings if their way in the world was fraught with corruption?

The antidote seemed airtight: women at home, where their influence could be valued most. Ellis' oratorical style carried the sentiment as well as the concept; English women had long been charged with "protecting the minor morals of life from whence springs all that is elevated in purpose, and glorious in action. The sphere of their direct personal influence is central, and consequently small; but its extreme operations are as widely extended as the range of human feeling." The loftiness and the essence of Victorian earnestness established here conveyed the key double point; despite their apparently subservient position, women's elevated sense of duty to put others before themselves made them paradigms of virtue. Ellis then defined what she felt made women valued: "I have little hesitation in saying—for her disinterested kindness. Look at all the heroines, whether of romance or reality—at all the female characters that are held up to universal admiration.... Have these been the learned, the accomplished women.... No, or if they have, they have also been women who were dignified with the majesty of moral greatness."[72]

The epistolary as well as governmental debate centered around the sentimental idealization of woman's role as explored by John Ruskin in his 1864 address "Of Queen's

Gardens" versus the more realistic dressing-down of patriarchy that was the central thrust of John Stuart Mill's 1869 pamphlet, *The Subjection of Women*. Ruskin's "Of Queen's Gardens" placed heavy emphasis on the innate moral superiority of women, and Ellis was a subtext. Mill's *On the Subjugation of Women*, conversely, followed a far different "tradition" regarding women and education; his premise and examples are more reminiscent of Wollstonecraft. John Stuart Mill argued passionately for women's legal rights as part of his plea for reorienting male/female relationships along truly egalitarian lines, much like his own relationship with Harriet Taylor. In an insightful analysis of the psychological "imprisonment" of women, Mill claims: "All causes, social and natural, combine to make it unlikely that women should be collectively rebellious to the power of men. They are so far in a position different from all other subject classes, that their masters require something more from them than actual service. Men do not want solely the obedience of women, they want their sentiments."[73] Mill's answer to Rousseau was unmistakable, as was his support of Sand's perspective. The other voice here was Harriet's. In "The Enfranchisement of Women" (1851), Taylor had combined ideas on freedom and self-determination present in her earlier works. In this essay she redefined "sphere": "The proper sphere for all human beings is the largest and highest which they are able to attain ... what this is cannot be ascertained without complete liberty of choice." Another salient point she made here was that the earlier distinctions between masculine and feminine behavior, particularly regarding violent displays as recreation for men, had diminished, so she asserted that in her own time home was more and more the center of interest for men and "they have now scarcely any tastes but those they have in common with women, and for the first time in the world, men and women are really companions."[74]

The female characters in Shakespeare are, according to Ruskin, the only heroic figures in Shakespeare. Ruskin also points to the Greek heroines of Homer and the Greek tragedians. In reading literary history, Ruskin foregrounded the steadfastness, virtue and "natural" rule of women.[75] Just as "naturally," Ruskin's analysis overlooked the misogyny and paternalism of the Greek models, which serves to underscore his own blindness for an astute reader/listener. One of his remarks actually named Joan of Arc as an example of a woman educated totally by nature; he uses this as evidence for his argument that women do not need the kind of thorough, formal education that men do. In Ruskin's readings of DeQuincey and Michelet, and possibly Southey, he has adopted their Rousseau-like position towards Joan's natural goodness. Ironically, Ruskin had chosen to focus on a heroine who rebelled against the very model of behavior he espoused. The essence of Ruskin's "celebration" of his feminine ideal concentrated on the distinctions between empirical knowledge and intuitive judgment, a pivotal nineteenth-century dichotomy: All such knowledge should be given her as may enable her to understand, and even to aid, the work of men. Yet it should be given, not as knowledge — not as if it were, or could be, for her an object to know — but only to feel, and to judge. It is of no moment, as a matter of pride or perfection in herself, whether she knows many languages or one; but it is of the utmost, that she should be able to show kindness to a stranger, and to understand the sweetness of a stranger's tongue. It is of no moment to her own worth or dignity that she should be acquainted with this science or that; but it is of the highest that she should be trained in habits of accurate thought; that she should understand the meaning, the inevitableness, and the loveliness of natural laws.[76]

Mill went on to counter Ruskin's position as he objected to the nineteenth-century "sentiments" about a woman's "ideal of character." He recognized that women were taught from childhood that they were opposite from men in all ways and must therefore be meek, submissive, and resign their own wills in deference to the men who determined their lots in life. How could they then develop regard for their intellectual powers? Since everything a woman wanted or needed was obtained through a man, "it would be a miracle if the object of being attractive to men had not become the polar star of feminine education and formation of character."[77] Here Mill challenged not only Ruskin, but a woman who had championed woman's sphere of private influence a generation earlier: Ellis.

Ellis, Ruskin and Mill wrote of woman in a general way, but their observations largely spoke of the middle to upper classes, since working-class women did not have the "luxury" of dependence. Mill did acknowledge the advantage taken of poor women by their men, who felt they had the right to assert their dominance in physical ways; Mill included this as part of his invective against the ideology. It was equally significant that women of the working classes dreamed of attaining the status of a lady, and those on the cusp of middle-class status subscribed to inexpensive family magazines that confirmed the "spheres" philosophy. These publications contained fiction as well as journalistic pieces, and were very widely read in the 1840s and 1850s. In light of Ellis' thesis, it is ironic that their large circulation came about because of the development of high-speed presses and the availability of cheaper paper at that time. Most prominent in the contents were stories that instructed the readers on the road to "respectability."[78] The predominance of examination of women was obvious here as well, especially in the "realistic" short fiction concerning young women and their lifestyles. In these, the protagonists were attractive models that demonstrated "to the woman of narrow means that ladyhood is not dependent on income, nor destroyed by the necessity of working, but lies in manners and bearing."[79]

For very different reasons, then, both perspectives on the woman question could find corollaries in the figure of Joan of Arc. In the fifteenth century, the lines between social classes were even less questioned than they were in the nineteenth, but there always have been people who see past these cultural determiners, if a higher cause/authority prompts their inner lives. Undoubtedly, Joan of Arc was such a person; she shrugged off breaches of convention that blocked the way to achieving her ends. This attitude was in keeping with Joan's clear-eyed and practical approach to her day-by-day decisions as well as her steadfastness to her mission. In turn, Joan's words and actions could be understood as both masculine and feminine.

For the reformers just coming to the fore in the 1850s, these disparate threads needed consolidation. No matter how great their private influence could be, there were still no laws to protect married women; they could not own property, nor could they keep money that they earned. Women concerned with making ends meet by their own labor faced worsening conditions and lower wages than men performing similar tasks. In the United States, the women's movement grew out of experiences at the 1840 World's Anti-Slavery Convention in London: women could attend, but not speak. Two women met there and decided to create their own movement: Lucretia Mott and Elizabeth Cady Stanton. By 1848, several women and men spearheaded the Woman's Movement at Seneca Falls, New York, working in conjunction with two major abolitionist leaders, William Lloyd Garrison and Frederick Douglass.

The "Declaration of Sentiments" that was approved by those in attendance covered legal and moral issues, just as its model, the "Declaration of Independence," had in 1776. Its other corollary was Olympe de Gouges' "The Rights of Women," composed in 1791. De Gouges devised 17 Articles to outline what women were entitled to, based on human nature and the revolutionary approach to government then underway. Its Postcript reminded women that the Revolution (in France) had lessened their power and rights, rather than placing men and women as equal beneficiaries in the new order. She urged them to "wake up" and asserted that their share in the new order was "more pronounced scorn, a more marked disdain," and laws that stripped them of dignity and control.[80] The American "Declaration of Sentiments" followed similar stances. Its overall message was the joint responsibility of both women and men for the betterment of society, one that required direct confrontation with the ideological factors that were detrimental: "*Resolved,* That woman has too long rested satisfied in the circumscribed limits which corrupt customs and a perverted application of the Scriptures have marked out for her, and that it is time she should move in the enlarged sphere which her great Creator has assigned her." Here the writers placed blame on the long-standing and presumably "natural" schism between men and women. A later resolution suggested cooperation: "*Resolved therefore,* That, being invested by the Creator with the same capabilities, and the same consciousness of responsibility for their exercise, it is demonstrably the right and duty of woman, equally with man, to promote every righteous cause by every righteous means...."[81]

By 1851, the work of the American movement had reached France, which had had its second political revolution in 1848. Two French feminists, Jeanne Deroin and Pauline Roland, wrote to the Americans at the Second National Convention in 1851. They were imprisoned because of their socialist affiliations and their attempt to gain public office. Their letter encapsulated the hope that labor and gender issues would combine forces and eradicate the obstacles. Men who opposed this way of thinking "evoke force to stifle liberty and forge restrictive laws to establish order by compulsion, woman, guided by fraternity, foreseeing incessant struggles ... makes an appeal to the laborer [in hope that he] recognizes the right of woman, his companion in labor."[82]

In the midst of the canonization process for Joan of Arc, the issues of equality for women and workers of France became disparate, yet each retained centrality in the popular imagination.[83] The Third Republic, begun in 1879, suffered because of fragmentation. As leaders advocated for the rights of the workers, the women of France voiced concern over their own economic and political disenfranchisement. At first it was the socialists who embraced the feminist cause. According to Claire Moses, what began as an all-inclusive concern quickly splintered into a schism between socialist aims and what became known as "bourgeois feminism." Why? The agenda of socialism sought egalitarianism, but asked women to defer their specific concerns. Women of the working classes cared more for economic survival than ideological purity. Part of the socialist ideology was the belief that gender would no longer be a factor if power were shared by all. At the Third Feminist Congress, held in Paris in 1900, the divergent viewpoints met head-on. Bourgeois feminists opposed a day off for servant women, and socialist feminists accused the bourgeois of participating in the oppression of the working classes in France. Only a handful of feminists claimed allegiance to both factions.[84]

Women needed to retain the advantages of their private sphere, as well as their clear-sighted moral vision, but they determined that the more public contexts that surrounded these could no longer be without their direct influence. A neat encapsulization of the method can be seen in Frances Power Cobbe's lecture 6 from her 1880 series, "Duties of Women." Cobbe's focus is on women's "entrance into public life and development of public spirit"; this was necessary because "women's duty is to promote virtue and happiness [not only through] the small powers they may find in their hands, but also to strive to obtain *more extended* powers of beneficence."[85] Sometimes politely asking, but more and more often gathering in public spaces, women from various social ranks made their presence felt, and rallied around Joan of Arc as their inspiration and visual icon.[86]

Perhaps more significant, however, in molding the modern conception of Joan were two biographies written around the time of her beatification: the two-volume *Joan of Arc* by Anatole France (1908) and its Scottish "answer," *The Maid of France* by Andrew Lang (1909). Each of these two writers presents a meticulously researched, minutely detailed description and analysis of the life and times of Joan. Both writers admire her openly and attempt to provide sufficient social context in which to view her and her accomplishments. What separates the works is the degree of autonomy granted to Joan; Anatole France insists in seeing her as one of a "type" while Lang emphasizes her genius and virtue. In Lang's view, A. France returns to the Enlightenment view of Joan as "puppet"; Lang, on the other hand, seems very determined to wrap Joan in the guise of a Victorian "Angel in the House."[87]

In the preface to the English edition of his work, Anatole France graciously acknowledged the English criticism of his work. His only harsh words are for the hagiographers who he said reproached him "not with any manner of explaining the

Above and Opposite: Sarah Bernhardt in male and female costumes—*Le Procès de Jeanne d'Arc* by Emile Moreau (1890). Sarah Bernhardt was middle-aged when she played Joan of Arc, but audiences believed in her portrayal, and these photographs attest to her extraordinary ability to transcend time. Each of these portraits shows Bernhardt as Joan, but the costume matches the gender identity as well as the status of Joan at different points in her life. Bernhardt's early success in breeches roles, and her famous Hamlet from this same decade, crystallize the link between clothing and the creation of personae (***Philip H. Ward Collection, Rare Book & Manuscript Library, University of Pennsylvania***). *Above*: Charles L. Ritzman (photographer), "Sarah Bernhardt," #190 *Procès de Jeanne d'Arc* by Emile Moreau. *Opposite*: Felix Nadar (photographer), "Sarah Bernhardt," #189 *Procès de Jeanne d'Arc* by Emile Moreau.

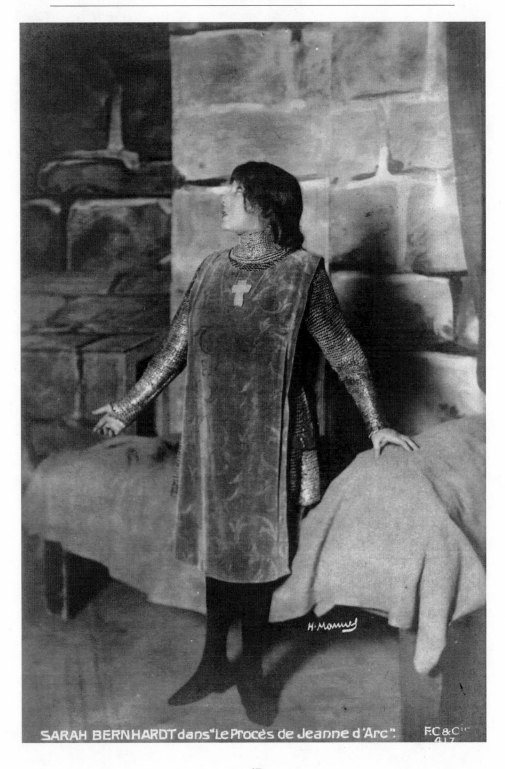

SARAH BERNHARDT dans "Le Procès de Jeanne d'Arc". FC&Cie 417

facts, but with having explained them at all.... They would wish the history of Joan of Arc to remain mysterious and entirely supernatural. I have restored the Maid to life and to humanity. That is my crime."[88] Before an appropriate assessment could be made of Joan and her actions by those in authority, however, the common people began to circulate reports of her doings, embellished by astonishment at and/or admiration for their uniqueness. After all, when had a commoner, let alone a young girl, ever commanded such attention? Anatole France recognized that rumors and legends have always been an integral part of Joan's story, adding layers of fascination as well as inaccuracy. He further noted that these skewed impressions can be detected as early as the fifteenth-century chronicles:

> At no period of her existence was Jeanne known otherwise than by fables, and that if she moved multitudes it was by the spreading abroad of countless legends which sprang up wherever she passed and made way before her. And indeed, there is much food for thought in that dazzling obscurity, which from the first enwrapped the Maid, in those radiant clouds of myth, which, while concealing her, rendered her more imposing.[89]

A similar tone recurs when dismissing the slanted evidence of the second trial: like that of a trial by the Inquisition, "it may represent the ideas of the judges [just] as much ... they have obviously been dressed up to suit the occasion."[90] Costume and pageantry, which would become public relations and marketing by the First World War, informed this part of the argument, just as crusaders for workers and woman suffrage were doing as this biography of Joan was written.

What remains clear from the preceding assessments is Anatole France's determination to strip away as much sentimentality as prejudice from this story. On the other hand, he aimed to showcase the image of Joan he claimed to be "restoring." Note that he had no trouble acknowledging her as a saint, but could not fathom her as an individual with political acumen, referring to her as the "fifteenth century's artless marvel."[91]

Lang, on the contrary, claimed that Joan did have military genius because she had the essentials needed to: "concentrate quickly, strike swiftly, strike hard, strike at vital points ... fight with invincible tenacity of purpose." Besides, he continued, if the method seemed more like heart or courage than science, so what?[92] Lang frames the whole story of Joan's rise and fall in emotional and psychological tones, emphasizing the moral shallowness of her own people who did not unilaterally recognize her outstanding gifts to her nation and her time. He complained that "even now among her own people, her glory is not uncontested."[93] Lang's unswerving admiration for Joan starts in the opening paragraphs of the book when he claims two causes for her glory: "She was the consummation and ideal of two human efforts towards perfection. The peasant's daughter was the Flower of Chivalry, brave, gentle, merciful, courteous, kind, and loyal."[94]

The Joan of Anatole France was not primarily a dreamy-eyed, simple-minded peasant; on the contrary, she was socially aware, imaginative, and a lover of stories, both religious and secular. The ardent churchmen of her region, he asserted, inspired her natural curiosity and it is due to them that Joan knew of the prophecy of the Virgin of Lorraine as saviour of the realm.[95] By the time Joan arrived at Chinon to meet the Dauphin, she had acquired her male attire and, consequently, began her more notorious public career in an outrageous way. France described her figure as full, although confined by the jerkin. She appeared robust, with a firm, short neck (long necks were considered beauty in her time), "but, beneath a woolen hood, her dark hair hung cut round in soup-plate fashion like a page's." Women of all ranks were careful to hide every lock of hair under elaborate headgear, so seeing Joan's hair was indeed shocking and strange.[96] When she recognized the Dauphin, despite his hiding from her, that was a sign of her power; the "difference" of Joan was doubled for the onlookers by her simple curtsey, and her removal of her cap in the Dauphin's presence.[97] Although captivated by Joan's manner and personality, Charles sent her to be examined by the theologians at Poitiers. Ordinarily, if seeking to determine divine/diabolical sources for claims such as Joan's, these men would have been relentless, but since they were loyal Armagnacs, and even "businessmen, diplomatists, old Councillors of the Dauphin," they were easy on Joan.[98]

Since both France and Lang were emphatic about the religious nature of Joan's mission, the distinguishing features between them emerged through style and manner of narration. Each of them "feminized" some of Joan's behavior, but Lang apparently had less trouble perceiving Joan as an individual young woman. Therefore, the clashes between France and Lang regarding Joan's behavior and role on the battlefield informed not only each writer's historical vision, but their stances on gender construction as well.

While A. France speculated on the spiritual issues in great detail, Lang delineated the specifics of her clothing: texture, color, and variety. He did not just announce that Joan went to Chinon in male attire; he said she was "so tall[99]" that she could wear a man's clothes ... when the Maid at last appeared before her gentle Dauphin, she wore a black *pourpoint*, a kind of breeches fastened by laces and points ... a short coarse dark grey tunic and a black cap on her close cropped black hair."[100] He addressed France's portrait directly in the confines of nineteenth-century standards of femininity when he stated: "In her was as much of chivalry as of sanctity ... now riding like a young knight, now leading in the deadly breach, Jeanne was not the *beguine*, or pious prude, of her latest French biographer!"[101,102]

For all the distinctions between these two biographers, one commonality is of the utmost importance: Joan of Arc was a "representation," in both the dramatic and literary senses of the term, to these writers. Attention was paid to her costume, gestures, posture, "props" and interaction with other people as if recalling scenes in a play. The same designations could be made of the women attempting to join the "ensemble" of public life and the world of business. As stated earlier in the chapter, actresses had become role models, and their power had grown over the course of the nineteenth century. By the time Anatole France and Andrew Lang wrote their biographies, actresses had expanded the kinds of roles they portrayed, and some were entrepreneurs as well as performers. But only one was "the most fashionable global celebrity of the nineteenth century ... [who] gave rise, in *fin-de-siècle* France, to much hand-wringing and soul-searching and deep ambivalence": Sarah Bernhardt.[103] "The Divine Sarah" was an actress, a businesswoman, a painter/sculptor, film star, and celebrity product sponsor. She was a phenomenon whose voice apparently touched the soul.

For others, she was an embodiment of hysteria. Worse still, she had many lovers, an illegitimate son, and Jewish heritage despite her Catholic upbringing. Her acting career really took off when she played breeches roles, beginning in 1869. Bernhardt adored these roles because she found them more "stimulating" to play. She also believed that an actress was better suited to play parts of young men because "a woman more readily looks the part, yet has the maturity of mind to grasp it."[104] Bernhardt's assessment here illustrates her recognition that the inner workings of the character relied upon the outward appearance, and vice-versa. The same could be said for any public figure with a message. By the time Sarah Bernhardt played Joan of Arc in 1890, in Jules Barbier's play with music by Gournot, she had shown the world she could play men and women from all levels of society. She played Cleopatra, Phèdre, and Camille, and projected the sufferings as well as triumphs of each of these women. Bernhardt could be fragile or ferocious. And she could play a nineteen-year-old Joan when she was middle-aged, and have the audience forget how old she was. By the time of this play, Joan was the darling of the New Women in the audience as well as the French Catholic right.

Bernhardt will be part of chapter 3's examination of visualizations of Joan of Arc and women from the 1840s to 1920. The era of images would be born at that time, and so the discussion will include paintings, drawings, sculptures, fashion, and graphic illustrations, and the new medium, film. All of these forms of visual representation revolved around the New Woman and the world of mass-produced art forms. But Joan of Arc was front and center in tableaux vivants, suffrage parades, posters, and film. Why? Sarah Bernhardt, in her memoir, *My Double Life*, offered this explanation:

> We do not want Joan of Arc to be a crude strapping peasant woman violently pushing away the young soldier who wants to joke, mounting like a man the broad-backed draft horse, laughing freely at the soldiers' crude jests, and subject as she was to the shameless lack of privacy typical of this still barbarous era, deserving all the more credit for remaining a heroic virgin. We want none of these useless truths. In legend she remains a frail being, led by a divine spirit. Her girl's arm, holding up the heavy standard, is supported by an invisible angel.... It is thus that we wish her to be. And the legend remains triumphant.[105]

3

Joan's Costume Changes: Wrapping and Unwrapping the New Woman

In the midst of reassessing the history, legend and mythology surrounding Joan of Arc in the last decades of the nineteenth century, a new persona appeared: the New Woman. Modernism spawned her, technological advancements in transportation and communication sped up the world around her, and mass production had given her more reading material, more popular culture, and clothing "off the rack." Her mothers and grandmothers may have studied fashion plates in a magazine, but she was shopping on her own, in stores as well as by catalogue, and was determined to pursue her own interests and avoid the confinements of previous generations. The New Woman went out in public with friends or on her own, and spoke her mind far more freely than young women ever had before. Commitment to social reform and service figured highly in her plans. The more radical among them were activists in the woman suffrage movement or labor union movement, or part of the second generation to attend college and pursue careers.

The previous chapter outlined the cultural factors that contributed to the push for the emancipation of women and introduced the disparate, yet interlaced, ideas and innovations that fostered this new generation's bold approach to life choices. What had given the younger generation the impetus to move so far afield from the separate spheres that supposedly kept society running smoothly, in public as well as in private? One answer is that there was a steady supply of written and oral arguments outlining the demands for change. Another is that, in addition to that impetus, several things happened in a short period of time that created the changed world. Yet another viewpoint combines the other two, and recognizes that each aspect of the cultural shifts began in the earlier nineteenth century and continued through the *fin-de-siècle* and into the early twentieth century. This chapter assesses the more specific cultural factors of dress and dress reform, the importance of visual appearance to platform speakers, and the connection among actresses, activism, and the iconographic importance of Joan of Arc.

To the older generations living in the 1890s and onward, the world had altered so much that it was almost unrecognizable. Young men and women plainly believed in more individual freedom; they likewise turned away from the stabilizing and clearly demarcated divisions between proper and improper behavior. This shift in attitude found both its touchstone and its hot spot in costume changes. Relaxed decorum was the mantra for the dress reform that characterized the appearance of the New Women. Whether in the name of freedom or health, the corset and its accompanying weighty garments became passé in the early twentieth century. In their place were long circle skirts, shirtwaists and ties, fitted jackets, and various kinds of hats; with the exception of the skirts, men's and women's fashions were quite similar. Women's shoes could be walked in, and could pedal bicycles.

Traditionalists, who felt threatened by sweeping social transformations, viewed technological advances, like telephones and telegrams, as unwelcome changes. They warned that reliance on speed in the nature of communications would lead to decreased regard for manners and individuals. Even those who applauded the marvels of industrialized society began to notice that the resulting mass culture was less personal. Mass culture's impact became magnified as more and more people moved to urban areas, in search of economic opportunities, as well as the cultural venues that cities offered. Advertising became an industry, and trends in fashion, popular music, and nightspots were visual emblems everywhere and in addition were reproduced through the increasing number of magazines and newspapers in circulation. Speed and convenience became the buzzwords for the decade of the 1890s ... at least for those who were ready for the shift. Trains and even automobiles had made their mark, but the bicycle craze that engulfed the popular imagination by 1896 consolidated the image as well as the nature of the times. Freedom to wander from home and yet return for mealtimes likewise added to the diminishment of the family as the center of the world. A quintessential visual representation of the predominance of this youthful lifestyle is the June 1896 cover of *Scribner's* magazine. Designed by Charles Dana Gibson, whose images of young women would define the more acceptable image of New Women, the white cover has one figure in its center: a young woman on a bicycle, wearing knickerbockers, a feminine blouse, and a smart hat.

Walter Besant, in *The Queen's Reign* (1897), wrote about the vast changes and improvements for women that had occurred in Great Britain since Victoria ascended the throne in 1837. Besant characterized the young lady of 1837 as someone incapable of reasoning, and prone to "carry shrinking modesty so far as to find the point of a shoe projecting beyond the folds of a frock indelicate ... [and who would] never even ... pretend to form an independent judgment." Even the proponents of women's sphere and the domestic ideal that accompanied it might have taken offense at such an extreme

Opposite: John Singer Sargent, *Mr. & Mrs. I. N. Phelps* (1897). According to the 2006 exhibit at the Newark Museum about New Women, "Off the Pedestal," Sargent's painting illustrated the boldness and newly defined sense of respectability for the New Woman. Mrs. Phelps is the dominant figure, while her husband is in shadow. The only odd point is the small size of her head. Her ensemble shows the way women's fashion borrowed from men's, and along with the clothing came the confidence (*Metropolitan Museum of Art, New York*).

SCRIBNERS FOR JUNE

statement; amazingly, Besant's next remark was equally extreme, albeit in another direction. A young woman of 1897 was educated enough to know about the workings of the body, and the gamut of academic subjects, which she "studies as the young man studies, but harder and with greater concentration.... She has invaded the professions."

Besant's use of "invaded" hinted at the disagreeable side of these changes for the men in the professions, but Besant dropped the subject and continued in his progressive tone. "These young women work, either out of economic necessity, or to pursue independence," which Besant defined as the "keynote of the situation.... The girls go off by themselves on their bicycles.... For the first time in man's history it is regarded as a right and proper thing to trust a girl as a boy insists upon being trusted." Most fascinating of all in this short discussion is that the most radical concept, trust in girls' independent judgment, betrayed no reservation on the writer's part. Things between the sexes were about to change; Besant predicted that women would no longer be considered fragile, incompetent, and ignorant of the world. He did not say what the men would substitute for the chivalric code, however. Despite Besant's apparent emphasis on expanded opportunities and changed attitudes towards women, he seemed determined to highlight the positive and avoid prolonged mention of any anxiety over this enormous shift in this portion of his text.[1]

The 1890s bicycle craze earned sanction by physicians as much as women activists. Healthy exercise was now deemed as essential for young women as for young men: "In women it is apt to overcome the impulsiveness and whimsicality which render so many of them unhappy.... Bicycling is no longer a mere fashion that may fall into disuse and give way to a new one. It is a wholesome and inspiring exercise, and has provided practical value as a means of rapid locomotion."[2] Bicycling and its benefits would be instrumental in sanctioning shorter skirts and other wardrobe essentials that would allow women to ride. Commentary in *Harper's Magazine* from 1896 captured the ardor surrounding the issue: "Women may ride in tights, but it is certain that men will never adopt the skirt. It is too dangerous. Man has not courage to risk the complications of an overthrow in a skirt. But whatever costume women may finally settle on for this arena, it is certain that they will not be driven from the wheel."[3]

Besant and other observers of social change would have noted the increase in women's civic activity during Victoria's reign, activities the queen herself fostered. The women's clubs that existed in Europe and the United States in the second half of the nineteenth century extended the boundaries of their supposedly private influence when they spearheaded the social mandate to make public spaces as safe and inviting as private spaces. More than a clever use of woman's "acceptable" role of creating

Opposite: Charles Dana Gibson, *Scribner's for June* (1896). Another key motif from the Newark Museum exhibit was women on bicycles. This magazine cover demonstrates the popularization of the Gibson Girls' activity via the bicycle craze that peaked in the 1890s. Women's determination to be freer and yet maintain a dignified appearance could not have asked for a clearer validation (*Library of Congress*).

livable environments, it was, as Susan Ware puts it, strategic in design. American "women strove to fuse politics with their domestic ideals.... The responsibilities that instruments of government increasingly took on for improving the social welfare of citizens testifies to women's impact."[4] On both sides of the Atlantic, women were increasingly in the public eye, individually and in groups, and the advent of more comfortable, functional clothing by the era of the New Woman encouraged their movement away from female helplessness, and their self-reliant attitude made it clear that women's push for freedom was by no means half-hearted. The appalled response to their changed looks reflected the fixity with which women's clothing signified their status, and how the physical weight and restriction of the garments were fundamental to the notion of women as the "weaker sex."[5]

An 1896 article in the *Englishwoman* made the changed costume choice seem a true ruination of a woman's chance for domestic happiness. The male writer couched his argument in melodramatic style when he claimed that wearing knickerbockers rather than skirts detracted from a woman's sex appeal because in this costume she becomes "insignificant in size, and robs herself at once of those subtle points and qualities wherein her vast power and *danger* lie." Because of the women's changed outlook, competition (for husbands, one presumes) increased and they might "wonder what it is they lack, and why life is such a miserable failure, despite all their advanced liberties, pleasures, and advantages.... Time may answer these doleful and unexpressed queries when they grow dissatisfied with their sex emancipation and man-like costume, with their robust health, open-air exercises and equality of struggle." The writer remains convinced that women need male protection, which they will never receive without wearing skirts.[6]

Exaggerated as the argument may have been, the degree of alarm shown at women's physical prowess in a public forum reconfirms once again the reasons for Joan of Arc's inevitable tangle with the authority of her time, as well as the perpetuation of similar reactions centuries later. By the 1890s, however, the occasional deviant woman had infiltrated middle- and upper-class society. The folly of those who thought they could stem the tide of deepening social change by concentration on woman's bodily appearance and costume came to the fore in the drawing-room comedies of Oscar Wilde. In his 1895 play *An Ideal Husband*, Wilde's genius for presenting inversions in gender roles lay in his adherence to the structure and conventions of both comedy and "well-made" plays. Dialogue combined serious commentary on the controversies of the day and sparkling wit, which first amused and then shocked the audience. The germ of the plot is the attempt to blackmail a peer in the House of Lords. Sir Robert Chiltern has an impeccable reputation, both in Parliament and at home: thus the twist on the play's title. The play's antagonist, Mrs. Cheveley, is a ruthless woman trying to stay afloat both economically and socially; she was also a schoolmate of Sir Robert's wife, Gertrude, but their relationship was not one of friendship. Gertrude is active in women's social reform, but her love for her husband lacks breadth of vision: he is as perfect to her as an idealized wife was to a husband. In Act 2, Sir Robert confides in his best friend, Lord Goring, who knows all the players well; he was once engaged to Mrs. Cheveley, and adores Gertrude.

Lord Goring's remarks carry both sides of Wilde's critique: "I should fancy Mrs. Cheveley is one of those very modern women of our time who find a new scandal as becoming as a new bonnet, and air them both in the Park every afternoon at five-thirty." Sir Robert's worry over the blackmail centers on his wife's finding out; he panics, like many heroines of nineteenth-century novels and plays: "Oh! I live on hopes now. I clutch at every chance. I feel like a man on a ship that is sinking. The water is round my feet, and the very air is bitter with storm. Hush! I hear my wife's voice." His past mistake involved the less-than-scrupulous use of knowledge about funds and governmental projects in order to launch his political career: the antithesis of his reputed integrity. Yet Lord Goring treats moral reproach with the same regard as fashion. He reminds his friend that there is as much fashion in people's pasts as there is in clothing. Once Gertrude enters the scene, her own commitment to her social causes and disregard for women's supposed preoccupation with clothes accomplishes the kind of circularity that ensures Wilde's inversion.

Lord Goring presumes she has been at the Park, and admires her hat, sorry that she is about to take it off. Gertrude's snippets of information about her political meeting deflate any expectation for her to be a character of aristocratic leisure, which Lord Goring proudly is. Despite the light tone, the dialogue makes it clear that she represents the New Woman's perspective:

> LORD GORING: It is so pretty. One of the prettiest hats I ever saw. I hope the Woman's Liberal Association received it with loud applause.
>
> LADY CHILTERN: [With a smile.] We have much more important work to do than look at each other's bonnets, Lord Goring.
>
> LORD GORING: Really? What sort of work?
>
> LADY CHILTERN: Oh! dull, useful, delightful things, Factory Acts, Female Inspectors, the Eight Hours' Bill, the Parliamentary Franchise.... Everything, in fact, that you would find thoroughly uninteresting.
>
> LORD GORING: And never bonnets?
>
> LADY CHILTERN: [With mock indignation.] Never bonnets, never![7]

Gertrude's "mock indignation" concludes the subject by both acknowledging and disregarding the suffragettes' recognized use of bonnets and other ladylike attire, but only as a means to their end of active rather than passive influence on social legislation. The acute awareness of what these women wore epitomized their anxiety over women's seeming desire to eradicate the boundaries between male and female capabilities and visibility in public spaces.

Elaine Showalter's study of *fin-de-siècle* eras foregrounds the anxiety that dominates them; the late nineteenth century was fraught with worries, especially about the removal of the very bastions of domestic conservatism that Besant noted in 1897. The mercurial attitude of the same writer was unmistakable, as he had published a flagrantly anti-feminist novel in 1882, *The Revolt of Man*, in which the entire patriarchal system was envisioned in reverse, and sympathy lay with the disempowered men. Showalter attributed Besant's attitude to the precise anxiety that characterized the late Victorian era. Women appeared bent on becoming men, and any gains toward equality led to the melodramatic resolution that men were becoming women. Actual ground gained by the women's movement was hard to measure in the 1880s. But the emotional swings associated with it had far from abated. Those opposed to women's rights acted as if women would take the world over completely any day; however, as Showalter notes, "the fin-de-siècle rhetoric of invasion was out of proportion to the reality." In Britain, the decade became known as 'the doldrums years,' Showalter emphasized. Although more than 40 percent of people elected in 1880 were pledged to support a women's amendment, the Reform Bill of 1884 went through without one; Gladstone and his Liberal party opposed its inclusion. "After the amendment's defeat, woman suffrage was more or less a dead issue until the beginnings of militancy in 1905."[8]

Not only was the Woman Question at the core of this fear; Showalter also pointed to the 1880s and 1890s as the time when "the emergence and medicalization of the modern homosexual identity" occurred, and the trial of Oscar Wilde for his homosexual affairs and embodiment of the "male aesthete" was, for many Englishmen, a "certain sign of the immorality that had toppled Greece and Rome." The larger framework squarely centered on the crisis, not only between masculine and feminine roles and identity, but also within them. If women could do what only men had been thought capable of, would that mean the end of marriage and childbearing roles for New Women? The backlash that ensued put both feminism and homosexuality as danger zones on the front burners of the morality campaigns to reinforce the family as the center of life.[9]

Wilde had an all-encompassing perspective on the gender issues, partly from his own life, but more from his observation of individuals' pronouncements on the gender questions that continued into the 1890s. His most familiar work, *The Importance of Being Earnest* (1895), places the critique of both men and women into the speeches of the two young women, Gwendolyn Fairfax and Cecily Cardew. When Gwendolyn arrives, Cecily presumes she was one of the elderly women of her Uncle Jack's acquaintance: women active in philanthropy. Cecily did not like such women; she felt they were "so forward." Such an attitude marks her momentarily as believing in women's domestic sphere.

Gwendolyn enters, introduces herself, and is satisfied when Cecily has never heard of her father, since, for Gwendolyn, the home is the "proper sphere for the man. And certainly once a man begins to neglect his domestic duties he becomes painfully effeminate, does he not? And I don't like that. It makes men so very attractive."[10] Here Wilde blithely inverted gender spheres in an upper-class family introduced as conservative. Gwendolyn's mother, Lady Bracknell, best represented the reality underneath the form, as she fulfilled both parental roles due to an ailing husband. Wilde's joke on the stereotype, this time neurasthenic rich women, couldn't have been clearer. Gwendolyn travels alone to counteract her mother's opposition to her engagement; like her mother, she acts on her own behalf, with even less fuss. Within moments of arrival, Gwendolyn immediately decides she likes Cecily, as her first impressions are "never wrong," and insists that they will be on intimate terms ... until she finds out Cecily is the ward of her fiancée and is far too young and pretty.

In this scene, women are criticized by young women at both ends of the spectrum, which can seem like a nod to traditional misogynistic notions of women's flighty and disloyal natures. Again Wilde has another perspective to impart: appearance as false barometer of quality, and assumptions about the need to exude quality through surface action. On more serious subjects, Cecily has no qualms about critiquing the gap between the educational exercises her governess assigns her versus true mental acuity. When she remarked that the Reverend Dr. Chasuble was so obviously intelligent because he had written no books at all, Wilde commented on the plethora of verbiage that he felt plagued his era, and also on the kind of education that resulted in glib assertions passing for reflection. Cecily's ability to think and act of her own volition obviously had more to do with her individual understanding of relationships and behavior than with rote memorization of key historical dates.

Barely eighteen, Cecily has certainly benefited from private tutoring because she has the confidence to think and act for herself. Even if their actions reveal the ways in which women used the spheres system to their own advantage rather than a desire to work for social causes, both young women represent the new generation of women who unsettled the domestic agenda. Their propensity towards judgmental attitudes mirrors those of the older women in the play. Despite the vast disparity of their social positions, Cecily's tutor/governess, Miss Prism, and Gwendolyn's mother, Lady Bracknell, share imperious attitudes towards what they term immoral behavior and wish to protect the younger women. As Besant had noted in "The Queen's Reign," the generation of New Women saw things their own way. Wilde's vision of the change in society focused on the inner rather than the outer manifestations, thereby illustrating the reality of a time in transition. A key visual artist of the same period, John Singer Sargent, captured the feeling of the New Woman in portraits of well-to-do women. One of his most famous, "Mr. & Mrs. N. Phillips Stokes" (1897), is a very large canvas, yet one which focuses squarely on Mrs. Stokes. She evokes the Gibson Girl in her long circle skirt, white blouse and black "tie," and a straw bowler hat in her hand. Mr. Stokes is obscured and obviously overshadowed by his elegant, vivacious wife.

Oscar Wilde may have written comedies, but his plays bring attention to a point easy to overlook: the gender debate illustrated the era's taste for melodrama. The extremes of sentiment associated with women's supposedly fragile natures versus the need for men to act without hesitation was ever-present in dramas or comedies that used and reinforced these stereotypical figures. Since neither women nor men in these plays were rounded, this can be seen as a barometer for an era that wanted to force gender issues into fixed categories, or, put another way, put them under glass for collection and casual observation. Wilde's plays took full advantage of his audience's familiarity with and preference for these stock characters, and then showed them as shams by mixing the masculine and feminine elements within his characters. Oscar Wilde did not write a Joan play, but his lucid representation of masculine, feminine, as well as "deviant," notions of gender, infiltrating upper-class society, helps us see how the puzzle of Joan of Arc's gender performance remained a slippery slope into the twentieth century.

Unlike her late–nineteenth-century counterparts, Joan of Arc never had the benefit of education, but her faith in her cause had given her the independent determination she needed to get the job done, and to include both men and women in her inner circle. Joan had no more tolerance for traditions that blockaded the role she believed God sent her to perform than the young women of the 1890s had for conforming to precut patterns of appropriate behavior or dress for women. Therefore, Joan's social iconographic status as both the independent and virtuous young woman of authority as well the representative of the masses matched the era quite well. Wilde's plays managed to include both halves of women's activities.

Simultaneously, however, the Church was working towards canonizing Joan of Arc for factors not related to the foregoing description of women's changing roles in the 1890s. Its aim was to work against increasing secularization, particularly the socialist governments that opposed the Church's power, as well as iconoclastic individualistic disregard for patriarchal authority.[11] While the left-wing causes of feminism and workers' rights dovetailed with the original push to canonize Joan of Arc earlier in the nineteenth century, the right-wing political institutions aligned themselves with the Church, bringing royalist sympathies and ecclesiastical traditions together. By the *fin-de-siècle* of the nineteenth century, the two "halves" of the Hundred Years War dispute of the fifteenth century had formed an alliance, and "the people," the peasant classes that stood by Joan of Arc in her own time, now rallied to her story and image in the modern era for fresh reasons.

One way of considering this apparent contradiction within these more modern associations with Joan's legacy is to recognize the blurring of the lines. On the conservative side, the right-wing political supporters and Church hierarchy had clearly gone past the rationale that condemned Joan of Arc for heresy largely on the bases of her cross-dressing and individualized spiritual connections. Like the secular apologists for Joan's changed status, the Church could sanction the cross-dressing and the "special case" identity they needed to assign to Joan in order to transmogrify her status.[12] Therefore, the era of the "New Woman" and labor organization apparently was the inevitable time to consolidate the iconographic as well as ecclesiastical importance of the French adolescent leader of the fifteenth century.

In the United States considerable interpretations of Joan of Arc came between 1895 and 1929; in many ways, the various images of Joan constructed during this period emblemized the consolidations that had occurred in the nineteenth century as a whole and that would continue her legacy past the canonization date for Joan of Arc. Joan was represented in sculpture, fiction, drama, and film; in almost all of these works, she is seen as the combination of both the sentimental heroine of American literature and the New Woman: wise, caring, selfless, athletic, and daring. While both images of women's role maintained that women were morally superior to men, there was hardly consensus that women also needed male protection. This dichotomy was not confined to literature; rather, it was an overall cultural response to the threat of feminism.[13]

The first major American representation of Joan of Arc coincided with Oscar Wilde's plays: Mark Twain's fictionalized biography, *Personal Recollections of Joan of Arc* (1896). This text interweaves historical data, melodrama, and the sentimental novel. The fictitious author for the book, "The Sieur Louis de Conte," serves as Joan's page and secretary. Twain also supplies a translator, Jean Francois Alden; the latter provides an impassioned preface for the work. He calls Joan's century "the brutalest, the wickedest, the rottenest in history since the dark ages," while Joan is characterized as a "miracle ... product from such ... soil"; "a rock of convictions in a time when men believed in nothing and scoffed at all things"; and "perhaps the only entirely unselfish person whose name has a place in profane history."[14] The appellation "entirely unselfish" betrays Twain's bias for traditional feminine images, in contrast to the first two accolades, which are not associated with either sex exclusively; this combination view becomes even more apparent in his depiction of Joan's accomplishments and indignation over Joan's treatment by Charles VII:

> A mere child in years ignorant, unlettered, a poor village girl unknown and without influence, found a great nation lying in chains[15] ... and she laid her hand upon this nation, this corpse, and it rose and followed her. She led it from victory to victory, she turned back the tide of the Hundred Years' War, she fatally crippled the English power, and died with the earned title of DELIVERER OF FRANCE, which she bears to this day.
> And for all reward, the French King, whom she had crowned, stood supine and indifferent, while French priests took the noble child, the most innocent, the most lovely, the most adorable the ages have produced, and burned her alive at the stake.[16]

Such remarks encapsulated what Americans found so important, so endearing about Joan's story. She was "self-made," a product of "the people," and a victim of a repressive ideology. As a young woman she personified the virtues of the nurturing healer, pure moral leader, and innocent child: the patriarchal/protector's view of a young woman. Nonetheless, the warmth Twain's novel evokes is its overriding strength. The opening portion, entitled "Domrémy," sketched a picture of Joan as a spirited, selfless, spiritual child: a picture very much in keeping with the testimony given by Joan's friends and family at the 1456 Trial of Rehabilitation. But in the true spirit of the nineteenth century, Twain pointed out her personal magnetism as well as her natural superiority, which reflects the modern change in "honor" from inherited to earned. He stated this directly when he reported her first meeting with the Dauphin and Court: "Joan charmed them every one with her sweetness and simplicity and unconscious eloquence, and all the best and capablest among them recognized that there was an indefinable something ... that testified that she was not made of common clay."[17]

Twain recognized Joan's uncanny presence of mind when he recounted her meeting with the ecclesiastical judges at Poitiers, whose approval had to be secured before the Dauphin would allow the Siege of Orléans. He perceived that she was: "as sweetly self-possessed and tranquil before this grim tribunal, with its robed celebrities, its solemn states and imposing ceremonials, as if she were but a spectator and not herself on trial ... [she] disconcerted the science of the sages with her sublime ignorance."[18]

No matter how glorified and feminized Joan becomes in this work, it was to Twain's credit that he read all of the major historical/biographical works of his time; he even consulted the biography highly regarded by his contemporary women writers, Janet Tuckey's *Joan of Arc, the Maid* (1880). Twain matched the Romantic European writers Robert Southey and Friedrich Schiller (see chapter 2) in his portrait of a rarefied child of nature, yet his rhetoric is more reverential than revolutionary. This depiction revealed Twain's recognition of the theatrical elements inherent in Joan's story, although this passage does not show her taking advantage of costume and spectacle, as the historical Joan was prone to do according to biographers Andrew Lang and Vita Sackville-West. But perhaps Twain was working in another direction: to show that those in command, who knew full well all the "tricks" of military attack, chose to foil Joan's instinctive decision to starve the English out of their fort by closing off their communications in order to expedite the Siege of Orléans. Because no one could be expected to take seriously the "command" of a seventeen-year-old "general," especially one who was a girl, Joan was easy to deceive. But, as Twain emphasized, all of this happened before the Bastard (General Dunois) met Joan. As Shaw would later dramatize in *Saint Joan* (see chapter 5), Joan was to deal as directly and effectively with the Bastard as with everyone else. He was so struck by Joan's manner that he gave in to her demands, recognizing the wondrous aura that surrounded the young girl.[19]

Conversely, Twain glorified Joan's "feminine" virtues in ways that would never occur to Shaw. Twain praised Joan for not gloating over her victory with Dunois, and then showed the theatrical savvy of Joan of Arc, specifically her splendid sense of symbolic gesture: "taking her little plumed cap off to somebody," "patting [someone] on the head with her gauntlet." The description concluded with the following note: "Joan of Arc had stepped upon her stage at last, and was ready to begin."[20]

Twain maintains a consistent view toward the corrupt fifteenth-century authority figures as well as the dignity, nobility and awe that he believed belonged to Joan. At the beginning of the book and again at the end he claims that the world will not see her like again for thousands of years; only One (Jesus Christ) could surpass her qualities and worth. His ideology is contained in concrete details as well. A prime example is a footnote decrying the reinstatement of Domrémy's taxes after the French Revolution. A portion of this note contains the essence of his attitude:

> Joan never asked to be remembered, but France has remembered her with an inextinguishable love and reverence; Joan never asked for a statue, but France has lavished them upon her; Joan never asked for a church for Domrémy, but France is building one; Joan never asked for saintship, but even that is impending. Everything which Joan of Arc did not ask for has been given her, and with a noble profusion; but the one humble little thing which she did ask for and get has been taken away from her. There is something infinitely pathetic about this.[21]

The rhetoric is reminiscent of Antony's "Friends, Romans, countrymen" speech from Shakespeare's *Julius Caesar*, as is its obvious intent. French authority glorifies itself in the eyes of the world. The "pathetic" epithet says it all. Twain uses a similar tactic in disparaging the Trial of Condemnation's obsession with Joan's male attire. He calls this: "shabby work for those grave men to be engaged in; for they well knew one of Joan's reasons for clinging to the male dress was ... better protection for her modesty than the other."[22] In sharp contrast, Twain ultimately sums up Joan: "Her words were as sublime as her deeds, as sublime as her character; they had their source in a great heart and were coined in a great brain."[23] At last Twain's Joan transcends her boundaries of gender to become an individual worthy of emulation.

Since Joan was depicted pictorially in both male and female dress during the entire canonization era, it was apparent that the nineteenth and early twentieth centuries could choose Joan's costumes as part of her iconographic representation, and the lack of dispute surrounding the clothing of "The Maid" suggests that the actions of Joan far outweighed her outward appearance. For the left-wing factions, the shift in perspective had moved farther to the right, as portions of the conservative stance on "woman" (as chaste, motherly, "ladylike" figures) were incorporated into their written, visual, and spoken rhetoric in order to attract and retain substantial popular support. Here again, this attitude both goes along with and confronts the concurrent debates over appropriate costume choices for the modern women. Why was this open-mindedness and ability to go beyond physical appearance possible only in retrospect? Why was it that dress reform efforts on behalf of women in the mid-nineteenth century had incurred such wrath?

Ironically, a primary sticking point in Joan's lifetime, her clothing, became the weapon that the women used to invert the traditional judgment against activism in women. By the mid–1850s, the public presence and multi-tiered demands of the woman suffrage movement had stirred backlash, particularly when the "Bloomer costume" surfaced. Anne Hollander in *Sex and Suits* argues persuasively that the suit for men was perfected by the early nineteenth century, thereby widening the gap between masculine and feminine attire. Women wearing trousers of any kind outside their homes was coded as deviant throughout the nineteenth century, which gave the behavior of

French writer and proto-feminist George Sand added emphasis. Hollander asserts that Sand's conspicuous appearance in men's suits was offensive not because she was trying to be a man, but rather because she wanted the privileges of a man within the self-determined lifestyle of a sexually active woman.[24] As Sand was the symbol for women's "acting out," in England and the United States as well as France, it is no wonder that the bloomers topped by a short skirt invoked outrage. The ensemble became the visual embodiment of gender blending and bending.

More specifically, Amy Kesselman's analysis of feminism and dress reform traces the ways in which dress hampered or helped feminist causes: "The reform dress became a symbol of everything that was threatening about feminism: women shaping their lives in accordance with their own needs, women declaring independence from male approval, women doing or wearing what had been traditionally reserved for men."[25] At first, reactions to the dress reform costume ranged from satirical cartoons to "abusive jingles" on public streets and even to hecklers surrounding women wearing the garments. Suffrage leaders persevered for awhile, then slowly gave up the garb-as-gauntlet. Elizabeth Cady Stanton concluded that the "physical freedom enjoyed did not compensate for the persistent persecution and petty annoyances suffered at every turn." Susan B. Anthony reported that attendees at her public speech concentrated "upon my clothes instead of my words."

Within a few years, a new kind of understanding emerged within the leadership; as Kesselman notes, Lucy Stone articulated it best when she determined that woman's "miserable style of dress" "was a consequence of her present vassalage, not its cause." Stone recognized that the socio-political changes would have to precede the entire overhauling of the social construction of femininity.[26] Hardly a signal of demise, this juncture can be read as a change in tactics for the women's movement. If appearance was the semiotic game, the women would lure the audiences via womanly wardrobes and even styles of décor at their conventions. The question was whether or not resistance to early dress reform by the power structure became internalized by women, who disregarded their own physical and psychic discomfort in the bargain. Charlotte Perkins Gilman asserted as late as 1886 that women did not wish to change their costume because it matched their acculturated personae: to serve others and neglect themselves. The next piece of her argument centered on women's mental rather than physical consciousness:

> the pleasures and pains of the heart and mind are far more important to her than those of the body ... true and reasonable dress means perfect ease and health and beauty of body, with the freedom of motion and increase of power and skill resultant therefrom. But it also means long combat with one's own miseducated sense of beauty, and fitness ... an uneasy sense of isolation and ... loss of social position, constant mortification and shame.[27]

Despite new cultural associations for Joan of Arc, assertive women were still denigrated in ways similar to those that had been used against Joan: namely, references to inappropriate clothing, and moral "looseness" as a "logical" ramification of her "unnatural" public roles. As Gilman pointed out, cloth is a "social tissue"; in other words, it serves as a means of identifying people as members of groups, or as distinctive from groups. It is therefore both an individual and an emblematic marker. Distinctions between men's and women's costume rules reflect norms that apparently came out of nowhere. Modesty, a pervasive virtue of the age, controlled body language as well as skirt length for women. They were always to look down, and yet, Gilman emphasized: "Why it should be 'modest' for a woman to exhibit neck, arms, and shoulders, back and bosom, and immodest to go bathing without stockings, no one so much as attempts to explain.... We have attached sentiments of modesty to certain parts of the human frame ... that is all." Her conclusion must have startled her contemporaries: "So 'modesty' in dress, as applied to that of women, consists in giving the most conspicuous prominence of femininity."

Men did not escape the absurdity of fashion trends either; Gilman maintained that the bane of their existence was starch. Ironically, this is the one element of men's dress that was not only symbolic (that is, of no utilitarian function) but also was contrary to free movement of the body. Starch was emblematic of wealth, as working-class men could not have performed their work with starched collars. Full evening dress was the worst, as Gilman humorously put it: "One might as well hang a dinnerplate across his chest, as the glaring frontlet so beloved of the masculine part."[28] The theatrical language used here should not be disregarded; costume was an everyday part of social life, especially among the more affluent, and their appearances at social functions apparently resembled theatrical roles. Interestingly, theatrical representation of gender continued to move back and forth between conventional and unconventional costume and attitude.

Once the "woman question" was open and prominent in the public eye, the visual display of women posing as men was causing more discomfort in the nineteenth than it had in the eighteenth century, when women had been considered imperfect men. The visual semiotics transferred as well. Approaching the subject from a different vantage point, Lenard Berlanstein analyzes the connection between cross-dressing by women in the theater and its cultural discontents. He characterizes the theater as:

> synonymous with worldliness throughout the nineteenth century.... Even the elite flocked to see performers assuming the identity of the opposite sex.... Nonetheless, audiences did not tolerate ... blurring of sexual identity ... there was a correspondence, if a rough one, between conventional gender understandings and the characterizations that audiences would accept on the stage.[29]

Since George Sand had both "passed" as a man in her role as arts reviewer and writer, but never fully hidden her identity as a woman, and since she had written about public performance, her display became doubly important. She became prominent in the 1830s, just on the brink of change. Public women, particularly actresses, had been pigeonholed as morally weak, and therefore inappropriate role models, until the 1840s. By the second half of the nineteenth century, the pendulum swung and actresses were symbolic of alternative possibilities for women, in England and the United States as well as France. According to Christopher Kent, this reversal was important to Victorian women since these individuals had "striking opportunities for independence, fame, and fortune, and even for those outside it, the stage incarnated fantasies ... [a world apart from] the normal categories, moral and social, that defined woman's place."[30]

Theatrical representation intersected public as well as private imagination throughout the nineteenth century, and its manner of behavior affected the way audiences would also behave. That is one reason why women's appropriation of theatrical spaces became emblematic of new possibilities for women — of all classes. In 1809, London experienced a "price war" in theatres, which sprang from the alteration of the seating arrangements; suddenly, the lowest-priced ticket holders found themselves distanced from the stage, and could barely hear the performance. Prior to this, there had been a long and open upper gallery, which had none of the restrictions. More than a concern over money, it was the visual demonstration of the tiers in society reflected in the tiered seating that reserved the box seats for the wealthy. Even though the situation was relatively short-lived, it bore a far-reaching change in theatrical venues: melodrama. While the dispute between old and new styles of theater management raged, only two theaters were deemed "legitimate," so other houses turned to this hybrid form of entertainment, one that often contained musical interludes. Elaine Hadley's argument about melodrama's significance centers on the provocative and disruptive aspects of the new genre. Rather than represent lofty material, melodrama depended on gothic elements, and was a staged picture of the political terror that had plagued Europe in the aftermath of the French Revolution. But, more importantly, the genre: "publicized itself; its emphasis on the visual, the emotive, and the audience aside thematized the importance of the spectators, not only as observers of the action but, perhaps most significantly, as participants in the plot." Baser human motivations and actions also became more public as a result of melodrama's focus on these in its visual and almost interactive mode of performance, "transferring relationships among private interests to a transparent public sphere devoid of class demarcations and the divisions between private and public identities."[31]

Widening the sphere and extent of public performance had been an essential part of early-nineteenth-century popular culture, initiating the time of the radical celebrity artist. The writer George Gordon, Lord Byron, and the composer Ludvig von Beethoven, became international figures: one for his flamboyance as well as his politics, and the other for his music's unmistakable expression of the depth and breadth of human emotion. Simultaneously, actors and actresses became "stars," spurring the cult of personality. The term originated in England in the 1820s and was applied to David Garrick and Mrs. Siddons, and then applied to Rachel Felix and Talma in France.[32] Rachel Felix was the first truly international star, with adoring fans in London and the United States. Like George Sand, whose work and life dominated the popular imagination, Rachel was both a performer and a public persona. As her biographer,

Rachel Brownstein contextualizes these labels: "Stars are remarkable for doubleness above all; perhaps they represent doubleness.... A problematically public woman, the star is accessible to all, but also entirely self-possessed."[33]

Poor and Jewish, Rachel nonetheless was considered a royal presence onstage, and her renown began when she was only seventeen. Best known for her portrayals of Racine's heroines, her physical as well as psychological impact was enormous. Despite her designation as a "mock Queen" of the stage, Rachel's waif-like physique and face bore the marks of poverty, which only added to the intrigue of the audience. Brownstein claims that Rachel "flamboyantly mocked" her cultural classifications, yet "seemed to flaunt the fact that she was a fiction and a fabrication, someone making herself up." Such an encapsulization could just as easily apply to Joan of Arc, as would a significant portion of the following remarks by Brownstein:

> Rachel eluded stereotypes and evoked them. She inflected and combined images that were already compelling to the popular mind ... stage queen risen from the gutter, the virgin and the virago. As a woman, an actress, and a Jew, who commanded respect and made large sums of money, she focused and braided together a set of anxieties about sex and power, about national and sexual as well as personal identity.[34]

Rachel's unhidden background apparently vied with her enormous talents for her place in the hearts and minds of the theatrical public. Joan had a similar mixed background accompanying her rise to prominence. The humble origins that would become so attractive to modern interpreters of her story and legacy were an almost opaque barrier to her mission while Joan lived. Long before the cult of personality, however, Joan of Arc was either born with or cultivated an impassioned charisma. The female saints who lived in the centuries preceding Joan had behaved in strident ways, so Joan's religious background gave her ready-made models. Joan also understood the importance of spectacle for its impact on the popular imagination. From the letters she dictated to her behavior at the crowning of Charles VII at Reims Cathedral, Joan employed the performative rituals of a military commander as well as a religious activist. She clearly enjoyed the spotlight, even as she constantly viewed her actions as part of a higher chain of command. A young girl, she and her devotees relished her costume and props. Hollander observes that Joan "looked immodestly erotic in her men's gear ... she didn't just look soldierly and practical, especially since in her private moments without armor she was something of a dandy. At court, she seized the male privileges of going bareheaded and showing off her legs and figure with attractive tailoring ... without hiding the fact that she was a woman."[35]

However distinct their actions or contexts, both Joan and Rachel aroused similar combinations of anxiety and reprehensibility. Since Rachel neither performed breeches roles, nor was overtly sexual onstage, two common points of attack vanished. Her danger, apart from social class and ethnicity, stemmed from her acting style: a physical and psychological representation of inner states of mind that electrified and disturbed spectators. Rachel's performativity linked the traditional view of women as appearance-driven objects of praise or blame on the one hand, and the essence of nine-teenth-century heightened consciousness of the multi-dimensional selves that lay underneath outward appearance.

By the 1840s, Rachel was beloved in London as well. Queen Victoria and Prince Albert attended the theater often, and helped dispel its *déclassé* status. English and American writers, including Charlotte Brontë, George Eliot, and Henry James created fictional characters based upon their individual interpretations of Rachel as actress and persona. Brownstein also suggests that, particularly in Bronte's *Villette*, a kind of dialogic relationship existed between the actress, the fictional character, and the writer, each of them a woman becoming conscious of the roles she played internally as well as externally, and the social and psychological aspects of these everyday performances.[36] These fictional characters could reach a wider audience than the theatrical ones, which makes them important. What makes them more significant, however, was their place in a genre known to portray the everyday concerns of middle and working class char-acters. Through them, the novelists gave voice and tangible shape to the notion of gen-der as social construction, and to the fluidity that was apparent and possible in modern life. Reading novels also bridged private and public imaginations, as people often read them aloud as evening entertainment, especially those serialized in the periodicals of the day. Even those who would never attend a theatrical performance became accus-tomed to actresses as cultural presences.

Rachel was likened to a statue for her physical presence as well as her classical roles, and also a pythoness because some of the women she represented were danger-ous to men; therefore, Rachel visibly represented both variations on the theme of woman. Apparently, she selected roles accordingly, and played women who were tra-ditionally feminine, but also those who were motivated by more masculine mindsets. Then in 1846 she portrayed Joan in Soumet's *Jeanne d'Arc*, for which she wore a "cun-ning costume of metal and cloth." The costume was elaborate, and the combination of the visual imagery, the celebrity of the actress, and her impassioned performance onstage mesmerized audiences across class lines and caught the attention of painters and writers as well. One intimated that Rachel performed in an inferior play[37] in order to become a living embodiment of the famous statue of Joan, the Maid of Orléans, sculpted by Princesse Marie, daughter of Louis-Philippe.[38] The contemporaneity of the visual as well as performative styles suggests that Rachel chose her vehicle wisely. Within a year, Michelet's biography of Joan of Arc would appear, and by 1848, France would again become a republic.

Rachel's importance as a national figure was cemented in what the *Jewish Ency-clopedia* sees as her greatest popular triumph. During the 1848 revolution she sang the "Marseillaise" nightly at the Comédie Française, then rechristened "Théâtre de la République." Night after night the theater was crowded, and each night the workmen in the audience subscribed for her bouquets. Rachel always considered this a far greater triumph than her success in *Phèdre*; but by common consent *Phèdre* was considered her masterpiece, and has been described as "an apocalypse of human agony not to be forgotten by any one who ever witnessed it."[39] Brownstein expands this notion when she remarks that: "Images of other celebrated women impose themselves on a star, blurring and also aggrandizing her. The individual becomes generic, history melts into metaphor, fictions and their creators become one."[40]

By the time Rachel died in the late 1850s the women's movements in Britain and the United States had begun, with demands for suffrage and other legal and political rights. Images of Rachel as Marianne in paintings and even stamps continued to emerge, and these denoted her continued importance to French constructions of feminine ideals that went beyond the strictures of class designation.[41]

Unfortunately, it would be another half century before consciousness across class lines would finally emerge. The situation for working-class women worsened over the course of the nineteenth century, as more and more people came to the city to live. For many, work and home had one major commonality: deprivation and grime. The hope many clung to was the possibility of future "respectability," and the fundamentally traditional gender roles that went with it. London's "penny weekly" family magazines included what they termed "realistic" short stories about women who attained respectability because of their inner grace as much as their behavior. In an article on what she terms the "forgotten women" of the Victorian period, Sally Mitchell writes of the adherence this group had to essential mores of the age, especially the "fusion of upward mobility with notions of class" as internal. The magazines enjoyed the widest circulation of any periodicals ca. 1840–1860, especially among families on the cusp of middle-class status. The characters they read about in these magazine stories were "attractive models because they demonstrated to the woman of narrow means that ladyhood is not dependent on income, nor destroyed by the necessity of working, but lies in manners and bearing."[42]

Stories such as these implanted their values into working-class women, who dreamed of being on the pedestal their wealthier counterparts longed to be freed from, but it would not be until the twentieth century that disparate classes of women would connect. A woman journalist who saw the sharp divide among women was Fanny Fern. In a brief but biting essay that she wrote in 1868, Fern began by claiming that: "Nowhere more than in New York does the contest between squalor and splendor so sharply present itself.... Particularly is this noticeable with regard to its women. Jostling on the same pavement with the dainty fashionist is the care-worn working-girl." She was quick to say that neither class of women had an enviable life; the affluent woman lacked sufficient occupations as well as her husband's company, and the working-girls worked thirteen-hour days, "with only half an hour at midday to eat their dinner of a slice of bread and butter or an apple, which they usually eat in the building, some of them having come a long distance ... the roar of machinery in that room is like the roar of Niagra [sic] (Falls)."

Sadder yet, these young girls made the hoop skirts fashionable women wore daily without a thought for those who labored tedious on their construction. Fern contrasts high fashion with the working-girls' attempt to duplicate, within the limits of their income, a sense of style. Fern prefaced the description by reminding her readers that the young women lived in rooms that lacked ventilation and "no accommodations for personal cleanliness"; these remarks framed the rest flawlessly: "...their dress is flimsy and foolish, and tawdry; always a hat, and feather or soiled artificial flower upon it; the hair dressed with an abortive attempt at style; a soiled petticoat; a greasy dress, a well-worn sacque or shawl, and a gilt breast-pin and earrings."[43] Even if the clothing was soiled and flimsy, it represented an attempt to be stylish. And those who made high fashion happen for those who could afford it knew only too well what accessories could do to make the ensemble. The young working-girls probably would have felt wounded by Fern's calling their attention to these details "foolish," but they would have missed the larger irony and point: their psychological rather than physical pleasure, to return to Gilman's terms, meant even those who were on subsistence wages sacrificed in the name of fashionable appearance.

On both sides of the Atlantic, dressmakers had been exploited for decades, and their plight represented in paintings exhibited in London's Royal Academy from the 1840s forward and staged by women playwrights in the era of the New Woman. Victorian painters chose to portray the workers neatly arrayed, but isolated in rooms that bespoke deprivation. Dressmakers were at the mercy of aristocratic women and their social calendars. Oftentimes, they worked through the night to retain the favor of their clients, an outrage the artists felt would appeal to "manly virtue" as a call to reform. In England, Thomas Hood's "Song of the Shirt" appeared in *Punch* in December of 1843; that was the same year of R.D. Grainger's parliamentary report for the Children's Employment Commission. Numerous journalistic exposés had followed. But it was Edith Lyttleton's 1906 drama *Warp and Woof* that gave the genre its widest audience; although it was essentially a three-act tract, the production starred the pre-eminent Mrs. Patrick Campbell, an actress who would go on to star in Bernard Shaw's *Pygmalion* in 1913, at the height of the suffragettes' radical street actions.[44]

4

Ready-to-Wear: Joan as Iconographic Public Woman

Perhaps the most apparent need and use for Joan of Arc in the nineteenth century was as a prototype for women crusaders. No longer willing to remain background "window dressing," women from middle- and upper-class backgrounds began to step forward and address audiences from the mid-nineteenth century forward. Two professions served as models for platform speaking: preachers and actors. In a popular culture that came to expect interactive experience, it was easy to see why politics and theater borrowed freely from each other. Helene Roberts' article on clothing and the image of Victorian women points to William Thackeray's *Paris Sketch Book* of 1840 for his observation that clothing transformed Louis XIV into the imposing figure he came to represent. Roberts cites the *Quarterly Review* of 1847 and its declaration that dress as symbolic language became "a kind of personal glossary — a species of body phrenology ... every woman walks about with a placard on which her leading qualities are advertised."[1]

Once women determined to add audible and idea-laden voices to this "placard," it was essential to design every aspect of its appearance and resulting appeal. Despite the unmistakable physical as well as psychological confinement of women's dress in the nineteenth century, its very presence on public platforms ensured audiences and media coverage. The American organization that succeeded splendidly with this formula was the WCTU (Woman's Christian Temperance Union) under the leadership of Frances Willard. She even commissioned a specially designed "Willard Dress" to ensure the rhetorical opportunity for women speakers, according to Carol Mattingly. Mattingly cites a write-up from Annie Miller that "clearly equated women's dress with ethos." Mattingly quotes Miller's note that "Dress is all important, for it marks the refinement of character as unmistakably as does the behavior or conversation ... and by dress I mean clothing the body so that the integrity of natural functions shall be considered in connection with the picturesque effect." Miller's advertisement also offered a free pattern of the "divided skirt" for anyone ordering the dress.[2]

Willard paid even more attention to her own constructed appearance and consequent image, and she gained steady and positive press coverage as a result. Willard emphasized her natural appearance through a combination of "modest dress," "simple hairstyle" and avoidance of "flashy or elaborate decoration." These efforts

American World War I Poster. James Montgomery Flagg, *Stage Women's War Relief* (1918). The combination of theater, social commitment, and stylized gesture shows how this single figure had multiple parts to play, and she was respectable in all. The nursing uniform underneath the fur coat implies the virtue and character under the costume of stage character and possible celebrity (*Library of Congress*).

pre-disposed audiences to "hear and be sympathetic to her messages. Would-be cynics found her sincere in promoting her cause rather than in seeking notoriety for herself, placing her within appropriate feminine conventions.... She constantly reminded the public that she and other members of the WCTU were 'womanly' women."[3] Such a designation was essential, as detractors of "sensible dress" (the later incarnation of dress reform) saw simpler clothes for women as the end of womanliness.

Frances Willard expanded the work within the WCTU with the same vigor she used to maximize the organization's positive press coverage. Although temperance legislation remained its top priority, the organization participated not only in middle-class causes, especially suffrage and political engagement, but also in the struggle for workers' rights. Willard's own indefatigable energy became reinvigorated with the invention of the bicycle. Willard's own book on her experience with bicycles, *A Wheel Within a Wheel: How I Learned to Ride the Bicycle* (1895), expressed how riding released the suppression of her spirit that had been taken away on her sixteenth birthday, "when the hampering long skirts were brought, with their accompanying corset and high heels; my hair was clubbed up with pins, and I remember writing in my journal, in the first heartbreak of a young human colt taken from its pleasant pasture, 'Altogether, I recognize that my occupation is gone.'"[4]

By the time she learned to ride a bicycle, Willard was fifty-three, so it was not so easy. But she persevered, not only for her own physical well-being, but because she believed the bicycle was one way to give women a "wider world, for I hold that the more interests women and men can have in common, in thought, word, and deed, the happier it will be for the home." Willard's remark could have served as an antidote to the misnomer that equated women's emancipation with men's emasculation and the end of family life! The description of her "bicycling costume" was likewise phrased in a mollifying yet straightforward style: "This consisted of a skirt and blouse of tweed, with belt, rolling collar, and loose cravat, the skirt three inches from the ground; a round straw hat; and walking shoes with gaiters. It was a simple modest suit, to which no person of common sense could take exception."[5] An endorsement for bicycle riding for women of this kind was important; as it came from one of the most respected public American women, it was even more powerful. But most significant of all was Willard's appeal to women of all ages to bicycle, or to at least give up their cumbersome Victorian dress. Helene Roberts points to a British bicycle advertisement with a similar theme, in more visual fashion. It contrasted the "wheel of the past (the spinning wheel) with the wheel of the present (the bicycle) and the long-skirted woman of the past seated dutifully by the hearth with the unencumbered, independent, new woman wheeling into the twentieth century, not wholly emancipated, but liberated from her actual and symbolic encumbrances of long skirts and tight lacing."[6]

Yet femininity had not gone out of style; the blouses featured lace trims, and the high collars framed the increasingly bouffant hairstyle made famous by Charles Dana Gibson. His drawings, posters, and magazine covers created a sensation: Gibson Girls.

Not only was there a "look" associated with this designation, but there was also a tacit understanding of the personality that went with it. Demure on the one hand, on the other hand athletic as well as confident and comfortable in the outside world. They had spunk as well as style. Only some of them went to college, but the look and behavior was spread among the various ethnicities, races, and social classes thanks to ready-to-wear garments and mass advertising campaigns in newspapers and magazines throughout the country.

As the NWSA (National Woman Suffrage Association) in the United States corroborated the WCTU efforts, the press grew even more interested. An unfortunate twist occurred when the focus turned to fabric and jewelry choices by the speakers: expensive silks and genuine gems became semiotic cues for ladies of high purpose. The organizations' emphasis on feminine methods of presentation —flowers and banners— gave a public space a home-like quality, but also unwittingly added to the elitist frame of reference.[7] The suffrage campaigns in Britain and the United States combined a mollifying visual impression to capitalize on the belief in the domestic ideal and its accompanying perception of the "innate" moral superiority of women. The slogans, posters, and emblems of the movement (i.e. buttons, pins, even decks of playing cards) reminded the population at large that the push for suffrage was a push for better mothers, who would instruct their children more wisely than ever about their moral values and social responsibilities.[8]

Both the suffrage campaigns and labor unions borrowed styles of clothing and rhetoric from actresses, and coupled these with the visual look and known appreciation of their private theatricals: *tableaux vivants*. In this stylized form of entertainment, women were allegorical figures, holding poses like artists' models. The historical figures portrayed embodied ideals of virtue and strength already associated with women, and yet routinely represented women's successes over the centuries in non-traditional leadership roles for their material. In this one venue, women dominated; male characters were background figures, and men in the audience were in the passive rather than active role.

The genre was far more significant to the development of women's and later feminist consciousness than its simple definition of impersonating figures or abstract concepts in frozen poses would suggest. In actuality, these theatricals reinforced the concepts of the public platform, and writings about women's nature and roles that permeated nineteenth and early twentieth-century life. Monika Elbert argues that the practice of women trying on a "variety of personae" became a project of "self-fashioning" that "invited them to envision themselves in idealized roles, and as they did so, they were learning how to integrate their identities as public and private figures. It was a lesson that would not be lost on future generations of women." The lesson was two-fold; first, the *tableaux vivants* raised awareness as to what was true of women over the course of time versus what was deemed appropriate for a given time period, and second, the genre gave the spectator true involvement. Just as women shrewdly used more feminine style to attract support for their social and political platforms, women learned to both identify and conceal the empowerment they gained from the roles they played. As Elbert puts it, the entertainments were like still photographs, capable of capturing "moments of interiority from woman's private sphere [that] then iconographically translate that personal experience out into the public arena."[9]

Plays and novels from the late nineteenth and early twentieth centuries make use of the *tableaux vivants*; an especially notable example is from Edith Wharton's 1905 novel, *The House of Mirth*. The novel's heroine, Lily Bart, begins life in the upper classes, but her family fortune dissipates and she has to sustain herself and her image, sometimes through gambling, and at other times by courting favor from more affluent acquaintances. When the *tableau vivant* occurs in the novel, Lily's position has begun to waver, and Wharton's use of this genre allows the character to reveal more than she could have done in conversation. Wharton reminds her readers that the effect of these entertainments relies on more than lights and gauzy costume; they also depend on "a corresponding adjustment of the mental vision ... to the responsive fancy they may give magic glimpses of the boundary world between fact and imagination." Among the spectators is Lawrence Selden, whose attachment to Lily likewise wavers. When Lily chooses her character for the *tableau vivant*, she wisely decides to portray a Joshua Reynolds portrait: an uncanny likeness to herself. The narrator remarks that Lily had shown her "artistic intelligence in selecting a type so like her own that she could embody the person represented without ceasing to be herself." Selden's response is even more telling: "for the first time he seemed to see before him the real Lily Bart, divested of the trivialities of her little world, and catching for a moment a note of that eternal harmony of which her beauty was a part."[10] Momentarily, Selden sees the way life slips by as we get caught up in the trivialities, but Wharton has more in mind; through the male gaze, she tells the reader that women appear most appealing when frozen, in an artist's frame.

In painting and in poetry, the trope of the woman in repose or death dominated the Victorian era. Robert Browning's last Duchess hangs on the wall, and Dante Gabriel Rossetti's poetry is equally filled with images of sensuality and death. His sister Christina composed the sonnet that captured the male artists as surely as they had captured their female models: "In An Artist's Studio." The poem's speaker gives the reader a tour of a painter's obsession, as seen through a repetitious series of portraits. The biting tone is even more pronounced because Christina Rossetti did not attempt to obscure the fact that it was her brother's studio and his destructive feelings she designated. Beginning with the same face and figure that belonged to a model "hidden just behind those screens" (line 3), Rossetti turns next to the painter's gaze: "That mirror gave back all her loveliness" (line 4). Yet the model was "A nameless girl in freshest summer-greens,/ A saint, an angel: — every canvass means/ The same one meaning, neither more nor less./ He feeds upon her face by day and night" (lines 6–9). The woman in the paintings gazes back at the artist in one way only: as he desired her to be. The concluding lines read: "Fair as the moon and joyful as the light:/ Not wan with waiting, not with sorrow dim;/ Not as she is, but was when hope shone bright;/ Not as she is, but as she fills his dream."[11]

Visual representations of women throughout the nineteenth century and into the twentieth exemplified the spectrum of opinions regarding the woman question, but almost universally focused on the female as body —clothed, or nude. Allegorical figures of women as abstractions of virtues and ideas retained their centrality, and the fervent psychosocial works of Eugene Delacroix intersected many of these categories. A favorite among these is his 1830 painting "Liberty Leading the People." In this vast canvas, Liberty is a large and earthy figure, albeit with a clearly spiritual as well as political role to play. She is bare-breasted because her garments, the same color as the sun-infiltrated dust in the background, have slipped off her shoulders in the fray of battle. She holds a tricolor standard above the crowd in her right hand, and a musket in her left, thereby bringing the allegorical and the present moment jarringly together. Stephen Eisenman adds further insight into the painting by concentrating on the unnatural pose, especially of the figure's head. The head turns to present a "flattened outline" of the scene to the viewer. Eisenman argues that "Delacroix makes Woman the link between matter and understanding, the medium of passage from fact to meaning and back again."[12] Yet, as Eisenman points out, Liberty is also a "robust plebian — sunbrowned, barefoot, and careless of all modesty ... she belongs to all ages and classes represented among the living and the dead.... If she were the least bit more idealized ... the painting would revert to a curious juxtaposition of reportage with arbitrary allegorical accompaniment."[13]

Obviously, the combination of archetypal and contemporary referents in the work was both potent and incomprehensible. These shocking and yet inspiring aspects of the painting kept it out of public view for decades. According to Carol Duncan, this particular censorship decision was multi-dimensional in purpose. The 1830 event did not extend privileges to the people as a whole, so Delacroix's figure of Liberty was a "frightening and offensive specter of democracy to good bourgeois citizens" even when seen, at the artist's instigation, at the 1855 World's Fair. Critics in the 1850s as well as the 1830s complained of the "commonness of Liberty and her unclean friends." The work was not on more permanent display until the more liberal political mood of the 1860s.[14] Duncan here points to both the repetitive dismay over a powerful and "unladylike" woman, and to the class issues that were on the front burners in early nineteenth-century Europe.

Three of the vastly different and collectively fascinating depictions of Joan of Arc in fine art produced between 1850 and 1880 are Jean-Auguste-Dominique Ingres' "Joan of Arc at the Coronation of Charles VII" (1854), Dante Gabriel Rossetti's "Joan of Arc Kissing the Sword of Deliverance" (1863), and Jules Bastien-Lepage's "Joan of Arc" (1879). If Delacroix's "Marianne" female figure of Liberty can be seen as a nod to the historical French precedent, Joan of Arc, the actual paintings of Joan likewise solidify the physical strength as well as spiritual presence of "The Maid," and place her in a particular scene of her inspiration or triumph. For all their commonality, however, the three images represent Joan's body very differently. Regine Pernoud explains the categories that underlie French visual representation of Joan of Arc. Unlike most historical subjects, no accurate drawings or paintings were preserved, so artists have been able to conceive her according to their own individual tastes, and/or those of the era they lived in. Pernoud identifies three traditions that have prevailed: "shepherdess to whom the saints appear (visionary); female soldier carrying armor, the sword, and the standard (warrior); the saint at the stake in Rouen (martyr)."[15]

Ingres costumes Joan for one of her most lofty occasions: the coronation of Charles VII. She appears tall and solidly grounded in the scene, with her left hand resting on the table holding candles, and her right hand raised to hold a brilliantly colored standard with a red staff. Her armor covers her bodice, is tightly fitted at the waist, and then drapes over her hips and onto her red patterned full skirt. A sheath for her sword lies below Joan's left hip. Ingres included all the accoutrements to depict Joan as warrior. Joan's hair is long, but pulled back almost in the style of eighteenth-century gentlemen, but a barely discernable halo and her transfixed eyes remind viewers that Joan was no ordinary person. More to the point, on that day her rapt attention was on the fulfillment of her divine commandment.

Dante Gabriel Rossetti's depiction of Joan was commissioned in 1862. The image differed remarkably from his idealized women figures. The only Pre-Raphaelite trademark in this image is the long flowing hair, but even here there is distinction: it is off her face and down her back, but out of the viewer's sight. Her garments are richly patterned medieval designs, befitting a knight, and the scene he chose was Joan discovering the sword of St. Catherine in a remote church. Rossetti showed Joan as androgynous, almost masculine, particularly given the visible Adam's apple in the throat and the large, muscular neck. Her face, in profile, is raptly attentive to her prayers, but of course it could be argued that here Rossetti conformed to his idealized dreamy female faces. Either way, Rossetti's Joan remains a figure intent and purposeful, with wonderfully expressive and intelligent facial features.

Jules Bastien-Lepage's "Joan of Arc" (1879) captivates the viewer even before he or she can take in the whole of this vast painting. The figure of Joan at the moment that she hears her Voices, which suddenly emerge into view when we "read" Joan's face, represents her at her most spiritual and most earthy self. This is precisely why this painting often is the quintessential image of Joan for many people. Bastien-Lepage's Joan has bared arms, which show her strength, and hands that have obviously just been in the soil. Her clothing, peasant-style down to the kerchief in her hair, blends into the scene, leaving the face, and especially the eyes, to gaze through the viewer to the spiritual message. Painted after the humiliating defeat in the Franco-Prussian War, this painting inspired the French to regain their national pride, and yet was housed in the Metropolitan Museum of Art in New York by 1889.[16]

Between 1890 and 1910, several factors converged regarding costume, public women, and the molding of Joan of Arc's feminized persona. Less radical than blatantly masculine dress was the aesthetic movement, which derived from the Pre-Raphaelite painters' depiction of women in diaphanous gowns that skimmed rather than defined the body. Roberts suggests that these styles "helped to provide an acceptable alternative to fashionable dress" because they retained their feminine emphasis while allowing freer movement. Prominent actresses, particularly Ellen Terry and Sarah Bernhardt, joined the wives of the painters, e.g., Lizzie Siddal Rossetti and Janey Morris, who eschewed the corset in favor of "a fluid style of dress with simple lines, based on a vague medieval model, that became something of a fad in more fashionable circles."[17] Terry and Bernhardt were models of bohemian and outrageous lifestyles as well as independent professionals who ran their own careers.

Artists' visions of women ranged from the ethereal to the lascivious from the eighteenth century to the twentieth. While attitudes toward women's sexuality underwent extreme changes during the nineteenth century, what stayed constant was the medieval Eve/Mary designation of female figures, labeled by Carol Duncan as Eve/Salome/Sphinx/Madonna. By the 1890s, the slots shrank to "virgins and vampires," and by the 1910s the allegorical contexts dropped, yet women remained objects rather than subjects for male visual artists working in high culture. Duncan confirms the era's preoccupation with men and women, but sees the response of painters as much more conservative than literary or theatrical arts, where feminist voices and principles began to take their place.[18] Theatrical women knew how to command attention as well as lure an audience into accepting a new way of thinking. Within a hundred years, actresses had gained enormous financial, cultural, and personal power, especially those who performed in "high art" rather than burlesque.

One of the most complex artists of this era was Sarah Bernhardt; her acting style was clearly nineteenth-century, but her use of publicity and business savvy placed her squarely in the early twentieth century. Bernhardt was born five years before photography became an art form, rose to prominence when advertising and then neon lights lined the boulevards, and lived long enough to make films. Bernhardt was also immortalized in Belle Époque posters by Mucha and Grasset for her roles, including Jeanne d'Arc. Bernhardt herself painted and sculpted, and was influential in jewelry design.[19] Her magnum opus was herself. In her memoir, *My Double Life*, she distinguished between greatness in an actress and an artist; the former is impressive, while the great artist, according to Bernhardt, required that a personality emerge to be identified with the performer's name. A great actress who is not a great artist has not "created a being, a vision, that will evoke her memory. She puts on the gloves of others, but inside out...."[20] Bernhardt's stage performances were mesmerizing, but not in the way that Rachel's had been. The focal points were the combined effects of her exquisitely modulated voice and her obvious sensuality, made even more pronounced by her modern dress. She used melodramatic gestures and overacted in twentieth-century terms, but those who admired her proclaimed her the greatest living actress. Freud kept a picture of her in his office after seeing her perform. He did not think much of the play, but Bernhardt's effect on him is worth noting: "After the first words uttered in an intimate, endearing voice, I felt I had known her all my life. I have never seen an actress who surprised me so little; I at once believed everything about her."[21]

Bernhardt's own criteria for actress and artist are readily apparent in her description of how she prepared for roles, particularly for Joan of Arc. The translator's introduction to the memoir notes that Bernhardt made sure the public knew what she herself presented. Larson emphasizes that the memoirs are surprisingly novelistic, and they point to how consciously Bernhardt wished to represent herself: the book "does not so much tell us the 'facts' of Sarah's life, but rather fashions a persona for her, transforming her life into drama and her self into a character ... [for example] her insistence on her early religious mysticism creates a stereotypical Jeanne d'Arc–like image of fragile, innocent vulnerability." Despite this image as a fragmented aspect of her life, the double consciousness that the title states is particularly important because of the many historical and classical literary figures that she portrayed. Here is Bernhardt on fact vs. legend:

> On occasion I have tried, along with the dramatist, to force the audience to return to the truth and to destroy the legendary aspect of certain characters whose true nature modern historians have revealed; but the audience has not followed me. I soon came to the realization that legend always triumphs over historical fact.... We throw ourselves into pursuit of them in the ethereal heavens or in the infinity of dream. We discard their humanity as dross ... to leave them clothed in idealism and seated on a throne of love.[22]

Bernhardt's insight applied to her own time as much as any theatrical epoch. Because the conceptions of "woman" had been so rooted in containment of physical motion and intellectual limitations, the need to be both gracious women and paradigms for the future became infused with a new kind of self-assurance as leadership in suffrage and labor causes passed to a younger generation of women. Their methodology differed sharply. Perhaps more impatient for results, or perhaps just more in tune with the pace of the twentieth century, younger leaders worried less about affronting patriarchal structure. More to the point, they learned from the most dominant examples of public women around: actresses. Bernhardt had showed them that a feminine costume could still embody a more aggressive individual who stood not only for the betterment of others, but of herself. As Susan Glenn suggests: "The enabling condition for Bernhardt's radical rewriting of the female social script was ... the emergence of a modern urban transatlantic culture of spectacle that she helped usher in."[23]

Regardless of the apparent mixed message, something else emerged absolutely from their public personae: they would no longer brook confinement. These pageants showcased moving, speaking women, who were using the allegorical representations

99

to imply that modern women embodied all of the virtues visual and literary artists had celebrated, but they were actual individuals who wanted to be nobody's window dressing. Glenn characterizes their multi-dimensional image as: "mother, worker, consumer, 'municipal housekeeper,' womanly woman and modern girl—feminine, stylish, fashionable and pretty."[24] Like Henrik Ibsen's Nora Helmer, these middle-class women were slamming the door on the "doll house" and asking men to accept them on equal terms.

An American actress known to Bernhardt was Julia Marlowe. Like her French counterpart, she was renowned for her Shakespearean roles, including breeches parts. Marlowe was another actress who worked in London as well as the U.S., and she was acquainted with the powerful Mrs. Patrick Campbell. All of these threads would converge when she and her husband, E. H. Sothern, became partners with an American playwright and poet who wanted to bring American theater into the tradition of poetic drama: Percy MacKaye. The vehicle for their collaboration was a play about Joan of Arc. This version, *Jeanne D'Arc*, brought them together and caused a breach that would make the play fall into obscurity. The issue was over the way the play had to be cut down: MacKaye's emphasis on the inner qualities did not mesh with Marlowe's wishes. She held the power in the contract, and despite successes in Boston, Philadelphia, New York and London in 1907, refused to perform it again and would not allow anyone else to do so either. This decision was odd considering the reviewers' acclaim that Joan was one of Marlowe's finest roles.[25]

MacKaye wrote his play in 1906, knowing full well that the country was enamored of Joan as a person of great strength and spirituality. His emphasis was on Joan as the romantic child of nature, as Twain's had been. Yet, the two representations had great differences; MacKaye was more interested in the poetic truths of the story than in the politics. His first act is in Joan's birthplace, Domrémy, and places Joan in the midst of her peer group, at the Fairy Tree. MacKaye introduces Joan's relation to her friends and family, but also makes it clear that her friends know about her spiritual connections, and the Prophecy of Merlin is mentioned. His portrayal of the Voices scene includes wording from Joan's answers at her Trial of Condemnation. Echoes of Schiller's emphasis on Joan's virginity as the substance of her vow to St. Michael likewise appears. MacKaye also has St. Michael's voice emerge through a stained glass window.

Treatment of the Dauphin and Court are largely accurate, although the scene lacks the humor and energy Shaw will bring to it. Mrs. Patrick Campbell had given MacKaye the Murray translation of the Trial Transcripts that Shaw would also use. Yet, MacKaye veered away from historical accuracy, possibly in the interests of conveying the image of Joan as a vulnerable young woman, which suited his own era's evolving image of young women as both morally purer than men, and capable of public functions. Joan's military actions are here, along with the horrific insults from the English at Orléans. The combined, and therefore limited, characterization MacKaye gives Joan ultimately disappoints.

Rather than focus on Joan's relationship with the commander of the French Army, Dunois, MacKaye shifts focus to one of her followers, and makes him an ardent admirer. D'Alecon is enamored of Joan, and it is he rather than Brother Martin who helps her regain her faith before she is burned. Yet he recognizes that he loves the young girl rather than the inspired leader — and wishes to marry "Jehanette," which cannot occur. At the same time, he connects Joan to great women of antiquity, especially Hippolyta, "virgin-queen of Attica"; afterwards, he remarks in solitude: "A child! And her clear eyes, upturned to Heaven, shall influence the stars of all the ages."[26] Thus the play concludes with the warrior-saint, bridging both halves of the canonization-era feeling about Joan of Arc and her continued cultural importance.

In a striking way, the radical suffrage parades that lined the streets of New York and Washington in the 1910s would combine theatrical performance and feminine virtue via costume and slogans on banners.[27] These suffrage parades featured women dressed as Liberty, while someone rode a horse carrying a banner — like Joan of Arc. Since their demands were considered radical, they shrewdly chose costumes that were anything but "mannish" — they presented themselves as well-dressed, respectable women. This new generation of suffragists also recognized that they needed to work against their anti-feminine image, so the softening of their own came with that of Joan of Arc. As Glenn puts it, Joan was "the heroic symbol of woman's willingness to right and sacrifice for a righteous cause" and through Joan, the female militant could be "translated" into a "powerful and affirmative figure."[28] Unlike Joan, they did not need to wear male attire to occupy male space. Looked at from this perspective, their "womanly" dress code was in their best interests, and through it they controlled male as well as female gaze. The costume gave them entrée so the work could be done.

Beginning around 1907, American suffrage leaders began to follow the methodologies of the British suffragettes, who not only disrupted meetings, but also got themselves arrested and went on hunger strikes. Commitment was total: "Joining the WSPU was akin to joining a spiritual army. The language, iconography, and behavior ... were in terms of an army at war with society.... Members were encouraged to wear the WSPU's colors (white for purity, green for hope, and purple for loyalty)" when they gathered in Hyde Park or sold copies of their magazine, *Votes for Women*[29]; a figure dressed like Joan of Arc was on its cover, and pins of Christabel Pankhurst also resembled Joan.[30]

Bernhardt's American tours gave American suffragists the chance to engage with her directly. In 1910, Bernhardt was about to revive her 1890 *Jeanne d'Arc* role; a group calling themselves the "Joan of Arc Suffrage League" greeted Bernhardt and presented her with flowers and, although she would not speak, Bernhardt agreed to become an honorary member of their society. Three years later, Bernhardt's tour coincided with the New York Woman Suffrage Party's attempt to get the franchise on the state ballot. Bernhardt arrived on May 4, 1913, in time for a scheduled suffrage parade, and told

Hilda Dallas, British poster advertising *The Suffragette* newspaper, 1912. The Museum of London comments: "A suffragette [Christabel Pankhurst follower] dressed as Joan of Arc, patron saint of the suffragettes. The increasingly militant tone of the latter stages of the campaign is demonstrated by the use of this image, illustrated using the suffragette colours of purple, green and white" (*HIP/Art Resource, New York; Museum of London*).

reporters: "I believe in the independence of women. I am for the vote. Perhaps the methods of the militants in England are necessary ... women who starve themselves to death for an idea are not objects of ridicule. They interest me; they touch me very much!"[31]

The schism in the woman's movement that had existed between middle and upper-class women and their push for suffrage and legal rights, and working-class women who struggled for fair labor practices, finally gave way by the 1910s. The only painful irony was the cause of the low-priced goods that seemed to be so important for women's improved status: sweatshop labor, which paid workers by the piece at a rate that was barely subsistence level. Many of these workers were immigrant women who brought their clothing skills as well as their determination to America. Like the earlier generations of working-class women, they yearned for what they deemed the privileged status of their customers, some of whom worked on behalf of suffrage but had ignored the plight of garment workers. In effect, these twentieth-century women became the corollary to the overworked dressmakers of the elite.

The Triangle Shirtwaist fire in 1911 led to the garment workers' strikes where, for the first time, middle-class feminists joined their working-class counterparts. The young women who were virtually imprisoned in this factory were recent immigrants to the United States and had no voice in their own working conditions. When scraps of fabric caught fire, the workers found themselves locked in because the foreman, himself on a break, did not trust them to go out to the restroom and return to their sewing machines. The mistreatment became even more horrifying once people realized that the fire authorities had been after the company for months (as reported in a series of articles nine months earlier in the *New York Times*), to remove the excess fabric and unlock the doors during working hours before the fire actually occurred.[32]

The tragedy of the Triangle Shirtwaist fire reveals the connection to Joan's story at its most obvious; Joan was cognizant of the limitations of her social class and gender but, owing to her belief in her Voices and God as well as her right to follow their commandments, also recognized that traditions were merely forms, not absolute laws. Her decisions and actions thus confirmed notions of the individual making her way in the world, regardless of conventions. Not only did the fire receive journalistic exposés, but also a public forum. Spearheaded by the labor organizers for the garment workers, it was held a few weeks later at New York's Metropolitan Opera House. Rose Schneiderman spoke eloquently and bluntly about the reprehensibility of workers' treatment in factories, and poignantly about the workers' plight. Her speech, "We Have Found You Wanting," became a rallying cry for solidarity, similar in impact to Joan's speeches among the people in the towns. Schneiderman's words encapsulated the travesty: "This is not the first time girls have been burned alive in the city. Every week I must learn of the untimely death of one of my sister workers. Every year thousands of us are maimed. The life of men and women is so cheap and property is so sacred. There are so many of us for one job it matters little if 146 of us are burned to death."

"Suffrage parade" (March 13, 1913). (*Inez Milholland Boissevain, Washington, D.C.*).

Schneiderman clarified the moral grounds and gave the gauntlet to the workers, who would have to work on their own behalf in light of the spilled blood of the Triangle and other labor sufferings.[33] This event brought them together to bring these inequities into public discourse, via the lecture circuit, pamphlets and magazine articles, fiction, or the theater. Interestingly, this event was not the only one that used a performance space for political gatherings. Once suffrage speakers began drawing large crowds, their speeches were promoted and rehearsed, similarly to other forms of public perform- ance. Women speakers were considered "headliners" like entertainers. Many venues grew to perpetuate the trend, from newspapers to theater to amusement parks and fairs.[34]

Radical women, especially Emma Goldman, were big names in the popular imag- ination. Susan Glenn quotes her as saying "it is more important to do propaganda with one's personality than with words." Elizabeth Gurley Flynn, a powerful Socialist speaker, was described by American novelist Theodore Dreiser as "An East Side Joan of Arc" for her "eloquence, her youth and loveliness."[35] Both of these women were asked by theatrical producers to appear onstage, but the women knew that the theater and activism were not synonymous. Glenn's explanation of the distinctions is first-rate:

> Theater licensed female transgression so long as it could sell it as entertainment. Female activism, however it might take on the look and feel of theater, had vastly different agen- das.... Nevertheless, Hammerstein's invitation to Goldman and Belasco's summons to

German actress Hedwig Reicher wearing costume of "Columbia" (March 13, 1913). This photograph and the one on page 104 were taken at the same event, and reflect the sophistication of suffrage parades. The expansiveness of the pageantry, and the use of theatrical spacing as well as *tableau vivant* costuming, posing, and expression, demonstrate the complexity and impressiveness of these outdoor public events (*Library of Congress*).

Gurley Flynn symbolized a broad cultural shift in which acting and activism, theater and politics, began to blur. As women on both sides of the footlights were making spectacles of themselves in public, being political and being theatrical became mutually reinforcing aspects of a new style of femininity.[36]

Although the activists did not want to be considered "an act" in the vaudeville sense of the term, they were savvy enough to take advantage of the public's love of big moments, suspense, and publicity stunts.

Just as nineteenth-century women activists had done, early twentieth-century feminists would capitalize on society's belief in the moral superiority of women. Their message reached the public through a variety of media, including political cartoons and war posters. The social historian J. C. Furnas provides a thorough, balanced discussion of the mood as well as the facts of the World War I era in America. In 1914, at the onset of World War I, *Life* magazine featured a cartoon of Kaiser Wilhelm dragging Europe away from civilization; Europe was depicted as a girl being dragged by the hair.[37] To underscore their resistance to the idea of war and the propaganda's depiction of women, American women, under the leadership of Jane Addams, founded a Women's Peace Party in 1914.[38] When the tide of public opinion turned and the United

Howard Chandler Christy, *Gee!! I Wish I Were a Man. I'd Join the Navy* (1917–18). Here the tension among current images of young women is readily apparent. A vamp-like pose on a cross-dressed body demonstrates the flapper influence. Conversely, the poster's slogan nods to the nineteenth-century sentimental tradition, with the woman wistful for a role that can only belong to a man (*National Archives/NARA Still Pictures Branch*).

States entered the war in 1917, leaders of this peace party were ostracized, and a split occurred within the ranks of the American suffrage movement about shifting priorities.

One of the most audacious acts of the suffragists was the demonstration outside the White House. Some of the public was outraged that the women would picket during wartime, but that was precisely the point. How could the president say he was fighting for democracy when half of the nation was left out of American democracy? Needless to say, the police stepped in and made arrests, and were victorious when they captured the leader, Alice Paul. However, the authorities did not realize that "they had also jailed the inspired reformer, the martyr-type, who dies for a principle, but never bends or breaks." The parallel between her and Joan of Arc was unmistakable, and not ignored even then. The prisoner announced that her arrest was not due to her supposed offence of blocking traffic, "but because I pointed out to President Wilson ... that he is obstructing the progress of justice and democracy at home while Americans fight for it abroad."[39] During her seven-month imprisonment, Paul was force-fed, and when she was weak enough to be sent to the hospital, a police Commissioner and alienists examined her there; their purpose was to uncover her mental instability. Yet another parallel to Joan emerged here. When asked to speak about the work of the suffrage movement, Alice Paul was only too willing, which went against the theory that she suffered from the mania of persecution. After it was finished, one of the examiners reported: "'There is a spirit like Joan of Arc, and it is as useless to try to change it as to change Joan of Arc. She will die but she will never give up.'"[40]

Some other American women continued to fight for peace, but they also began to use the wartime labor shortage to their own advantage. According to Maurine Weiner Greenwald's study, *Women, War and Work: The Impact of World War I on Women Workers in the U.S.*, women banded together to raise salaries and break gender boundaries of certain jobs. They joined more unions and used the strategies of walkouts and collective bargaining more often and more effectively than ever before in American history. Women also used the propaganda of the war, reminding industrial bosses of the idealistic slogans of the war and their moral obligation to live up to them. These efforts emphasized that the women thought of themselves as "people first and common laborers, machine tenders, or clerks second."[41]

The wartime home front environment sought to glorify more traditional, domestic virtues: thrift, sacrifice, and moral protectiveness. The propaganda reached dramatic proportions. Greenwald notes the divergent messages of the federal government's posters. One was entitled "Will you have a part in Victory"; it showed a young white woman draped in an American flag planting a vegetable garden. Another was a plea for women to become stenographers. A secretary, seated at her desk, sees a shadowy image of a soldier. An opposite message was in a recruitment poster for the Navy. A woman, dressed as a seaman, proclaims: "GEE!! I WISH I WERE A MAN. I'D JOIN THE NAVY."[42] Once America entered the war, the U.S. government swiftly responded, appealing to all citizens to contribute to the war effort by buying Liberty Bonds and War Savings Stamps. The messages were truly inflammatory. The Liberty Bonds posters carried the ideology, i.e., "HUN OR HOME? BUY MORE LIBERTY BONDS," while the war stamps were linked to the home effort of thrift and sacrifice for the troops: "HELP THEM: KEEP YOUR WAR SAVINGS PLEDGE."[43]

Most intriguing is the enormous proliferation of iconographic uses of Joan in

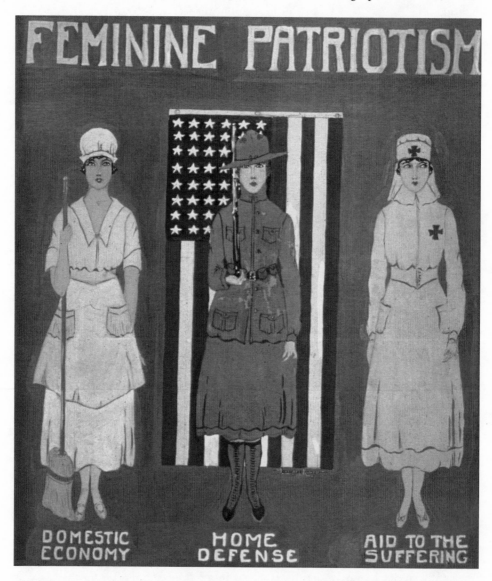

Feminine Patriotism (American, 1917–18). Almost an alter-ego, here the women's figures are appropriately attired, yet clearly engaged in war-time efforts that have enlarged their sphere for the common good (*National Archives/NARA Still Pictures Branch*).

108

light of the "mass culture" of the industrial age, first via print media, and followed by the advent of photography, and film. Joan of Arc was immortalized in a war stamps poster from the United States Treasury Department.[44] The artist, Haskell Coffin, created a vampish, yet spiritual, image for Joan. She has curly red hair under her helmet, blue eyes respectfully pointed toward heaven. Although clad in armor, her figure is curvaceous. The dichotomy continues with her raised, clenched fist holding up her sword. She looks determined, but contented, and she is smiling. The two major gestures, eyes and right arm up, correspond to the legends of "The Maid," as well as to other visual portrayals, while the glamorous hair and body have nothing to do with historical accuracy.[45] The wording on the poster calls upon the noble, selfless nature of women. The headline, written above Joan's head reads, "Joan of Arc Saved France." The balance of the wording, below Joan's hips, announces: "WOMEN OF AMERICA/ SAVE YOUR COUNTRY/ BUY WAR SAVINGS STAMPS." The British government issued their own poster, with the same wording; the difference was in the casting of the figure of Joan: uniformed in the colors of the Union Jack, her strong, androgynous figure is more reminiscent of Rossetti's portrait from 1863.

World War I was the first war to be supported by public relations and propaganda. The main target was Germany and its atrocities. In his declaration-of-war speech to Congress, President Wilson emphasized the cruelty of the Germans and their broken promises. His specific topic was the haphazard, ruthless sinking of ships, regardless of military involvement. Wilson reminded the legislators that: "Even hospital ships and ships carrying relief to the sorely bereaved and stricken people of Belgium" were subject to random attack.[46] In the eminent young people's magazine *St. Nicholas* there were countless stories about "a heroic little French girl helping a soldier or a sturdy American boy smelling out a submarine hideaway."[47] Furnas also claims that by 1915 American newspaper readers knew that "the soul of France resided in a slim figure in fancy armor named 'Jona Vark.'"[48] One particular World War I Liberty Bond poster was especially significant: "LIBERTY BOUND OR LIBERTY BOND: U CAN CHANGE IT." In this very large pen-and-ink drawing by James Hart, Liberty is wearing a flag-like robe, with a cap perched askew, similar to the one Joan wore to the stake. And Liberty is indeed tied to the stake. Other World War I posters featured strong representations of American women, with reminiscent *tableaux vivants* imagery, ironically linking two political forces then in opposition: suffrage parades and patriotism. Charles Dana Gibson's poster for the National League for Woman's Service depicts a Gibson Girl in feminine military garb.

Clearly, American popular culture had embraced Joan, not only as an historical heroine, but as an archetypal individual well-suited to American conceptions of courage and charisma. Two years prior to the war stamp, Anna Vaughn Hyatt had sculpted a bronze figure of Joan, in armor and on horseback, in New York City. Although other sculptures were erected in Philadelphia and Washington, D.C., Hyatt's represented true authenticity, according to the American Society of the French Legion of Honor,

Charles Dana Gibson, *Help Her Carry On: National League for Woman's Service* (1918). Here is "Miss America," in military garb, with a tailored skirt substituting for the trousers, but tie, hat, and boots like a soldier. All of the confidence and competence associated with the "Gibson Girl" shines through this design, especially with its inclusion of official language expressing war-time need of women's services (*Library of Congress*).

Inc. Their records show that research was done to ensure the correctness of Joan's military costume, and stones from Rouen were purchased as part of the statue's base. Even a piece of Reims Cathedral, demolished by the Germans in 1915, was obtained and set into one of the base's panels.[49]

Then, in 1917, Joan of Arc was again a prominent aspect of American culture; Cecil B. DeMille produced *Joan the Woman*, a film greeted with great enthusiasm by audiences. Joan was portrayed by world-famous opera soprano Geraldine Farrar. DeMille was inspired to make the film because of the Joan of Arc vogue as well as Americans' interest in the fighting in France. But the film critic Vachel Lindsay was disappointed by DeMille's inclusion of Joan's sudden love for an English soldier, taken from Friedrich Schiller's *The Maid of Orléans*, and with the visual image of Joan as well. In his review for the *New Republic* he noted that: "Joan the Saint had disappeared to be replaced by a beautiful, buxom Amazon in armor."[50] DeMille's film, with screenplay by Jeanie MacPherson, focused squarely on Joan as the "people's saint," in the way the Socialist French government saw it. The frame of the film was the discovery of Joan's sword by an English soldier named Lionel (the name in Schiller's play) during World War I. He is terrified of what he believes will be his suicide mission. When he "sees" Joan, she transports him back to her own time. Joan has no voices except for in one small part of the film, which adds further emphasis to Joan as a prototype of the virtuous worker/soldier. Joan refers to herself as a "Petticoat General" on the one hand, and a "Milkmaid of France" on the other.

Joan's leadership role is shown clearly during Orléans. She gets her wound, but, more importantly, is shown as a hero/ine and cheered by crowds in the streets. To lead the Dauphin to the coronation, Joan wears a white dress with armor and carries her standard, and when she sees him crowned, melodrama appears: Joan clutches her breast ecstatically. The rest of the rise and fall are uneven, but what DeMille does very well is keep the politics consistent. When Joan is shown the instruments of torture, there is Ku Klux Klan imagery, which is especially interesting in light of D.W. Griffith's racist pair of films from the same years: *Birth of a Nation* (1915) and *Intolerance* (1916). The villain in this film is definitely Cauchon; when the end is near, the scene is named "The Last Move in the Game" and Cauchon orders the "worst ruffian" to guard her. The World War I frame concludes the film, as Lionel awakens from his dream vision of Joan of Arc and is ready to sacrifice himself for his own cause.[51]

Coffin's image of Joan from 1917 embodies the archetypal pose and facial expression of earlier artistic interpretations, and complements the graceful, feminized look of DeMille's film. Since it combines these popular, if incongruous, representations, the poster could serve its intended political purpose. The aspects of her character and her story then flourishing were those that were palatable to the more conservative elements of society; she was idolized as nurturing, compassionate, spiritual: an individual ever ready to combat the forces of evil. The 1917 American song "*Joan of Arc They Are Calling You*" pleads with Joan to return as helpmeet to her bleeding country and

War Stamps Poster. Haskell Coffin, *Joan of Arc Saved France: Women of America, Save Your Country* (1918). Coffin's image epitomizes the great interest the United States showed in Joan of Arc during the canonization era and during World War I. Despite her feminized and modern hair and cosmetics, she is in armor, sword raised, in a classic "Joan" pose. The confidence and conviction of the young women of the 1910s blends naturally with the medieval costume and slogan here (*National Archives/NARA Still Pictures Branch*).

countrymen. The song asks: "Her heart is bleeding;/ Are you unheeding?/ Come with the flame in your glance;/ Through the Gates of Heaven,/ with your sword in hand,/ Come your legions to command."[52]

The *New York Times* article from 1920 also reminds its readers that one of the great Allied victories in 1918 was fought on the very ground (Compiègne) on which Joan of Arc was captured in 1430. By the time of the Great War (World War I), the spirit of Joan resurfaced as, once again, France faced invaders. Despite the recurrence of elitist interests as the basis for World War I, there was unanimous reverence for "*La Pucelle*" (The Maid). Part of the explanation for this was the strengthening of the Third Republic, which rallied as protector to all of France. Joan's canonization was already a reality, so depictions of her became increasingly saintly, even in graphic art.[53] Because the war was longer than predicted, and because its horrors—mustard gas and airplane bombing—were theretofore unknown, suffering was as acute as it had been during the Hundred Years War, and morale among the troops just as low.[54]

At the time of the beatification of Joan of Arc in 1909, a canonization date was set for 1931, the five hundredth anniversary of her burning. Surprisingly, the process was accelerated; as the *New York Times* article from the date of the canonization casually states: "The great war may have had something to do with hastening the final date."[55] Logical though this may sound, a different scenario had also contributed to the change: the breakdown of relations between the Socialist French government and the Holy See between 1895 and 1905. A conservative (royalist) political organization worked for Joan's canonization, so as to hinder the government's desire to use Joan's new status for purely political reasons. Conflicting reasons for declaring Joan of Arc a saint had at last come to fore. Yet, it was the shameful Dreyfus Affair that cemented the royalists' claim on Joan as their icon. The accused and convicted "traitor" was a Jew. Despite abundant evidence of Dreyfus' innocence, the Army refused to reverse the verdict, claiming that such an action would shake confidence in the Republic. The breach between the Republic and the Church grew as a result. The Army's decision was reminiscent of the position of Joan's judges at her Trial of Condemnation, but it was the protectors of the *status quo* who used Joan as their representative since she had become associated with official French positions in her role as national symbol. When the sentencing was announced there was a cry: "Down with the Jews! Down with the Masonic Republic! Long live Joan of Arc!"[56] Fortunately, by 1899, Dreyfus was pardoned, and by 1906 completely exonerated.

Such decisions revealed the conflict between church and state, which climaxed in 1905 with the passage of the laic laws, separating their powers for the first time in French history.[57] Frolich neatly encapsulates the settling of 1920 as a date; the war was over, the French were on the winning side, and the "Holy See was willing to give them their saint if the French [Socialist] government would reestablish diplomatic relations."[58] Marina Warner provides a more ecclesiastical explanation. She believes the process of canonization for Joan of Arc was stymied by more than the

Franco-Prussian War and World War I. The debate still was ongoing at the time of her beatification and focused on one issue: "was her allegiance to God, above all other loyalties for her, or was her type of heroic virtue of this world?" This question was posed in 1888, and then withdrawn in 1920, clearing the way for the sanctity of Joan of Arc. Warner's assessment of the canonization process identifies its other unusual feature: Joan was designated a Virgin rather than a Martyr, which means that Joan's death is not considered dealt by the hands of enemies. Apparently, the Rehabilitation Trial furnished more of the materials for their deliberations than the Trial of Condemnation.[59]

The text of the official pronouncement of Joan's canonization reflects the evolution of Joan's image succinctly and powerfully. Rather than saying so directly, the pronouncement attributes the change in thinking to the "design of Divine Providence," specifically linking Joan's requests for pontifical hearing during the Trial of Condemnation in 1431 to the approval of her sanctification. Joan's request to be taken to the pope had been denied, but no matter: "this very appeal, although it did not suffice to stay her cruel punishment, was nonetheless destined to exercise a power and evoke an effect beyond all expectation." The conciliatory and elegiac tone carries all the way through. Part I characterizes Joan of Arc as "the bravest maiden within the recollection of men and the most innocent"; the tribunal which convicted her is officially branded "unlawful" and her condemnation labeled "unjust." The political iconographic value of Joan is not ignored, but subsumed. The official representation of France at the canonization ceremony is acknowledged with approval, as the pope states: "this noble nation's lively devotion to Joan of Arc, the venerable savior of her country, will be of great spiritual benefit to her." Part III focuses on Joan's beneficence to the entire Catholic world: "May the whole Catholic world hear, and just as it has come to admire her brave deeds in defense of her country, may it now and henceforward venerate her as a most brilliantly shining light of the Church Triumphant."[60]

Joan of Arc's connections to the social issues of the canonization era and World War I consolidated the iconographic uses for both "The Maid" and "Saint Joan." Regardless of ecclesiastical designation, she grew increasingly important as a symbol of spiritual commitment, social and political leadership, and a visual as well as psychological image of a young, powerful woman. What the conflation of the domestic-angel ideology and the modern, capable woman accomplished for twentieth-century ideology was both applauded and avoided by the next generations, in public and private life and the arts. But the influence of Joan of Arc as internal advisor continued to grow.

5

So Well-Suited:
Joan and Her Shavian Sisters

From its boisterous opening line: "No eggs! No eggs!! Thousand thunders, man, what do you mean by no eggs?" to its heart-wrenching closing line: "O God that madest this beautiful earth, when will it be ready to receive Thy saints? How long, O Lord, how long?"[1] Shaw's *Saint Joan* poses more questions and tolerates far more ambiguity than its title predicts. Because Shaw's play was written three years after the canonization of Joan in 1920 and labeled a chronicle, audiences and critics had a right to expect a portrayal that would show the glory of a saint and the issues surrounding the controversy as settled definitively. Instead, Shaw places Joan on his continuum of characters known as the "unwomanly woman," female representations who engage in the ongoing struggle for recognition beyond prescribed social class and gender roles.

Joan's inclusion in this Shavian category is neither accidental nor insulting, but it *is* indicative that Bernard Shaw posited that official ecclesiastical recognition of Joan's saintly acts had no particular bearing on the acceptance of twentieth-century New Women and their radical agenda for gender equality. As a result, Shaw develops Joan's character as a complex, multi-layered archetype of the outstanding individual. As his Preface to the play makes clear, Shaw aligned the situation that Joan confronted with those of Socrates and Florence Nightingale; his discussion of these historical soulmates conveys his attitude that iconoclasts, whether men or women, have always been, and will always remain, forsaken among us. Shaw's treatment of the patriarchal ideology that framed Joan's world is critical and ultimately comic in its fundamental sense: social critique. The text clearly shows how and why the fifteenth and the twentieth centuries are more alike than different; the removal of historical distance prevents the audience from enjoying the satisfaction of being beyond reproach. We are implicated in Joan's story.

A further dimension to Shaw's judgment of history can be seen in his original concept for writing a play about Joan of Arc. When he visited France in 1913, he wrote to Mrs. Patrick Campbell, explaining the vision of the story he would tell:

> I shall do a Joan play some day, beginning with the sweeping up of the cinders and orange peel **after** her martyrdom, and going on with Joan's arrival in heaven ... have God threaten the English with eternal damnation for their share in her betrayal and burning, but Joan would stay the judgment by bringing forth a fragment of burnt stick. "What is that? Is it one of the faggots?" God would ask, and Joan would reply, "No, it is what is left of the two

Women of Britain Save Your Country: World War I National Savings Committee poster (ca. 1914–1918). Joan is part of this graphic design, and yet retains her commanding presence form. Allegorically posed, with sword raised in classic "Joan" ways, her fervor and power emerge through the androgynous figure and her "no-nonsense" approach to the dangers at hand (***HIP/Art Resource, New York; National Archives, London***).

sticks a common English soldier tied together and gave me as I went to the stake; for they wouldn't even give me a crucifix; and you cannot damn the common people of England, represented by that soldier, because a poor cowardly riff raff of barons and bishops were too futile to resist the devil."[2]

Initially, then, Shaw intended to show that the power of Joan's personality was undaunted, even in the presence of God. His interest lay in emphasizing the goodness as well as the strength that makes the figure of Joan so appealing. The clarity of her values would be shared by the soldier who performed a spontaneous act of kindness in the face of "official" atrocity. Even before the canonization process was completed, Shaw recognized that the important message of Joan's story was not her martyrdom itself, but the ruling forces that cause such tragedy, and the permanence of this situation in human history. At the same time, Shaw still believed in the ability of well-intentioned individuals to create a new and better world with the proper leadership, and to sweeten the most devastating moment with unexpected gifts. The "cinders and orange peel" are the remains of Joan and the picnic lunches that were consumed during her burning. Sweeping these scraps up together makes them equally important (or unimportant) as well as inextricably linked. In the case of *Saint Joan,* paradoxical as it may seem, time clearly did make a difference; by 1923, Shaw's heretofore pervasive belief clearly had been smashed. The text we know reveals a very different vision.

As the following scene-by-scene explication of *Saint Joan* reveals, very little of Shaw's original vision remains ... at least in terms of the play's structure. Chronology is much stricter, and the Epilogue, while retaining its post-martyrdom stance, has now been reduced to a dream sequence in which the other characters' woes, rather than Joan's glory, are emphasized. Most sobering of all, Joan's powers remain diminished when she offers to return to earth; even after the sanctity was granted, she is still too much to handle. The text of 1923 shows more potential than success for any outstanding individual. The apparent inevitability of such a conclusion was also reinforced by the Great War.

While "the common people of England" of his original plan for the play are represented by the soldiers in World War I, Shaw understood that their interests were not. Not only had the peace of the nineteenth century been an illusion, but its end was marked by weapons of greater capability for destruction than had ever been seen before. Worse still, there was no "Joan" to bolster their morale or fight against the absurdity of the battle, which accounts for the elegiac treatment of Joan of Arc during the Great War. In his analysis of *Saint Joan* that appeared in the 1920s, the Russian critic A. Obraztsova concurs that the indictment against authority in Shaw's text was equally operant for the powers of his own time, particularly so in Shaw's treatment of Joan's judges:

the grave crime[s] committed by them ... were the ideas which they defended and in which they piously believed. The hostile ring tightening around Joan in Shaw's play is a ring of hostile ideas.... He created his courtroom scene in order to explain the thinking of similar courts in all times.... The allusions to the world war are a constant undercurrent in preface and play.... Medieval justice proved specially significant in the perspective of the situation of postwar Europe. The judgment upon Joan reflected the fear always experienced by the Church and the secular power, for they are always being tested by the people.[3]

The Epilogue of *Saint Joan* is the clearest evidence for Obraztsova's perspective. The English chaplain, De Stogumber, who has not yet shaken off the horror of her burning and his role in the event, cannot acknowledge that it is "Joan" who addresses him. Interestingly, it is the executioner who convinces him of her veracity. In addition to the historical accuracy of his statement, this speech also offers a tribute to Joan's ennobling power that can be considered a nod to the sentimental Victorian ideal of a woman's special power. In its context, the survival of the heart can reflect the true saintliness of Joan, her transcendence of petty concerns and actions. The executioner explains: "She is more alive than you, old man. Her heart would not burn; and it would not drown.[4] I was a master at my craft: better than the master of Paris, better than the master of Toulouse; but I could not kill the Maid. She is up and alive everywhere."[5]

Within the play, there are two illustrations of this essential quality: Joan's concern for others' pain when she herself is wounded in battle, and the compassion shown her at the stake by the soldier who hands her a cross made of sticks to console her when she needs comfort most. But "heart" also means inner strength and gumption, which Joan shows in Scene V, aka the "Cathedral" scene in which she makes it clear that the Voices are her inspiration. She claims that without them she would "lose all heart."[6] Such an insight illustrates a modernist's recognition concerning the relation of past to present moments: understanding of the implications of her own actions gives Joan the strength to face her consequences on her own.

While examination of the text of *Saint Joan* illustrates its incorporation of considerable wording from the trial transcripts, it is also clear that Shaw capitalizes too on the theatrical power of Joan's costume and its significance in the trial. At the same time, the overriding characteristics of Shaw's "Saint Joan" bear striking resemblance to "pieces" of his predecessors' conceptions of Joan's character. Herein lie both the fascination and the frustration with the story for modern observers: Joan's character is better known to us than the intricacies inherent in the network of forces that condemned her. Shaw's Joan remains the savvy, quick-witted leader of Shakespeare's *1 Henry VI*; she is as blunt and loquacious as the moral force in Voltaire's mock-epic *La Pucelle*; her passionate idealism is as stirring as Johanna's in Schiller's *Die Jungfrau von Orléans*. But while the earlier images of Joan foreground singular, exaggerated aspects of her character, Shaw presents a complex and realistic individual. Her humor and practicality merge with her wit and fervor, as Joan's rise and fall are foiled by equally complicated, contradictory authority figures. Because the play emphasizes the full examination of the self-interest and prejudice of those who betray and condemn her, especially concerning her transvestism and feminism, Joan's own heroic actions are both more admirable than those of her adversaries, and also more astonishing.

The exaggeration of the domineering master/deferential servant in the egg-laying of Scene 1, for example, is excellent preparation for the arrival of Joan and her country manner and mother wit. Furthermore, the "magical" transformations contained within this scene — changing de Beaudricourt's mind, Joan's "winning over" important allies, and the hens "laying like mad" at its end — introduce the upheaval of form and expectations that were to follow Joan's rise to prominence and power. The interruption of the "natural" rhythm of egg-laying, a feminine trope, is complemented by the softening of de Beaudricourt, who appears to embody the medieval masculine codes of honor, virtue, and authority.

There is another sub-text to consider here as well: the popular culture of the World War I era. A staunch pacifist as well as a renowned satirist of contemporary manners and slang, Shaw lived up to his reputation on both fronts in *Saint Joan*. The opening line of Scene 1, "No eggs...," and its seeming resolution in the last line of the scene, "The hens are laying like mad," can also refer to a popular expression used during World War I: "Eggs-a-cook." The expression originally referred to "boiled eggs sold by Arab street vendors. It was later used by Anzac soldiers when going over the top."[7]

The colloquial speech in the scene reinforces the popular culture context as well. The steward, in his attempt to shift the burden of Joan's dismissal to his superior, refers to Joan in traditional, paternalistic fashion, as "only a slip of a girl." Yet, twice Joan has refused to obey de Beaudricourt's orders to his soldiers that she be sent home to her father "for a good hiding." Here Shaw is faithful to historical documentation, but he is also extending the incident to the issues of authority and gender roles of his own time. The steward turns the tables on de Beaudricourt in true Victorian fashion, suggesting that his "strong character" might be able to "frighten" the girl. When de Beaudricourt then accuses the steward and the others of fearing Joan, the servant disagrees. He claims that she is just "so positive ... she doesn't seem to be afraid of anything." Next the steward claims that the men are afraid of de Beaudricourt, not Joan, because "she puts courage into us."[8] Shaw's evident pleasure in both reinforcing and confronting the New Woman questions about gender roles and performativity is unmistakable.

At this danger signal, Joan's assumption of these very masculine and higher-class traits, de Beaudricourt calls down to Joan from the window, ordering her to come in. She appears, dressed in the historically accurate red wool dress of her class, greets de Beaudricourt, who believes she is delusional, and then Joan issues her demands. By this merging of masculine and feminine behavior, Shaw's Joan is introduced; Shaw's description of her voice reinforces the impression. Joan is unruffled when she replies: "They all say I am mad until I talk to them, squire. But you see that is the will of God that you are to do what He has put into my mind."[9]

In this one statement Shaw has dismissed the notion that Joan was "cracked." Here is a link to Florence Nightingale, who suffered a similar reputation. In his preface, Shaw cites Nightingale's religious devotion as a means of comparison, and points out that Nightingale had a mind "so exceptionally powerful that it kept her in continual trouble with the medical and military panjandrums of her time." Like Joan, Nightingale's sanity had been challenged in retaliation for her insistence on an active life rather than a leisured one and her investigation of medical conditions in the military. Such parallels reveal how little had changed, especially in terms of tolerance. Later in his preface, Shaw claims that if the events of 1431 occurred in the London of the 1920s, "[Joan] would be treated with no more toleration than Miss Sylvia Pankhurst ... or any of the others who cross the line we have to draw, rightly or wrongly, between the tolerable and the intolerable."[10] Joan's triumph in Scene I illustrates the appeal of the outstanding individual as well as the disruptive power of this kind of personality.

Scene II contains the historical miracle of Joan's recognition of the (disguised) Dauphin and includes a discussion about the nature of miracles, which completely deflates the conventional power of such a scene. The archbishop explains to La Tremouille that Joan will be able to pick out the Dauphin because he is "the meanest-looking and worst-dressed figure in the Court." When La Tremouille complains that would not be a miracle at all, the archbishop admonishes him, and says that miracles' true value lies within, since those who perform them don't consider them grand necessarily; their real function is to create faith in those who observe them.[11]

The Archbishop's perspective reinforces the characterization of Joan as an intelligent, down-to-earth person, despite the miracle he expects her to achieve. A key motif in this scene is clothing and its symbolic function in public images. In this scene, Joan appears dressed in a soldier's uniform, as the historical Joan had been. It is the first time she is seen in a man's clothing. The Dauphin is dressed shabbily; Joan's consternation over this reinforces the power of costume in her eyes. Yet Shaw's very point in the scene is to belie the importance of appearance and to focus on the inner process of consciousness and recognition. In her meeting with the Dauphin, Joan illustrates the archbishop's point herself. Just as she was unruffled by de Beaudricourt's skepticism, she is equally undaunted by the Dauphin's desire for her to show him magic. What does perplex and annoy her is his stubborn lack of ambition. When he refuses to be enthusiastic, Joan, who already calls him "Charlie," tells him he must do his duty. In essence, she tells him that even kings put on their trousers one leg at a time, and that he must rise above his fears and laziness. She does admit that she can offer him one real feat, the crowning in Reims, but she calls it "a miracle that will take some doing, it seems."

In Scene III Shaw once again infuses the historical Joan's manner and wording to provide his comedy. Upon reaching Dunois she asks him: "Be you Bastard of Orléans?" She is forceful, yet friendly; Dunois is the same. It is clear from the outset of their meeting that he will teach her and let her inspire him and his troops. For his part, Dunois has no trouble incorporating Joan's aura, mystical or practical, into the cause. Confident in his own role, he can see how Joan's central position will be more symbolic than strategic. Her assumption of power does not threaten him, even if it does invert relationships within accepted codes. To foreground Joan's confidence, Shaw calls for her to be attired in showy armor, madly rushing to lead the charge, when she realizes she is on the wrong side of the river. For the first time in the play, Joan has lost her cool; Dunois has it. He is as blunt with her as she with him; he sees through her bravado and understands its origin. When she offers to inspire him to remove his fear, he laughs and says: "No, no my girl: if you delivered me from fear I should be a good knight for a story book, but a very bad commander of the army. Come! let me begin to make a soldier of you."[12]

This is a fascinating reversal on several levels. On the surface, Dunois seems to be assuming the "mentor" role that so many men have for women in nineteenth-century fiction and drama. Conversely, he is the first male authority figure to accept Joan as a person, with attributes and weaknesses. While he will not accord her military prowess or storybook courage, he does begin to teach her how to become a soldier. He is neither afraid of her, nor is he truly condescending. He really does teach her what she needs to know and gives her credit for what she can contribute. When Dunois accepted her, so historical legend goes, the wind changed direction, which allowed the Siege of Orléans to begin. Shaw accepts this, and also sees this moment as engendering the collaboration of Dunois and Joan. The give-and-take between them develops for several scenes, modeling the more egalitarian relationship fostered by feminists of the time.

Scene IV, the "tent scene," is infamous for its length as well as for its intention: stripping away the mask of conventional validation for the *status quo*. Here Shaw condenses the "under the table" kinds of tactics used to seal Joan's doom for expediency's and greed's sake. The characters are what Andrew Undershaft in *Major Barbara* would refer to as "good customers" for his armaments. But while that 1905 play believed as much in re-visioning the world as in labeling it, *Saint Joan* reveals only the harshness of the vision, and the spirit and some details of the original charges brought against Joan in 1431. Although many of the key issues under discussion in this scene belong clearly to the fifteenth century, i.e., the emergence of nationalism as a threat to feudalism, and the distinction between a witch and a heretic, a considerable amount of the scene's wit and irony emanate from sprinklings of more modern vernacular. This language characterizes not only Joan but her surrounding authorities. The chaplain, among his other insults, refers to Joan as "a drab from the ditches of Lorraine"[13]; the Burgundian nobleman realizes that persuading the Bastard of Orléans will be "a harder nut to crack."[14]

But it is Cauchon, the bishop of Beauvais, who blends classical theological rhetoric with modern put-downs when he reminds the authorities that Joan's victories were not likely to be viewed as sorcery by the French. He calls for heresy: the English hothead chaplain impatiently asks what the difference is. Cauchon speaks with amazement that such a clear and vital distinction can be blurred, declaring that the English are "strangely blunt in the mind."[15] Cauchon recognizes the same definition of miracles as the foregoing one by the archbishop, a fine piece of dramatic irony that becomes even more apt when we consider Cauchon's self-interest on the one hand, and his solid understanding and application of ecclesiastical dogma on the other. Shaw's rendering of this meeting of authorities to seal the doom of this religious and political pawn reports historically accurate conclusions with the immediacy of *au courrant* expression; this earned him the contempt of 1920s critics, who failed to understand or acknowledge that Shaw's intent was not to distort history, but to reveal the historicity of the decision.

Jeanne Foster's scathing review contended that neither the play nor the character of Joan brings "for a single thrilling instant ... the peasant maid.... We cannot even think of this 'flapper' as the Joan of Bastien-Lepage." T.S. Eliot declared that Shaw could never "devote himself wholeheartedly to *any* cause.... Hence the danger, with his "St. Joan," of his deluding the numberless crowd of sentimentally religious people who are incapable of following any argument to a conclusion.... Mr. Shaw's "St. Joan" is one of the most superstitious of the effigies which have been erected to that remarkable woman."[16]

It can be further argued that in Shaw's text, the contrast between Joan and her judges is molded by these unchanging factors. If, as Cauchon admits, it was a "masterstroke" of Joan's to crown the Dauphin at Reims,[17] the same could be said of Shaw's conclusion regarding Joan's continuing iconographic importance. The lesson of Joan's character becomes a fundamental part of Shaw's plea for toleration and hope in the play. A brief interchange between Joan and Dunois opens Scene V; it takes place immediately after the coronation. While Joan is still beautifully dressed in male attire, the ceremony is not shown to the audience. Instead, Shaw continues his pattern of concentrating on the behind-the-scenes action which surrounds great events. The conversation between Joan and Dunois illustrates that Joan has not yet completely let go of the trappings of storybook "should be" scenarios, as she fails to see why those in power find her great achievements disheartening and offensive. Joan tells Dunois that her actions have brought them honor; all she asked for herself was tax relief for her village. Dunois replies: "Sim-ple-ton! Do you expect stupid people to love you for shewing them up? Why, I should be jealous of you myself if I were ambitious enough."[18]

Only one expected "ingredient" is missing from Dunois' listing: he never focuses on Joan's gender. It is a very obvious omission, foregrounding the others' rather obsessive focus on precisely that issue. This same scene, widely known as the "cathedral scene," reveals Joan's own weaknesses, particularly her effrontery toward church authority, but also showcases her courage when she recognizes that she, like France, must stand alone. It is especially important to note that Joan's expression of the nature of loneliness conveys a classically pure religious perspective, and reflects the separateness of saints on earth.

Thanks to Dunois, Joan understands her position more clearly, although she forgets herself far too often. She defies the king and the archbishop in her relentless quest to push towards Paris. This behavior, in combination with the discussion in Scene IV, confirms the impossibilities of the situation. The king closes this scene with a mundane, yet emotion-packed, misogynistic remark, wishing that Joan be silent or literally disappear from his world by returning home.[19]

The brilliance of Scene VI, the "trial scene," operates on many levels. Dramatically, it is the one the audience has waited for, yet in the wake of scenes III and V, suspense is removed. For it is important to note that none of the three "big" scenes in Joan's career — the Battle at Orléans, the coronation, and the burning itself — are shown onstage in *Saint Joan*. Shaw has relied on costume changes instead of large-scale pageantry to encode Joan's rise and fall. For the trial scene, her appearance is as shabby as her treatment. Since so much of the dialogue is among the other characters, Shaw manages to turn attention to the repercussions of what has happened and what will happen (in preparation for the Epilogue).

The ultimate choice made by Joan in the trial scene to explain to her judges that they cannot fully understand her position deconstructs their ideological framework and intensifies their desire to condemn her. They were knowledgeable, powerful, authoritative; how could an ignorant peasant girl know more than they? The key speech is taken largely from the historical Joan's testimony towards the end of her trial, May 9, 1431: "If you tear me limb from limb until you separate my soul from my body you will get nothing out of me beyond what I have told you. What more is there to tell you that you could understand?"[20]

Even in her most desperate hour, Joan of Arc retained her commonsense understanding of human motivation. While it is a cynical remark, it serves a purpose at the pinnacle of drama: it prepares Joan to accept death rather than degradation. By the time Joan speaks her final word to them, shock has been replaced by exhaustion: the audience has almost assumed Joan's own role in the scene. There is no miracle here. Joan's last speech in *Saint Joan*, known by actresses as the "Light your fire" speech, consolidates Shaw's portrait of the heroic archetype; the allusions to both the situation of Sophocles' *Antigone* and the attitude of its heroine are likewise unmistakable. When Antigone learns that she is to be buried alive in a cave rather than executed, she recognizes that for all her lofty ideals, removal from the world and the beauty of nature is more than she can bear. Antigone remains steadfast in her mission, convinced that the authority she obeys is the highest. Joan, in contrast to Antigone, values her life on earth as well as God's laws and expected her Voices to save her. Yet, when faced with the ultimate choice, Joan, like Antigone, goes to death with strength and defiance intact. While Antigone refers to the gods, Joan alludes to the treatment of iconoclasts in the Bible.[21]

Here she becomes the "Saint Joan" the audience has anticipated all along. But Shaw concludes with an unexpected twist: she condemns her judges, calling their "gift" of life in prison for her or any other human being proof that their counsel is of the devil. Antigone, too, recognizes that her condemnation was unjustified, though the

Chorus disagrees. They remain convinced that Antigone's willfulness and the sins of Oedipus are the cause. While she sees the truth in this, Antigone asks:

> What law of heaven have I transgressed? What god
> Can save me now? What help or hope have I,
> In whom devotion is deemed sacrilege?
> If this is God's will, I shall learn my lesson
> In death; but if my enemies are wrong,
> I wish them no worse punishment than mine.[22]

Antigone is led away after she resigns herself to death with honor. In *St. Joan*, Joan comes to an understanding similar to Antigone's when she tells those assembled that she accepts her death as God's will, so that she can be removed from people who offer her nothing but pain. Joan is dragged to the stake, but the burning itself is handled diegetically, both to deflect melodramatic attention to the tragic suffering and to force the audience to concentrate on the reactions of the judges to their fatal mistake.

Perhaps to reinforce the classical echoes on the one hand, while returning to the mood and critique of his present moment, Shaw set the Epilogue in 1456, not 1431. This was the date of Joan's Rehabilitation Trial, a re-examination prompted by Joan's mother to clear her name, and by Charles VII to remove the connection between his coronation and the actions/influence of a suspected witch and heretic. Even more surprising is the treatment of the canonization in the Epilogue: it merges with the rehabilitation. Could the implication be that these further developments do not matter as individual events?

The anonymity and unceremonious coming and going of a messenger from 1920 accompanied by fleeting onstage glimpses of statues of Joan in Winchester and Reims, foreground the minimal impact of the supposed landmark moment. Likewise, the characters' bemusement over the gentleman's costume betrays their focus on the outer appearance rather than on the content of his speech. I also view these choices by Shaw as distinct Sophoclean echoes.

Like *Antigone's* sentry, the modern messenger is business-like and unmoved by his news. But his news is good, so, once it has been delivered, he is free to return to his world. Actually, he vanishes. It is precisely here that Shaw uses dramatic technique brilliantly: Joan's proposal of her miraculous possibility (return to life) is greeted by a darkened stage, through which Joan's indignant "What! Must I burn again? Are none of you ready to receive me?"[23] achieves a double layer of impact as the audience, along with the actors, are joined together by Oedipus-like blindness. More to the point, the reminder of the burning returns everyone momentarily to the mindset of the trial and the doom which has now been accepted as part of the record of the past.

Psalm 6 of David is one source of Joan's last question. In this text, the psalmist beseeches the Lord for healing, comfort, and mercy in the first five verses. Verses 9–11 are even more apt, as he asks that those who do evil against him should depart because the Lord has heard his petition. The psalmist asks then for the enemies to be made ashamed and confused.[24] But an even more pointed and contemporary reference extends Shaw's view of the circularity of history, and helps Shaw drive his point home. The stirring closing lines of the Epilogue — "...how long, O, lord, how long?" contains the title of a popular World War I poem by Robert Palmer, "How Long, O Lord":

> How long, O Lord, how long, before the flood
> Of crimson-welling carnage shall abate?
> From sodden plains in West and East, the blood
> Of kindly men steams up in mists of hate,
> Polluting Thy clean air; and nations great
> In reputation of the arts that bind
> The World with hopes of heaven, sink to the state
> Of brute barbarians, whose ferocious mind
> Gloats o'er the bloody havoc of their kind,
> Not knowing love or mercy. Lord, how long
> Shall Satan in high places lead the blind
> To battle for the passions of the strong?
> Oh, touch Thy children's hearts, that they may know
> Hate their most hateful, pride their deadliest foe.[25]

It cannot be overlooked that Joan had claimed her accusers were unfit for her to live among in Scene VI; in the Epilogue, when they abandon her anew one by one, she asks if she must burn again. The tone of this reminder is as important as its content. Scene VI portrayed anger derived from disappointment, whereas the Epilogue is the reverse. As she closes the play with its searing question, Joan reflects another level of awareness; she realizes that neither the passing of time nor a change in her official status could alter the human potential to attain true peace in the world, nor embrace the innately superior individual. The first part of the question is painfully rhetorical, since the world is unlikely to ever be ready to receive its saints. The sharper pang is in her final double question: how long, O lord, how long? Such a question conveys an adult longing for an answer, and a childlike fantasy that *someday* the answer will be possible. Yet, as Robert Palmer's poem revealed, these seem to be impossible longings.

Because the Epilogue is presented as a dream sequence and Joan has the power to visit the characters' consciences while they are asleep, it is likewise clear that Shaw is acknowledging the 1920s' fascination with and admiration for psychology. Conversely, Joan, being beyond human pride and suffering, is part of the set of ancient truths. Since she retains the capacity for emotions without repercussions, she is elevated to the role of a god. True enough, although Joan's behavior throughout the Epilogue reveals no elevated sense of herself, until she hears the official news. At this point, she "chuckles" as she hears herself declared Venerable: "rapt" when she hears herself proclaimed a saint. Joan also realizes she is now in a position to provide the miracles people had always wanted from her. While she dryly dismisses the verbal acclamations, "Woe be to me when men praise me!" she does wish them to transcend their weaknesses.[26]

Saint Joan's Epilogue is one of the most important contributions of Shaw's text to the image of Joan as a universal icon, not merely a historical figure. For the first time onstage, Joan's immortality is embodied, not merely glorified. The matter-of-fact tone of the other characters during the Epilogue is clear demonstration of Shaw's contention that human nature does not change. Joan's counterparts have achieved a deeper understanding of events and their causes, but this knowledge only confirms their notion that Joan's treatment on earth could not really differ. Certainly the suggestion that Joan return to those who mourn her as a living being is the ultimate chance to redeem past mistakes, yet the soldiers, and even the king, recoil at the prospect. One by one they abandon her again; they leave the stage recognizing their admiration for her attributes and accomplishments as well as their inability to co-exist with her. Joan is at once good-humored and resigned and disappointed in the responses that she makes to them, but Shaw's point crystallizes here: the change in Joan's official status influences only her iconographic significance. On the human level, she remains impossible.

This recognition is not new to the audience, however; the conclusion of Scene VI has set it up. When the burning is complete, Warwick is informed by the executioner: "You have heard the last of her." His seemingly rhetorical, almost comic, reply: "The last of her? Hmm! I wonder"[27] reveals the awareness that the burning had been folly all along, a conclusion acknowledged by the historical records as well. Yet how can this be reconciled? Can the post-canonization audience continue to re-envision a "what if...?" proposition? The ultimate question thus becomes, does the ending of the Epilogue of *Saint Joan* contain a degree of hope? J. L. Wiesenthal believes this is the case, precisely because so much historical time has been conflated from the end of Scene VI to the end of the Epilogue. Though idealistic, his view can be supported by the structure of Shaw's text:

> In one sense, the crowd at her execution saw the last of her. In another sense, the audience watching the end of the Epilogue has seen the last of her. If we look to the future, however, we can see the human possibilities she represents could flourish, and the earth could become ready to receive its saints. Unless one conceives of this as a possibility, then one's dramatic response to *Saint Joan* has been diminished.[28]

Margery Morgan's assessment of Shaw and history provides a useful link between the representation of universal behavior and events grounded in a specific historic moment. Morgan contends that Shaw's view of history emphasized "a coherent interpretation of the past as political determinant.... Not fact, but belief, is crucial."[29] It is this concept that underpins Shaw's choices regarding dialogue and consciousness of his characters. Therefore, Morgan continues, historical drama must be tied to the present: "[no matter how] ancient a fashion the costumes represent, the consciousness of the wearers is modern: they talk anachronistically, as with foreknowledge of modern issues. Famous names are attached to characters whose essence is the familiar, the ordinary. Such 'historical' drama is merely a special area of fantasy."[30]

Ultimately, this play's Epilogue makes it all too clear that the historical Joan never had a chance, not because the Middle Ages was "backward," but the inverse. *Saint Joan* thereby places the reader or spectator *inside* the ambiguity: sympathetic towards Joan and her situation, yet all too familiar, even comfortable, with a societal structure that condemns the iconoclast. Shaw's text deliberately runs counter to earlier ones regarding Joan's role as a leader. Several times in the written Preface to the play, Shaw recognizes that Joan's domain was in the "masculine" realms of politics and war. In fundamentally Shavian style he concludes: "If an historian is an anti–Feminist, and does not believe women to be capable of genius in the traditional male departments, he will never make anything of Joan."[31] Surely this comment is leveled not only at Shakespeare and Voltaire, Schiller, Twain, A. France, and Lang, but also at the drama critics who were prone to condemn many of Shaw's "unwomanly women."

Shaw believed in the ability of both men and women to improve the world's social condition through a reconfiguration of ideology. In these efforts, women had to confront society's challenges the way men did: head on. Only after they were successful in making their marks individually could they then go on to change the structure of the society that had pigeon-holed them into passive, submissive roles. It was essential, then, that Shavian hero/ines be known for their presumption, candor, intellectual savvy, and wit, becoming, in turn, "unwomanly." Barbara Bellow Watson notes, in *A Shavian Guide to the Intelligent Woman*, that Shaw's women characters announced a departure from expected female "types" in the theater. These women bore little resemblance to "the mooning ingénue, the vivacious soubrette, the whore with a heart of gold ... [or] to the malicious witch, the angel child."[32]

Each of these theatrical "types" posited female roles contained within the scope of Victorian gender distinctions. Precisely because Shaw was determined to rescue the literary image of Joan from what he considered the distorted legends of sentimental fiction, melodrama, and romance, he drew a portrayal of her startling individuality. So, naturally, his conception of Joan turns away from stock characterizations, particularly of women. In the preface to *Saint Joan* he derides Schiller's *Die Jungfrau von Orléans* (1803), claiming that Schiller's Joan "has not a single point of contact neither with the real Joan, nor indeed with any mortal woman that ever walked this earth."[33] This was a clear way for the playwright to communicate to his audience that Joan's stage history had been clouded by these theatrical conventions.

In terms of theatrical genres, Shaw may have turned to comedy for his models because the comic stage offered far more possibilities for women. More important to the interests of this study is the transvestite tradition underneath these genres. Unlike Elizabethan theatrical practice, the Victorian theater showcased more women portraying a range of male characters, while men played only satirical female roles.

A dominant presence in this aspect of the Victorian theatrical world was W. S. Gilbert; his representations, particularly of middle-aged, unattractive female characters ("dames"), may have scandalized some critics and viewers, but their impact was permanent. What Gilbert did was cross the boundaries of taste in his presentation of characters who saw through the treasured Victorian penchant for youthful beauty. It was apparently all right that "dame" characters like Katisha in *The Mikado* satirize middle-aged spinsterhood. So says Jane Stedman in her study of Gilbert, "From Dame to Woman: W.S. Gilbert and Theatrical Transvestism." In his works, Gilbert relied on the 'masks and faces' motif of Victorian times to admonish his audiences not to judge by surfaces. What Shaw did was more "offensive"; he attacked aspects of patriarchal structure, rather than remind audiences that medieval *fabliaux* should be considered *déclassé*. In this way he extended Gilbert's scope as well as his technique.

Victorian theater contained another classification of comic transvestite roles for women: principal boys. These roles had their origin in burlesques, pantomimes and extravaganzas; they were a variety of soubrette. The sexual appeal of some of these characters was heightened by the Victorian fascination with legs; in response, costumes rose from "near-knee-length in the 1860s to silken thighs in the 1870s." Other heroines were more boyish in appeal: impudent — insouciant rather than provocative."[34] By emphasizing her youthful, earthy side, Shaw's Joan uses and expands these criteria, particularly in her initial meetings with de Beaudricourt and the Dauphin (scenes I and II respectively). The dames (mature women characters) had been "remodeled" by Gilbert; Stedman cites Shaw specifically on this point: "Shaw, who objected to making fun of stout, mature ladies admitted that in creating such characters Gilbert had perfectly understood his public."[35] It is certainly to Shaw's credit that he included many positive models of middle-aged women in his plays.

Two of Shaw's earlier plays, *Major Barbara* (1905) and *Pygmalion* (1913), revolve around wise and sympathetically-drawn older women, as well as young women who have qualities Shaw consolidated in his portrayal of Joan. The older women in the plays, Barbara's mother, Lady Britomart; Mr. Higgins' housekeeper, Mrs. Pearce; and his mother, Mrs. Higgins, serve as touchstones to both the social *status quo* of the privileged classes and the reality underneath it; each is an intelligent woman, in true control of her life and fully aware of the environment she lives in. Thus stereotypical elements of "dames" (older women) and/or "principal boys" (spunky young women) have been absorbed into the more individualized, complex Shavian characterizations. These two works' protagonists deal with social roles and issues of class; they also use costume discriminately, cognizant of its semiotic value. Barbara Undershaft is a spunky, idealistic person of action; Eliza Doolittle is an ordinary girl from working-class origins who, like Joan, makes the most of her opportunities and struggles to maintain her sense of self.

Major Barbara is a play that combines stark social criticism and urbane drawing-room repartee; as a result, the audience is constantly poised between spontaneous response and pondering the implications of dialogue and action. Thus Shaw blends his new way of thinking about issues and behavior into the norms of comedy. Primarily, the characters try to get their own way via cajolery, deception, and/or direct confrontation. The issues of money, power, religious fervor, and conventional family relationships are woven both directly and indirectly into the arguments that comprise the conflict. Lady Britomart, whose name is borrowed from the heroine of Spenser's sixteenth-century epic, *The Faerie Queen*, represents an unusual tribute to her predecessor. She is a true Victorian lady, but not an object for courtly love. Although she has influence over her family members, and even her estranged husband, Lady Britomart knows that she is limited by her gender. Unlike Spenser's Britomart, she is not destined to affect great events. Nonetheless, she relies on her intellect rather than her charms to ensure dominion over the men in her life. This is shown plainly in the opening scene of *Major Barbara*, when she asks her son, Stephen, for his "advice" about inviting his father to the house.

Not only does Lady Brit manipulate Stephen's answers to suit her own agenda, but she also solicits male "approval" after the invitation has been made. As he would do in the opening scene of *St. Joan*, Shaw illustrated the reality underneath the façade of supposed gender role performance. Lady Britomart chides her son about his spineless attitude, obviously alluding to Ruskin's assessment of "educated" young men: "It is only in the middle classes, Stephen, that people get into a state of dumb helpless horror when they find there are wicked people in the world. In our class, we have to decide what is to be done with wicked people."[36] Due to Shaw's attack on "philistine" and "idealist" positions, the play opened to mixed reviews. Michael Holroyd presents a range of opinions. Desmond McCarthy is quoted by Holroyd as saying that "Mr. Shaw has written the first play with religious passion for its theme and has made it real." On the other hand, an anonymous critic for the *Pall Mall Gazette* found the play betrayed "an utter want of the religious sense." The *Morning Post* believed its offenses "against good taste and good feeling are of a kind not to be readily forgiven."[37] These objections are grounded in attitudes very similar to those of Joan's critics: orthodoxy must be upheld above all else.

An organization which found a prominent place in *Major Barbara* was the Salvation Army, founded in 1878 by William Booth to combat the evils of poverty. In Shaw's text, the Salvation Army is not perfectly good, nor is Andrew Undershaft's armament industry or Bodger's distillery thoroughly evil. Shaw's point is that all use money: the question is, how? While Barbara cannot live with the Army's acceptance of donations from Undershaft and Bodger, the General (Mrs. Baines) can, and does. Conversely, Undershaft cannot abide poverty for his workers, so he has created his own city where all can live decently. Most noteworthy was the donation of uniforms for the play by the Salvation Army and their attendance in the theater itself. Shaw, in his preface to *Major Barbara*, responded pointedly: "they questioned the verisimilitude of the play, not because Mrs. Baines [the General] took the money, but because Barbara refused it."[38] Despite its efforts and successes, as well as the Poor Laws, the number of paupers in London had risen rather than fallen by 1905. Shaw wanted to dramatize this paradox, as well as the more serious one of the dichotomy between England at the height of its imperial power and the numbers of native English people hovering at the brink of destitution.[39]

Perhaps even more than he admired its philosophy, Shaw applauded the Salvation Army's policy towards women. Sonja Lorichs notes that the Salvation Army may have failed to change the economic situation of the poor, but it provided a paradigm for feminist achievement. Lorichs states: "In the Army equality between men and women was a fact at least half a century before it was in the secular world."[40] The character of Lady Britomart is at once mirror-image as well as frame for the realistic perspectives of the female Salvation Army officers. She is clearly representative of her class in some ways, and Shaw's introductory description of her in the stage directions reveals a decided feminist bent. She is a controlling, capable matron, "limited in the oddest way with domestic and class limitations, conceiving the universe exactly as if it were a large house in Wilton Crescent."[41] Lady Britomart is a woman of practical sense and liberal-mindedness, just as Joan was. Separated from her husband because he refused to live by conventions of inherited wealth, she has always accepted his money for support of her children, despite its source (the armament industry). As a pragmatist, Lady Britomart uses a style that blends ideas from Ruskin, Mill, and her husband, Andrew Undershaft.

Barbara herself is contrasted with both her mother and her brother; she has defied the idle, decorative life of a woman of her class. Like her real-life activist counterparts, Barbara has rejected her "birthright" in exchange for social causes.[42] When Undershaft comes to call, at her mother's request, Barbara is fascinated by him and, showing her connection to him in temperament, wants to convert her father to her way of thinking. Undershaft, in turn, is quite taken, if also bemused, by Barbara's zeal. He proposes a bargain; he will visit Barbara at the Army if she will come to the cannon works. The frank admiration for each other's differing strengths that emerges here will repeat in the relationship between Joan and Dunois in *St. Joan.*

From the outset, Barbara demonstrates salient qualities that would also mark Shaw's Joan: cheerfulness, purposefulness, and largeness of vision. In dismissing the notion that people can be thought of as either "good men or scoundrels," Barbara claims:

> There are neither good men nor scoundrels: there are just children of one Father; and the sooner they stop calling one another names the better. You needn't talk to me: I know them. I've had scores of them through my hands: scoundrels, criminals, infidels, philanthropists, missionaries, county councilors, all sorts. They're all just the same sort of sinner; and there's the same salvation ready for them all.[43]

Such a speech is very like Joan's to the Dauphin (Charlie) in Scene II of *Saint Joan,* when the Dauphin is reluctant to discuss the realities of war with the English and wants to know if Joan has brought him any secrets. He confesses that his official duties plague him and he'd rather just mind his own business. Joan chastises him, saying:

> Minding your own business is like minding your own body: it's the shortest way to make yourself sick. What is my business? Helping mother at home. What is thine? Petting lapdogs and sucking sugarsticks. I call that muck. I tell thee it is God's business we are here

to do: not our own. I have a message to thee from God; and thou must listen to it, though thy heart break with the terror of it.[44]

Shaw himself had been involved in collective, public efforts in connection with the Fabian Society since the 1880s. He was drawn to their Socialist positions because of their emphasis on waiting for the right moment and then their resolve to "strike hard ... or your waiting will be vain and fruitless."[45] In 1884, he wrote a leaflet entitled *A Manifesto* (Fabian Tract No. 2) that encapsulated its goals, including the abolition of *laissez-faire* capitalism and its unequal distribution of wealth and accompanying division of workers by classes, and the establishment of equal political rights for men and women.[46] In his study and subsequent lecturing on economic topics during the balance of that decade, Shaw spoke out against Marx's class war, declaring that the real conflict should not be thought of in terms of workers and capitalists, but rather as workers of all classes against "such idlers as the aristocracy."[47] In this context, the positive outcome of *Major Barbara* becomes more important. The key to the reconciliation of opposing viewpoints is the mutual respect shown between Undershaft and his workers, his daughter, his wife, and his competitors. Shaw firmly believed at this point in his life that collective efforts could yield benefits for large numbers of people.

While more cognizant of distinctions among social classes, the same spirit of mutual understanding informs *Pygmalion* (1913). In his re-telling of the Pygmalion/Galatea story, Shaw subverts Ovid's romantic conclusion. Henry Higgins, the Pygmalion figure, is a confirmed bachelor; he doesn't detest women, but he also can't commit himself to a relationship. Eliza Doolittle, the Galatea figure, is a representative of the hard-working, downtrodden classes who live near Covent Garden but cannot partake of the cultural events that take place on its streets. But Eliza is by no means a statue-like "empty vessel" awaiting the patronage or protection of a man. On the contrary, she stays away from men and is self-supporting, if only at a subsistence level. To Shaw, there is an issue far more important than romantic attachment: mutual respect between individuals. What stands in the way of this are the artificial social barriers.

Pygmalion is a play that strips away the notion of class division by reducing the distinctions to costume, speech patterns, and manners. Of course Eliza knows that Higgins is her social superior and is physically stronger, but she also uses these "rules" to her advantage, tossing them in his face throughout the play, either to remind him of what she believes is proper or to invert them. This is an important element of Shaw's intention to turn the Pygmalion myth inside out in his play. By the end, the part of Eliza that is indeed Higgins' creation is reminiscent of the Victorian "mask" (her manner, speech, and costume), while the substantive inner changes are self-made, thereby representing the two diametrically opposed Victorian concepts of "face" and the "New Woman." It is this context that provides the fullest reading for Eliza's recognition of her changed status. She rejects a traditional "lady" role as readily as she had discarded the "flower girl" one, on the grounds of indignity. Eliza tells Higgins: "I'm a slave now, despite my fine clothes."[48]

The Pygmalion myth has been one of the most enduring ones, and Shaw inverts more than Ovid's ending in his play. In Ovid's text, Pygmalion falls in love with his creation and wants to possess her as a wife, a wish granted by Venus. Ovid's tale ends with Pygmalion's joy and gratitude towards Venus, and Galatea's awakening, and recognition of her bridegroom and Heaven in a simultaneous moment. According to Error Durbach, W. S. Gilbert wrote a play entitled *Pygmalion and Galatea* in 1871 and the same era saw a series of four paintings by the Pre-Raphaelite painter Edward Burne-Jones. Durbach doubts Shaw knew of Gilbert's play, but finds it intriguing nonetheless to point out Gilbert's typically Victorian, anti-feminist stance in its construction. Galatea not only falls on her knees to worship Pygmalion, but she gives him sovereignty over her. As Durbach characterizes it, Gilbert's play is "a curious blend of sentimental idealism declining sadly into a form of equally sentimental cynicism.... Here she is again—the Victorian domestic paragon, the Angel in the House ... a piece of property without the shred of a sense of self."[49] Shaw's depiction of both Pygmalion (Higgins) and Galatea (Eliza) are very far from this image. As for the series of paintings, completed in 1879, Durbach notes their authentic replication of Ovid's themes, and the worship of Galatea by Pygmalion in its final panel will show up in Shaw's retelling almost entirely.

Shaw infuses much of the struggle over gender in his own era into the relationship of Higgins and Eliza. Higgins can see himself as Eliza's father, teacher, friend, and even dependent, but never as her husband. Eliza has Barbara's determination, but none of her advantages. Yet Eliza turns out to have a great deal more inner strength, and a real self-identity that Barbara lacks. This connects Eliza more directly to Shaw's Joan. The two protagonists of this play meet on a rainy night, just as the theaters have let out. Eliza tries to sell her remaining bunches of violets to the crowd. In the bustle, a young man in search of a taxi runs her down, crushing some of the flowers. She then attempts to have someone else pay for the damage. Higgins, a professor of phonetics, writes down all she says. One of the people in the crowd warns Eliza, assuming Higgins is a plainclothes policeman.

While the opening is full of comedy, it is also the set-up for the play's lesson. We are not merely *what* we say, but *how* we say it. The moment Higgins tosses Eliza enough coins to do more than pay her bills at the end of Act I, she realizes that he has also given her options. Higgins had explained that people's speech patterns determine their place in society. This speech is not directed at Eliza, nor is Higgins aware that she has even heard it. But the power of Higgins' words is instantaneous. Eliza begins to take herself in hand; her situation becomes something she wants to change. She does allow herself the indulgence of taking a taxi, but she largely uses the money for important things (more heat in her room) and she makes a decision to take Higgins up on his boast to Col. Pickering to teach Eliza enough to pass her off as a duchess in three months.[50]

In Act II, when Eliza arrives at Higgins' home, it is obvious that neither of the men recalls the conversation at Covent Garden. Eliza comes to negotiate a deal for elocution lessons. She knows how much her friend pays for French lessons, and expects to pay less for lessons in her native tongue. At first, Higgins does little more than insult her. Even the proposed arrangement of having Eliza move in shows no consideration for the social criticism that would follow. Pickering, as the representative of a gentleman, is concerned that Higgins is treating Eliza without regard for her feelings. All of this shows that Higgins is more elitist than he would confess. Yet it is in this act that the "Pygmalion" myth surfaces. Higgins has Eliza bathed and dressed appropriately before he begins to work on her speech patterns. For months they work together, form an affectionate bond, and Higgins eventually introduces Eliza to society. She betrays her roots when divulging family secrets about alcoholic routs in the most rarefied speech patterns, thus proving Shaw's premise from an opposite perspective.

The "whole truth" *is* told in *Pygmalion*, by almost all characters; the most surprising of these is Eliza's father, Alfred Doolittle. His Dickensian name misleads the audience into believing him to be a conniving fraud, a melodramatic villain. However, Doolittle turns out to be the mouthpiece for the working-class "Everyman" that Charles Booth had studied, as well as the "answer" to prevalent misinformation about the viewpoints of the poor. When Higgins is outraged by a father's demand for five pounds in exchange for his daughter, in Act II, he accuses Doolittle of having no morals. The reply is accurate as well as witty: "Can't afford them, Governor. Neither could you if you was as poor as me." He goes on to describe himself as one of the "undeserving poor." Here is a reference to the Salvation Army's idealistic belief that it was serving the "deserving poor." Doolittle tears this concept apart when he explains to Higgins how it works:

> Think of what that means to a man. It means that he's up agen middle class morality all the time. If there's anything going, and I put in for a bit of it, it's always the same story: "You're undeserving; so you can't have it." But my needs is as great as the most deserving widow's that ever got money out of six different charities in one week for the death of the same husband. I don't need less than a deserving man: I need more. I don't eat less hearty than him; and I drink a lot more.[51]

Doolittle's critique of "middle-class morality" intersects the distinctions drawn between deserving and undeserving recipients of charity, as well as good versus "tainted" money as sources of charity. Hypocrisy and greed infect both sides. In his study (Volume II) Booth described Shelton Street, a neighborhood in London east of Soho and south of Bloomsbury. The majority of its tenants were Irish Catholics who were either porters in nearby Covent Garden or sold vegetables or flowers in the nearby market. Thus a factual basis for Eliza's origins underpins the humor and the argument of Doolittle's speech. Moreover, the informal marriage arrangements and loyalty claimed by Doolittle are borne out by Booth's work. As Fraser Harrison reports:

James Hart, *Liberty Bound or Liberty Bond: U Can Change It* (American, 1918). Here the political agenda, "the stake," as contemporary as well as historical referent, and the tradition of allegorical, large women figures all emerge in an ink drawing/poster. The outcome of the struggle was as vast as it was in Joan of Arc's own time — and the expression of appeal as well as pain vividly displays the prominence of the legacy of Joan of Arc during World War I (*National Archives/NARA Still Pictures Branch*).

the house-to-house surveys conducted by Booth and Rowntree suggest that fidelity between couples was the norm, not the exception, and that family loyalties and connections were sustained over many generations. The symbolic significance with which the middle classes had charged the institution of marriage carried less weight with the poor who, for excellent reasons, looked upon any binding contract between two people with extreme misgiving. Theirs was a world fraught with uncertainty; if anything was certain in it, it was that life tended to get worse, not better.[52]

By Act IV, Higgins accuses Eliza of being heartless when she confronts his elitism and assumption of her achievements. When Higgins strips Eliza of her dignity once again in Act IV, by ignoring her role in the "triumph" at the garden party while he and Pickering congratulate each other, Eliza retaliates. First she hurls Higgins' slippers at him, and then she removes her "hired" jewels. By emphasizing her inner power against the shallow appearance of the costume, Shaw reinforces his theme and allows the "created" lady to come to life. Eliza recognizes in Act IV that as a "lady" her options are certainly still limited. She tells Higgins after the triumph that when she sold flowers, she sold a product. Now that she has been transformed into a lady, she has only herself to "sell." Eliza claims her new education makes her "unfit to sell anything else."[53] Since she remains unwilling to bargain with her body, she says she will seek financial security through her language skills. With her new understanding she declares to Higgins: "If I can't have kindness, I'll have independence."[54]

This reversal continues in Act V when Higgins and Pickering find Eliza at Mrs. Higgins' home. Mrs. Pearce and Mrs. Higgins had both warned Higgins of the danger of his "experiment" with Eliza, to no avail. Even Pickering had been oblivious In a heated exchange that could vie with the much-touted wooing scene of Shakespeare's *Taming of the Shrew*, Higgins and Eliza trade insults and deny their affections for one another. More to the point, Eliza refuses to compromise herself in any way. She has learned to value herself openly, as Joan will do in *Saint Joan*. Eliza began the play by accepting her lot and maintaining her own dignity and morality, but has now learned that she cannot go back to this life. In a mood of outrage mixed with disappointment, one Joan experiences often in *Saint Joan*, Eliza leaves Higgins' house.

When Higgins finds her the next day at his mother's and asks her to come back, she asks him: for what? He has no ready-made answer because he's so used to his authoritarian ways gaining automatic acceptance. Yet Higgins does propose an egalitarian, albeit "no strings," arrangement wherein they would be free to come and go as they pleased, without romantic attachment. At this moment, Eliza bemoans the loss of her former sense of self when she asks Higgins: "Oh! if I only could go back to my flower basket! I should be independent of both you and father and all the world! Why did you take my independence from me? Why did I give it up?"[55]

Eliza's declaration encapsulates Shaw's positive outlook for the success of the militant suffragette position, not only regarding the vote, but also in terms of a genuine change in socioeconomic possibility for unmarried women. *Pygmalion* can be seen as a faithful, if indirect, representation of the class struggle as well. The economic independence sought by Eliza and her determined chastity are the very issues highlighted by Christabel Pankhurst in 1913. Although Higgins dismisses Eliza's moral concerns with "We want none of your Lisson Grove prudery here"[56]—Shaw's contemporary audience would surely have recognized the rhetoric; the Pankhurst slogan was "Votes for Women, Chastity for Men."[57] Higgins certainly is a confirmed bachelor and takes no undue advantage of Eliza sexually, despite the expressed concern of Pickering, Mrs. Pearce (the housekeeper) and Mrs. Higgins. What Higgins is guilty of, though unconsciously, is treating Eliza with disrespect, referring to her as "baggage" and "heartless guttersnipe." Higgins is totally blind to the sexual innuendos that would accompany Eliza as a young girl "living with" him.

Each of these Shavian heroines had indomitability, like the leaders of "The Cause." According to histories of "The Cause," Christabel Pankhurst was thought of as a maiden warrior and her followers wore emblems resembling Joan of Arc. The Pankhursts thought of their Women's Social and Political Union (WSPU) as a "spiritual army," according to Martha Vicinus. The "suffragettes," the name Christabel Pankhurst coined in 1913 to distinguish those who participated in militaristic tactics from those who would not, were often thought of as woman warriors. The other supporters of enfranchisement only she sarcastically labeled "suffragists."[58] The schism had developed in the short period from 1906 to 1913, approximately the same period of time that separates *Major Barbara* and *Pygmalion*. Shaw supported the militaristic faction because he recognized the essence of Fabianism in their thinking. Now was their time to "strike hard." In much the same spirit, Shaw explores the relations between Barbara and her father, Eliza and Higgins, and Joan and the Dauphin; how much give and take could there be in relationships between men and women that were bound by social and/or political conventions?

Shaw's texts illuminate what Joan herself could not reconcile: the world according to imperfect human parameters, not necessarily equal to God's design. This precise point captivated Bertolt Brecht, who saw the original production of *St. Joan* in Berlin. Brecht admired Shaw, and his main version of Joan's story, *St. Joan of the Stockyards* (1929), is reminiscent of Shaw's *Major Barbara*. The Brechtian representations and interpretations of Joan of Arc are the subject of the next chapter. The three plays Brecht wrote about Joan, in collaboration with others, pick up this final thread of Shaw's insight. In their extension of the concept, they launch a very different perspective on the meaning of Joan's story for twentieth-century audiences. The emphasis becomes the inevitability of Joan's failure, due to her political naïveté and romantic individualism. Brecht's socialistic vantage point was far more extreme than Shaw's, and far less optimistic.

6

Putting on Their Trousers One Leg at a Time: Brecht's Three Joans

The stirring closing of Shaw's Epilogue to *St. Joan* appears to be the antithesis of Brecht's renowned notion of instructive theater, but a glimpse at Brecht's criticism of Shaw belies this assumption. In an article written in 1926 as a tribute to Shaw for his seventieth birthday, Brecht offers praise for what he labels Shaw's "terrorism." Brecht notes that Shaw's terror is unique because "he uses an extraordinary weapon, that of humour. This extraordinary man seems to be of the opinion that nothing in the world need be feared so much as the ordinary man's calm and incorruptible eye, but that this must be feared without question. This theory is for him the source of a great natural superiority." Brecht's overview indicates that it is the classical comic sensibility in Shaw's characterization that carries the weight of his message.

In the Epilogue of *St. Joan*, salient principles of comedy prevail: human nature is flawed, and the power to change things rests in the characters' hands. The anguish of the final moment connotes the despair Joan experiences as she recognizes that most people are incapable of such change. As the Epilogue in Shaw's play emphasized, Joan offers to incorporate the official change into the everyday lives of the characters. They abandon her once again because they can only live with the *idea* of Joan. In life, she had been too difficult to control, too different, albeit saintly, for them to tolerate. Unlike Shaw's, however, Brecht's own treatments of Joan of Arc do not lament the tragedy of society's punishment of an outstanding individual; rather, they underscore the futility of these very qualities in a society which cannot accept change or difference.

Brecht's remarks about Shaw in 1926 emphasized "the ordinary man's calm and incorruptible eye" because this affirmation of innate goodness is something Brecht and his contemporaries could no longer confirm. The prevailing socioeconomic conditions of the late 1920s in Germany produced an aura of alienation and cynicism that was reflected in the works of writers like Franz Kafka and the expressionistic silent films of the same period. The combination of the sick economy, the psychological wounds of the Versailles Treaty, and the increasing anxieties brought about by modernization were the causes. Martin Esslin sees Brecht's generation as the precursors of the French existentialists of the 1940s. Each group was plunged into despair and prompted to seek an appropriate commitment because "the young intellectuals responded to a world in which the comfortable security of bourgeois standards and assumptions had been replaced by terror and violence, in a spirit of grim realism."[1]

The Shavian world highlights the appeal and danger of its individual characters; the Brechtian one foregrounds the oppressive nature of the system that condemns the unorthodox. While both playwrights rely on comic and satiric twists of dialogue and plot, Brecht refuses to reinforce any concept that reflects a comforting solution from the past. For him, the past cannot provide the impetus for improvement, since the present must stand on its own. What is immediately different about Brecht's representations of Joan is their modernity. Shaw sees the consistency between medieval and modern life, while Brecht perceives that twentieth-century events have precluded the relevance of history. While Brecht's early plays, like *Baal* (1918), reflected a proclivity towards the burlesque in their jaded view of human nature, their tone was more satirical than didactic. However, the plays written after 1929 show a marked tendency towards moral examination of society as a whole, aligning him more directly with Bernard Shaw. These later plays revolve around protagonists who recognize the depravity of their conditions and struggle, not as isolated individuals, but as participants in the social milieu they neither like nor trust. If these plays offer solutions, they are collective in spirit. Brecht invariably treats historical material as a present reality rather than as safely distanced events; this technique was part of the "alienation effect," Brecht's approach to theater that aimed ideas at audiences to think about, rather than connect to characters' situations on an emotional level.

While both Shaw and Brecht recognize the importance of history as a measure of understanding the human condition, their vantage points differ sharply. Shaw emphasizes the notion that human nature does not change, so changing history can occur only when traditions are analyzed and challenged. Brecht highlights the uselessness of the past as a guide for the present and future because conditions do change, necessitating new solutions to even universal problems. Brecht's texts deliberately update the situations of history in order to achieve their intention of spurring audiences to draw parallels to the events of their own time; Shaw's plays invite the audience to recognize the roots of present conditions in past situations.

Part of the originality of Brecht's style of instructive theater lay in its synthesis of drama, journalism, and the evolving art of cinema. Because Brecht aimed to disrupt the ancient Aristotelian convention of audiences to sympathize with onstage figures, he incorporated the newer forms of popular culture into the text as well as *mise-en-scène*. Performances served to remind people of reality outside the theater. Chapter 4 spoke of the significance of film's emergence in the canonization era for Joan of Arc; in particular, DeMille's popular epic from 1916 can be viewed as yet another barometer for the continued variation of uses for Joan's image. Most important were the French films, since they echoed the dichotomous roles for Joan as religious saint and political icon.[2] Carl Dreyer's 1928 film *The Passion of Joan of Arc* stands as highest achievement because of its intense concentration on the Trial of Condemnation shot as a series of close-ups. Dreyer's depiction of Joan as an individual who suffers, and the inhuman depiction of those who question her, manages to convey the totality of Joan of Arc's experience, and its inspiration for audiences everywhere. Brecht and Shaw illustrated the ways in which Joan's image was both understood and exploited; Dreyer focused on the humanity of the young woman. Kevin Harty notes that the director's choice to condense the twenty-nine sessions of the Trial into one day not only represented Joan as a classical tragic heroine, but also intensified each scene. Questions multiplied, the numbers of adversaries became that much more obvious, and Joan's heroism and sanctity merge as a result. The screenplay was a fusion of Dreyer's reading of the trial transcripts and Joseph Delteil's, whose influential biography of Joan appeared in France in 1925.[3]

Brecht was drawn to Joan's story three times. In 1929-30, *St. Joan of the Stockyards* was written in commemoration of the five hundredth anniversary of her burning and in reaction to the world-wide economic crises; it responds to Shaw's *Major Barbara* (1905) and his *Saint Joan* (1923). Several years later, Brecht adapted Anna Seghers' radio play, *The Trial of Joan of Arc at Rouen* (1935), a work that combines twentieth-century technology and style with a medieval setting and historically accurate materials. During World War II he collaborated on *The Visions of Simone Machard* (1942), a text that fuses portions of the historical material about the heroism and innate goodness of Joan of Arc into a story of the French Resistance.[4] The first play was completed as the Nazis rose to power, the second after Brecht lost his German citizenship following a trip to Moscow, and the third while he was in exile in the United States. Brecht's representations expand Shaw's assertion that Joan's personality and actions would lead to the same outcome in any historical era because *St. Joan of the Stockyards* and *The Visions of Simone Machard* have twentieth-century protagonists who suffer society's scorn and/or indifference when they, like their historical model, try to confront the power structure. These works were not produced onstage in Brecht's lifetime, due to the texts' blatant criticism of the status quo, first of capitalism, then of fascism. *St. Joan of the Stockyards* was presented in Germany on radio in 1932, directly preceding Brecht's flight to Moscow.[5]

Anna Seghers' radio play, *The Trial of Joan of Arc at Rouen, 1431,* which Brecht adapted in 1935, is remarkable for its authenticity. Many of the short scenes of the trial contain almost verbatim transcripts of Joan of Arc's trial. The selected portions highlight the plight of the iconoclastic, yet naïve, girl; these moments are contextualized by crowd scenes that illuminate the condemnation, indifference, and bloodthirsty desires recorded in the chronicles of the 1400s. Throughout, vernacular language is used to update the situation and emotions, reminiscent of Shaw's choices in *St. Joan.* The overriding tone of Brecht's adaptation is cynical and callous — qualities noted in the historical accounts of the mood at Rouen by Joan of Arc's biographers. It is not surprising that this adaptation condenses Segher's actual trial scenes to embellish the role of the crowd, the representation of Joan's audience and Brecht's own. In Scene 5,

"The Weekly Market in Rouen," a man selects a mackerel, referring to it as having "soulful eyes. No doubt she heard voices too! I suppose they advised her to take the bait." A peasant woman and a fishwife argue about whether or not Joan is really a witch. The peasant woman believes Joan is from the devil; the fishwife thinks if she is a witch, it's too bad, because Joan is against the English. Moreover, "her voices seem to say what we're all saying. I mean, that the English should get out of France."[6] The remainder of the scene has a bantering tone, revolving around Joan's sentence, her virginity, and the hypocrisy of the clergy. It includes a smattering of a popular song which lampooned Bishop Cauchon of Beauvais, the French church authority who condemned Joan. He is described as "an Englishman now, they say/ On sentimental grounds/ And for five thousand pounds."[7]

Two important notes from Brecht on this work illuminate his stance. Brecht perceives that Joan's ability to resist her persecutors is hindered most by "her isolation." Joan's temporary lapse is explained by Brecht as derived from "her own mistaken assumption as to the people's passivity."[8] The people's support was very important to Joan of Arc; this text emphasizes how devastated she was when she believed she had lost this. As a result, Joan recants. But when she regains her faith and resumes her fight, she is "less inclined to submit to its [the Church's] authority." Despite her refusal to accept her judges as "the Church," Joan still tried to fit into Catholic doctrine, asking to go to the pope, agreeing to answer certain questions in the context of confession. Viewing her isolation as a determining factor separates this Joan from Shaw's; in *St. Joan*, Scene V, Joan exclaims: "Do not think you can frighten me by telling me I'm alone. France is alone; and God is alone ... I see now that the loneliness of God is His strength: what would He be if He listened to your jealous little counsels?"[9] In the Brechtian world, the counsels are the predominant factor because they rule the moment.

A third image from Brecht also is a collaborative effort. *The Visions of Simone Machard* (1942), written after Brecht was in exile and had come to Hollywood, is the most radical treatment of the material in that it tries to fuse fifteenth- and twentieth-century wartime experiences. As the world situation had steadily worsened, Brecht's despair and disgust had deepened, and his belief that the past offered no viable solutions had strengthened. The original material for the play came from Leon Feuchtwanger's experiences in France in 1940. Simone Machard reads her book about Joan of Arc in an attempt to find solutions as well as comfort. Later, she converses with the Angel (St. Michael) in dreams; these contain the impetus for the play's central action. The text heightens the importance of Joan's innocence by making its protagonist fifteen years old. Simone sees only what is morally right; she has no understanding of corruption. The other characters' cynicism provides the perfect foil for Simone's attitude. In her second dream, the Angel tries to enlighten her. It is here that she asks the all-important question in this play: "Should we go on fighting even after the enemy has won?" to which the Angel replies, yes. He also tells her to destroy all things that will enable the conquering enemy to vanquish France.[10]

Judging by the meticulous ways *The Visions of Simone Machard* parallels and/or inverts details of the historical Joan's visions, pilgrimage, and course of action, it is clear that the hopelessly repetitive outcome points simultaneously to perseverance on both sides. The function of public opinion and the rigidity of mores have remained constant through the centuries. In this Brechtian representation, the obdurate still must be taught to bow to authority, no matter how corrupt. Clearly, in this sense, the play corresponds to Shaw's *St. Joan*, which makes sense because Shaw's play was performed in Vichy France. The greed and political expediency that characterized fifteenth-century authority figures and business people dominate much of the action of this play as well. Simone works in a hostelry[11]; the owners give provisions to the Vichy supporters. As early as Scene 1, it is clear that the war is morally bankrupt. Thousands of civilian refugees are roaming the countryside; Père Gustave declares: "The tanks can get through any ordinary bog, but a bog of people gets them stuck. The civil population seems to be a great liability in this war.... You have to abolish people or abolish war, you can't have them both." Similar sentiments are spoken by a sergeant, who says: "They're treating the army like an enemy in its own country."[12]

Like her historical model, Simone refuses to compromise her honesty, and admits setting fire to brickworks which housed the fuel for enemy tanks. She is fully aware that she will be considered a saboteur and subject to execution, but she will not deny her actions, which she believes is at the command of the Angel. The allusions inherent in this symbolic action abound: the fire itself is an inversion of the stake; the poster forbidding sabotage connects to the edicts throughout France disseminated through public posters.[13] The Patron of the hostelry affords Joan the opportunity to dodge her punishment, by telling the German authorities that she blew up the brickworks before she saw the poster, but she refuses to lie. In a trial scene that combines historical references and characters and the concerns of the present, Simone is not executed, but returned to her employers. They pack her off to St. Ursula's, a sanitarium for the retarded and insane, where people are still chained and beaten rather than helped. Simone's friends are outraged, but the Patron's wife, Mme. Soupeau, shrugs off their concerns by saying that the girl must learn law and order. Was this an act of patriotism on her part? Hardly. She was angry that Simone had destroyed their sweet deal with the Germans.[14] The expected Brechtian irony surfaces at the end of the play, when the refugees have set the village hall on fire. Brecht's biographer, Ronald Hayman, sees this ending as an ultimate praise of Simone's courageous actions, despite its opposition to Mme. Soupeau's speech and actions.[15] True enough, but since the burning of buildings and whole communities is more drastic than punishing an offending individual, the play foregrounds the overwhelming sweep of the problem, and the corresponding destruction that must eradicate it.

St. Joan of the Stockyards was the work representative of the fullest Brechtian interpretation of the enduring meaning of Joan of Arc's story. The historical issues that matter most are interwoven. In this way, Brecht's play continues the tradition of explicitly using Joan of Arc as part of an ideological agenda. The setting is Chicago in 1929 and the protagonist, Joan Dark, is already in an army of sorts before the play begins. The question of Joan Dark's membership in the Black Straw Hats, a Salvation Army–type of organization, becomes threatened only when she confronts the power structure. Thus, progress for women is obliquely recognized, while the fate of the iconoclast remains as it had been for centuries. Interestingly, Brechtian "Joans" have common-alities with Shavian "unwomanly women" (see chapter 5). The characterization of Joan Dark of *St. Joan of the Stockyards* contains striking parallels to Barbara Undershaft of *Major Barbara*, even more than to Joan of *St. Joan*. Shaw's Barbara and Brecht's Joan Dark both work as idealistic, religious leaders, Barbara in the Salvation Army and Joan Dark in the Black Straw Hats. Each believes in her work and her own abilities to improve the lives of people she encounters. Both understand, albeit intuitively, that physical needs must be satisfied before any appeal to the mind or spirit of an individual or group of people is feasible.

That both Shaw and Brecht emphasize physical need in their plays places their works squarely in their times. Shaw illustrates the apparent failure of the Army to succeed in its mission of "saving" those in need[16]; Brecht's text mirrors this position. But Shaw portrays an industrialist who understands that workers whose biological needs are met are more productive and loyal; Andrew Undershaft has created a planned community, incorporating his munitions factory and housing. By 1929, however, the world situation had grown so desperate that such a solution belonged to the realm of fantasy. Despite his comfortable, middle-class upbringing, Brecht was greatly influenced by colleagues who were either socialist or communist and whose leftist ideology highlighted the plight of the working class. To these committed idealists, the efforts of the Weimar Republic seemed little more than rhetoric, as more and more people struggled to find viable employment in an economy marked by inflation and overcrowding. Young people were particularly affected by the lack of opportunity because the birth rate had peaked between 1900 and 1910. Therefore, the usual rifts between generations were exacerbated and an aura of bitterness was dominant, especially in the crowded cities.[17]

St. Joan of the Stockyards reflects this situation accurately when it portrays large numbers of unemployed youths and a handful of ruthless, older bosses and authority figures. When the stockyards are closed due to falling prices, the workers gather en masse despite the bitter cold. As one police detective observes: "those crowds stretch further than the eye can reach. If a person called out for a Joan, maybe ten or a hundred would answer. They sit and wait and have no face or name. Besides, one man's voice alone cannot be heard."[18] If Barbara Undershaft learns not to judge people and actions based upon stereotypical roles, Joan Dark recognizes that no individual insight can penetrate, let alone alter, the brutalities of modern life, especially if the individual is a woman. In this play, if the men in power emblemize our evil inclinations, then the women attempting to infiltrate the power structure reflect the futility of our more noble intentions. Bowls of soup cannot mend broken lives, or alter the system that caused the inequities to begin with. As Albert Doolittle reminds Henry Higgins in Shaw's *Pygmalion*, Act II, the poor "cannot afford" middle-class morals. The female protagonists of these plays by Brecht have to understand this grim truth in order to rise above naïve notions of social service.

Peukert offers a further context for the play's position: the schism created by modernization. Populations concentrated in urban areas where the individual was superseded by the mass. The quality of life, within the workplace as well as outside of it, had become increasingly mechanized.[19] Because of the economic crisis, the entrance of more women into the workforce was interpreted as yet another way in which the comfort of tradition (the family) was threatened by the alienating industrial environment. At the same time, women workers were consistently paid less than their male counterparts. As was true elsewhere, German women were then struggling to gain entrance into fields heretofore closed to them. At the same time, the women's movement in Germany had become much less active and less radical during the Weimar period than it had been before World War I, due to economic necessities that forced women to accept positions that were less challenging and remunerative than they would have liked. The typing pool and department store sales positions Peukert mentions represent such compromises. Even the granting of women's suffrage by the election of 1919 did little to alter this mood.[20]

John Fuegi argues that Brecht also had deep-seated misogyny. In 1925, Brecht set down some notes about male/female relationships, placing them in the context of written contracts under which the man could demand a considerable amount, while the woman had to concede to him disproportionately, although she could seek retribution for such inequalities. Brecht believed this dynamic to be unchangeable.[21] His own private inclinations were given enormous support when he met the leading German Marxist economist, Fritz Sternberg, in 1926. Sternberg was an unabashed misogynist who summarily dismissed the role of women, not only in private life, but in world literature, citing Plato as his authority.[22] Joan Dark herself is a curious mixture of wide-eyed idealism and information-seeking realism. Her naïveté gets in the way of her success, but does not mask either her capabilities or her compassion. It's clear that this character does not fit the mold of the "ingénue" who needs the guidance of a man to realize her potential.

The anxiety over the implications of these changes created a cultural dichotomy between those who saw the new ways as progress and those who saw them as the doom of civilized life. Peukert claims that no one who lived through this time period could remain neutral on this issue. More importantly, this controversy was inseparable from that of "Americanism," which was held responsible for these lifestyle changes. The growing influence of the media cannot be confirmed more dramatically, as the movies had created the myth of the "vamp," who represented a glamorized and exaggerated version of the "new woman." In Peukert's words, she was: "a bit too independent to be true, armed with bobbed hair and made-up face, fashionable clothes and cigarette, working by day in a typing pool or behind the sales counter in some dreamland of consumerism, frittering away the night dancing the Charleston or watching ... films."[23]

Brecht's awareness of the gender and social class conflicts in both everyday life and the cinema informs the dynamic between Joan and Mauler: a delicate balance between empathic connection and competition. Joan makes expensive moral demands of Mauler; he cannot live up to these. He is drawn to her on a personal level, but his business sense prevails; as a result, he uses her image with the workers to further his own agenda of exploitation. Since Brecht represents a larger cultural image here, it is important to recognize his radical agenda. German culture may have been influenced by American films of this time, but German filmmakers of the 1920s were far more daring and innovative regarding political statements. Brecht's friend Fritz Lang produced *Metropolis* in 1927, a futuristic blockbuster that portrayed the rich industrialists living above ground in pleasure gardens while the workers live and work underground, surrounded by enormous machines. A spiritual and political leader named Maria tries to rally the workers; she is abducted and replaced by a robot that possessed everything about Maria except her soul. The false Maria is burned at the stake when her plan to save the workers goes awry: truly a Joan of Arc image. A similar scenario will play out in *St. Joan of the Stockyards.* Another part of Berlin's modernist culture was cabaret, a venue for biting social satire in which Brecht participated and which influenced the mise-en-scène of his own plays, no matter what historical era they concern. Cabaret put a range of cultural issues at the fore: fluidity of gender, dubiousness of personal as well as governmental liberalism in the Weimar Republic, and the increasing economic depression. In 1922, Brecht's friend Trude Hesterberg performed "Song of the Stock Exchange," by Walter Mehring. This number was a "satirical pastiche of business clichés ... as well as patriotic songs and religious hymns, slightly varied to acquire a capitalist bent."[24] Brecht's plays often include songs of similar style and subject matter. Because of Fuegi's perspective, differences between *St. Joan of the Stockyards* and *Major Barbara* seem weightier. One example is Joan Dark's refusal of "tainted" money from the meat-packers for the Black Straw Hats' rent. Like Barbara, Joan must learn to differentiate between moral purity and reality. Just as the Salvation Army would never refuse a donation, neither does the leadership of the Black Straw Hats. But this version is harsher: when Joan Dark chases the meat-packers away, she is fired and publicly chastised.

In Shaw's text, Barbara Undershaft comes to understand that the world is more complex than she had acknowledged and finds a place in it, albeit with the guidance of her father and the persuasion of her fiancé. The removal of the Army uniform provides further evidence. Barbara takes hers off in a moment of disappointment and spite, but it is her decision, just as it is Barbara who chooses to leave it off when she sees that she can be more productive in her father's industrial world. Joan Dark is ordered to remove her uniform and resume women's clothing when she chases the industrialists away. From this point forward in this play, Joan becomes more disillusioned, more physically debilitated, and ultimately fails in her mission. The depiction of physical illness, mistreatment, and defeat by the power structure turns the text's attention once again to Joan of Arc and her condition during the Trial of Condemnation. But here the parallel freezes, as *St. Joan of the Stockyards* does not have a trial scene per se. The Black Straw Hats do give Joan Dark her uniform again before her canonization and death. The text's cynicism is nowhere more apparent than here, with its inverted ordering of these two events.

In *St. Joan of the Stockyards*, women are factory workers, devoted missionaries, or housewives. Whereas Brecht was mesmerized by the kinds of media images described earlier by Peukert, Elisabeth Hauptmann, his collaborator, observed real women. This same sense of realism dominates the attitude of Joan Dark, who consistently seeks truth and understanding. Her knowledge of economics and business ethics may be scanty and cause her eventual failure, but her perspicacity regarding human nature lingers in the spectator's mind. In light of the complexity of the socio-cultural moment Brecht shrewdly observes, Joan Dark represents a view of the world hopelessly out of synch by 1929, and yet closely aligned to the radical labor movements of the late nineteenth and early twentieth centuries, symbolized by the "Internationale" anthem.

In some ways Joan Dark can be compared to Jurgis, the protagonist of Upton Sinclair's American novel *The Jungle* (1906), an exposé of the horrific working conditions of the meat-packing industry of Chicago. The novel had been translated into German and Brecht had also used it in his earlier play, *In the Jungle of the Cities* (1922), a play also set in Chicago. For Brecht, Chicago was a symbol of decadence for Berlin as well as America, whereas for Sinclair it merely represented the monster of industrialization. The clearest parallel between the novel and play is the incident of the worker falling into the vat: the epitome of the fate of the individual in a mechanized world. *St. Joan of the Stockyards* also includes the closing of the factories, which matches Sinclair's in concept: to arouse the protagonist to action. In *The Jungle*, Jurgis walks home with "his pittance of pay in his pocket, heartbroken, overwhelmed." One more bandage had been torn from his eyes, one more pitfall was revealed to him! Of what help was kindness and decency on the part of employers— when they could not keep a job for him."[25] The play takes this view as its starting point and shows how much worse things had become. Joan Dark's role as a missionary instead of factory worker adds a wider and deeper scale to the leftist message, showing the impact on a society larger than that of the novel. Like Jurgis, Joan Dark becomes involved in the collective movement, but while the novel shows his eventual failure as an individual as an evolving tragedy, the play assumes this from the outset. The play tries to show the meaning of the events from both sides, underscoring the hopelessness.

The link between the socialist aspects of Sinclair's novel and the limitations of the Salvation Army had been confirmed for Brecht and Hauptmann in 1928, when they visited the soup kitchens run by the Army in Berlin. According to Frederic Grab, in his introduction to Frank Jones' English translation of *St. Joan of the Stockyards*, at first they saw the worthwhile aspects of the Salvation Army. It was only when Brecht and Hauptmann saw that the attempt to stand "above" the battle resulted in their supporting industrialists (the status quo), that the idea that good intentions were not enough became dominant. Joan Dark embodies this evolution in her attitude towards the Black Straw Hats in the play. Moreover, the May Day strike in Berlin in 1929 accelerated the cynical view of authority found in *St. Joan of the Stockyards* and the plays that follow it. Before the day was over Brecht, watching from an apartment window, saw twenty people killed by the police. It was then that the Marxist stance on violence, its inevitability and expediency, became part of the Brechtian stage.[26]

While an individual cannot triumph in Brecht's world, the attempt remains admirable. The fault lies in the structure of society and its corruption by greed on the one hand and privation on the other. This position is very much in keeping with the socialist movement's platform in the United States in the early part of the twentieth century. A strong influence and possible role model for Joan Dark may well have been the labor organizer and orator Mary Harris "Mother" Jones, a friend of Upton Sinclair's. While neither Brecht nor Hauptmann mentions Mother Jones directly, certain parallels make the connection probable and enlightening. Mother Jones was a collectivist, but she was also an outstanding individual.

Several biographers of Jones liken her to Joan of Arc, as Mother Jones spoke what she felt to be the moral truth and stood in awe of no authority other than God. She worked tirelessly for the sake of the common people, sacrificing her private life, going to jail in adherence to her principles, risking her life in labor strikes. Like Joan Dark, Mother Jones went to the people to discover the problems and their solutions. Both women, one very young and the other very old, understood the importance of publicizing important issues and actions and knew how to dress for the parts they recognized as their roles. The one key distinction is that Joan of Arc's cross-dressing and Mother Jones' traditionally feminine "widow's weeds" approached the power structure from opposite directions. Each of them, however, chose her costuming with keen awareness of its semiotic function. As Mother Jones stated in her autobiography, dressing like an old-fashioned grandmother gave her entrance to places that would have been closed automatically to one who "looked like" an agitator.

If Joan was known for her standard, Mother Jones' trademark was her black bonnet. The bonnet, long associated with modesty and propriety, had gone out of fashion by the 1880s, when Queen Victoria revived it for her 1887 jubilee. The Victorian chronicler Asa Briggs notes in *Victorian Things* that by that time bonnets were associated with the old, while young fashionable women favored hats.[27] By the 1890s, bonnets were on the way out.[28] Yet Mother Jones wore hers until her death in 1930. As a dressmaker, she was certainly aware of fashion trends, so it stands to reason that she was making a statement by sticking to this outmoded fashion. Dale Fetherling notes that Mother Jones was quite aware that part of her appeal and power lay in her connections to the past as well as the future. Fetherling asserts that Mother Jones' "costuming," from the perspective of the worker, represented a link to his "desire for a new industrial freedom and his desire to hang on to the best and most familiar parts of the past."[29] The image contradicted the absurd rumor that Mother Jones had been a "madam," a classic misogynistic attack at a peculiarly sensitive time. Mother Jones' infiltration of their world via the safe costume of grandmother underscores her understanding of her opposition.

As Eve Merriam describes Mother Jones, she was a formidable, up-front woman who used "an umbrella for a sword." Despite the times that governors called the militia against her, "the only dangerous weapon in her possession was the hatpin that attached the flat-top bonnet to her curly white hair."[30] Ultimately, however, Mother Jones achieved notoriety as "the most dangerous woman in America." The editor of her correspondence, Edward Steel, encapsulates her image well:

> By 1900, when she became an official organizer for the United Mine Workers of America, Mother Jones had already established the persona which she was to maintain for the rest of her life: the mild-looking motherly figure who was metamorphosed into a Joan of Arc when she mounted the platform and converted an uncertain crowd into a purposeful group of unionists, or who worked among the women and children, comforting them in their hardships and organizing them in protest parades.[31]

The iconographic conception of Joan of Arc, according to the above passage, has two major components: firstly, charisma to persuade an audience to take action, and, secondly, compassion and willingness to reach out to those in need. *St. Joan of the Stockyards* alludes to both of these attributes in its treatment of Joan Dark's effect on Pierpont Mauler as spokesperson for the Black Straw Hats. When she boldly goes to see him to find out why he has locked the workers out of their jobs, Joan is told that she can ask no questions, but only answer his. Mauler is fascinated by her zeal and courage, especially since the Black Straw Hats earn almost no money for their work. It touches him and frightens him. He says: "it's almost more than I can stand/ that there should be people like this girl, owning/ nothing/ but a black hat and twenty cents a day and/ fearless."[32] Unable to face her any longer, he arranges for one of his subordinates to deal directly with Joan. Like Mother Jones, Joan Dark is undaunted by the apparent failure of her appeal. When Mauler asks the other meat packers to empty their pockets as contribution to the poor, Joan confronts him directly: "Mr. Mauler, you know this is only a drop in the bucket. Can't you give them real help?"[33]

A fine example of the clear moral high-mindedness of Joan of Arc, as well as her directness, emerges in *St. Joan of the Stockyards* in Scene IV, where Joan is supposedly enlightened about the "wickedness" of the poor. However, instead of accepting the authorities' viewpoint, Joan Dark perceives the circumstances as evidence of the people's helplessness. A woman comes to inquire about her husband, saying he hadn't been home for two days. The truth is, her husband fell into a boiler and was killed[34]; the factory never reported his death, not even to his wife. Rather than apologize, the factory offers her twenty lunches in return for her silence. The boss tells Joan that her acceptance shows her innate wickedness. Joan counters: "If their wickedness has no limits, their poverty/ has none either./ Not the wickedness of the poor/ have you shown me, but the poverty of the poor./ Now that you've shown how wicked are the poor/ I'll show you next the troubles at their door./ Brand of depravity, premature disgrace!/ Be contradicted by their stricken face!"[35]

The indignation that marks Joan Dark's interpretation of what she sees illustrates her ability to go beyond stereotypical images. The ideology behind her words matches that of William Booth and the Fabian socialists of Shaw's generation. Its discernment that poverty is the real evil of the world is the essence of the play's Marxist stance. The rhetorical method Joan employs here, arousing moral sensibility in hopes of positive action, was a trademark of Mother Jones as well. Although she was known as "the miner's angel,"[36] Mother Jones' most dramatic feat was her March of the Mill Children, 1903. Because the child labor laws were enacted on the state level, no uniform means of enforcement existed. Mother Jones was perplexed as to the seeming complicity between the parents of these child workers and the mill owners; her eyes saw only the suffering of the children. Since she believed that the system was bound to be corrupt more often than the majority of individual parents, she sought some answers.

One mother said that her husband was dead and without the money her ten-year-old brought in, her family could not eat. Mother Jones' anger was aroused, but she transformed it into creative, collective action. To publicize the plight, she went to the Philadelphia newspapers, who told her that the mill owners were stockholders, so the conditions in the mills could not be written up in their newspapers. Mother Jones took a representative group of children from Philadelphia to the summer home of President Theodore Roosevelt on Long Island to show the public their plight. Along the way, she gave speeches and won over the hearts of so many that food and shelter was donated to the cause.

Just as the widow in *St. Joan of the Stockyards* chose her survival over loftier ideals of remaining true to a dead husband, so too would the children in Mother Jones' "army." In Coney Island, she took advantage of the setting: the Roman Coliseum. In the empty iron cages which normally housed animals, Mother Jones placed little children, who clung to the iron bars as she told the audience that any of these children would trade their supposed highest dream, that of becoming president of the United States, for "good square meals and a chance to play." She then commented on the monkeys who were being coaxed to talk by professors: "The monkeys are too wise for they fear that the manufacturers would buy them for slaves in their factories."

St. Joan of the Stockyards embraces these same attitudes, but also, like *Major Barbara*, discredits the notion that the poor are immoral. Not only does Joan Dark say in Scene IV that the poverty of the poor, not their depravity, is what she sees, but she also recognizes that without sufficient funds, the poor lack the ability to rise above the animalistic survival mentality. In her speech of reproof to the meat packers she warns them:

If a man has to bash his neighbor's head in for a bit of ham on his bread, so as maybe to grab from him what are, after all, the necessities of life ... how can any feeling for higher things stay alive in the human heart? ... Where are their morals to come from, if morals are all they have? ... My dear sirs, there is such a thing as moral purchasing power. Raise that and you'll get morality too. And by moral purchasing power I mean something very simple and natural: money. Wages.[37]

The contemporaneous context of Mother Jones' campaigns complements the elements from Joan of Arc's story that the play represents. The army in this text can be considered either the organization of the Black Straw Hats, of which Joan Dark is a member but not a leader, or the proletarian workers struggling to organize collectively. When Joan Dark attempts to join this latter army, her own political naïveté and dire physical conditions render her impotent, a complete inversion of the role and circumstances in Joan of Arc's rise. The integral "recognition of the Dauphin" scene is here and its significance heightened: Joan spots Pierpont Mauler easily and has a decided effect on him as an individual. In the long run, however, this makes no real difference; he remains a ruthless capitalist profiteer.[38] Although he truly cares for Joan and her plight, this does not matter enough to change his modus operandi, and the shock of this truth for the audience is a key element in the alienation effect of the play.

Only one hint of the issues in the trial remains: Joan's clothing. When Joan Dark alienates the capitalists and their money, she is summarily dismissed and told to remove her uniform. The stage directions note that she returns dressed "like a country maidservant." The political lesson is at its peak, as the audience begins to understand that Joan's failure to enact change results in devastation for everyone at the stockyards. After she leaves the traditional world of social reform (the Black Straw Hats), Joan begins to experience the reality, rather than the conception, of poverty. Like Shaw, Brecht and Hauptmann see that the trappings of philanthropy are not only deceptive, but they are often more directly aimed at those who should be giving rather than those who are in need. The discussion of Mauler's donation to the Black Straw Hats crystallizes the schism between Mauler and Joan, despite her personal effect on him. Joan sees the money as belonging to the workers, whose paychecks have been stopped for the sake of raising Mauler's prices. Like Joan of Arc, Joan Dark will not recant; like her historical model she will remain true to her principles. The wishes and wisdom of her Voices ruled Joan of Arc, while Joan Dark is bound to the victimized people of the stockyards. She tells Mauler she will not eat or have money again until they do, until there is a way for her to get it honestly. As she leaves she judges him: "you, sir, who live on poverty and/ can't look at the poor and condemn/ something you don't know and arrange/ not to see what sits condemned/ abandoned in the stockyards, unbeheld."[39] Condemning and abandoning one who is different is precisely what led to the burning of Joan of Arc in the public square.

Hungry and cold, Joan Dark sees the limitation of her personal appeal to Mauler, and she begins to recognize how impenetrable the system really is. This kind of awareness never came to the historical Joan, who was also hungry and ill during her trial. Joan of Arc, however, blamed individuals, not their roles; she never understood that their official roles precluded their compassion. Shaw's Joan gleans the full truth about the system only in the Epilogue, set long after her death. Joan Dark sees nothing but the reverse of this. In the world of 1929 Chicago, even good uses of money, i.e., support of the work of the Black Straw Hats by the stockbreeders and packers, is motivated by greed and self-interest. Joan Dark likens the situation not to a vicious cycle but to a teeter-totter:

> It's a seesaw board, this whole system/ is a seesaw, with two ends that depend/ upon each other,/ and the ones on top/ sit up there only because the others sit below/ and only so long as the others sit below and/ they couldn't stay on top if the others came up/ leaving their place, so that/ they must desire that these shall sit below/ for all eternity and not come up./ And there must be more below than up above or else the seesaw wouldn't hold./ Yes, it's a seesaw.[40]

If Shaw challenged his audience regarding the impact of historical redress of wrongs, this text is even harsher in its response to the supposed comfort that official acts such as canonization prompt. After arousing interest in the historical story, the play follows up with no trial scene. Instead, the plot proceeds directly to the condemnation. Here the play seems to extend the criticism of Shaw's "Epilogue" in *St. Joan*. If Shaw's coupling of the Rehabilitation Trial and the canonization fuses in this obviously unrealistic dream sequence, the later play highlights precisely what Shaw leaves out: the complicity of the mob.

On the other hand, if tragedy aspires to stir an audience to a higher purpose, a vision of what could be, the closing scene of *St. Joan of the Stockyards* fulfills this aim, albeit in a new way. Rather than identifying Joan Dark as the inspirational figure to raise the consciousness and moral outlook of the audience, the play places the spectators in both positions. They need to extrapolate the meaning as well as its subsequent required action. That was the essence of the "alienation effect" and the less empathic, "gestus" style of acting in Brechtian theater. Joan Dark's behavior would be exaggerated and stylized, and the reactions of the others onstage would not appear congruent with hers. In this scene, Joan, Mauler, the breeders/meat packers, and the Black Straw Hats all contribute to the clarification of the individual's role in the larger design, and the moral dilemmas which are part of the combination.

At the close of the prior scene, Mauler, though personally affected by Joan's pleas and her plight, goes ahead nonetheless with his capitalistic, greed-oriented agenda, buying the other packers out and thereby circumventing the impending workers' strike. He ensures the re-opening of the packing houses and the activation of the work force, but at two-thirds pay. Shrewdly aware of the possible unrest these facts may incite, Mauler gives ample funds to the Black Straw Hats to allow them to continue the work that can "encourage order./ It's true that there ought to be people among you again/ like that girl Joan, who inspires trust/ by her mere appearance."[41] Through the antagonist, Mauler, the text conveys the practical benefits of cultural icons. Such a moment matters greatly in the contexts of Joan of Arc's canonization by the very power structure that centuries earlier had condemned her.

The closing scene, "Death and Canonization of St. Joan of the Stockyards," refuses to adhere to the unities of tragedy, or even allow catharsis to develop. If tragedy traditionally points out and upholds the merits of the status quo, Brecht's rendering of ideology as a repetitive, child-like game, turns this convention inside out. The subsequent drowning out of Joan's final speech to the people by those who would "saint" her and then turn their attention elsewhere, likewise mirrors the motion of the board. The present and past tense of the words "see" and "saw" represent yet another doubling and serve to remind us that the lessons of history are pointless unless we abolish the ideology that created the problems.

This set-up is followed through in the final scene by Joan Dark's initial shock at the news of the stockyards' re-opening conditions. Her condemnation of her own individual failure as well as her cynical assessment of the industrialists betrays the lack of heroic stature in any part of the past. In her own painful confrontation of these truths, Joan connects herself to the minds of the spectators as she cautions them: "Take care that when you leave the world you were not only good but are leaving a good world!"[42]

Joan's next speech continues the theme of shared responsibility between the individual and the world at large. She observes that the two worlds that are the halves of the seesaw are separated by a gulf so wide that neither side knows what occurs on the other. Further, "there are two languages, top and bottom/ and two standards to measure by/ and that which wears a human face/ knows itself no more."

If the individual who "wears a human face knows itself no more," the play reinforces its Marxist stance; no true society can exist until economic inequities are addressed. After Joan says this, the stage directions specify that packers and stockbreeders speak so loudly that Joan is "drowned out." It is at this point that the play begins its most telling and significant break with the tone and events of the historical Joan. The absence of a "trial" in this text is amplified by the merging of Joan's literal silencing, the granting of her canonization status, and her death, not by burning, but from pneumonia.[43] The power structure could canonize her, and Pierpont Mauler himself wants to keep her from starving, but with a price that Joan Dark, like Joan of Arc, could not pay: sacrifice of principles. Such treatment does more than extend the questioning evinced in the closing scene and Epilogue of Shaw's *St. Joan*; Brecht's Joan Dark, rather than reaffirming her own faith before dying, brutally disavows the comforting omnipresence of God. Although an "inaudible" speech, it contains the essence of the play's stand: a Marxist acceptance of the necessity of violence, and dismissal of religion as viable comfort:

> So anyone down here who says there is a God/ although there is none to be seen/ and He can be invisible and help them all the same/ should have his head banged on the pavement/ until he croaks.... And as for the ones that tell them they may be raised in spirit/ and still be stuck in the mud, they too should be tossed out/ heads down. It's not like that!/ Only force helps where force rules, and/ only men help where men are.[44]

Joan's last speech is overwhelmed by loudspeaker announcements of the horrors of the 1929 economic scene; these, in combination with the tone of Joan's words, dispel the loftiness and idealism, replacing these with the crudeness that befits the world of the slaughterhouses and insensitive government that supports them. Rather than the terror of comedy that he saw in Shaw, Brecht's text offers the bluntly prosaic commentary of high-tech. But then the scene takes the most unexpected turn of all, when the cast accepts both sides of the dialectic. Joan Dark, the sainted but failed heroine, is dead and Mauler has won. Even though he has attained perpeteia, he is neither lost nor remorseful. Instead, he describes his choice in an echo of Goethe's Faust's divided self: "A twofold power cuts and tears my miserable inner state like a jagged, deep-thrust knife:/ I'm drawn to what is truly great/ free from self and the profit rate/ and yet impelled to business life/ all unawares!"[45]

Joan Dark has died because of her own inability to penetrate the status quo; Pierpont Mauler continues to thrive. He does not look to the "Chorus" for wisdom; rather, the reverse is true: the Brechtian collective message embraces Mauler's position, and then transforms it: "Humanity! Two souls abide within thy breast!/ Do not put either one aside/ for life with both is best./ Be two in one! Be here and there!/ Keep the lofty and the low one/ Keep the righteous and the raw one/ Keep the pair!"[46] As Fritz Lang's film *Metropolis* had done two years earlier, Brecht offers the possibility of the head and heart working in unison for a common cause.

With the film parallel in mind, Brecht's modernization of the Chorus in his dramatic structure is both an extension and a contradiction of Schiller's vision of the "ideal spectator," the individual who would be inspired by the heroic protagonist and incorporate the values represented by the drama into his future actions. Schiller's theater was virtually emblematic for German audiences, despite its nineteenth-century sentimentality. Even though Brecht sees Schiller's vision as illusory, he likewise recognizes his predecessor's influence on European culture as ongoing. Therefore, in parodying the style and structure of Schiller, especially regarding choric elements, Brecht is both acknowledging the earlier interpretation while revealing its inadequacies for twentieth-century concerns and conditions. Conversely, it is important to note the distinction between Schiller's use of history and Brecht's; while the former distorts historical fact to suit the demands of the tragic form, the latter uses the same technique to foreground the patterns of social response to issues and individuals.

In 1939, Brecht wrote a play about the most memorable female protagonist in his canon: Mother Courage. Like Schiller's trilogy *Wallenstein*, *Mother Courage and Her Children* is about the Thirty Years War, as well as the struggle between self-preservation and fidelity to a cause and/or leader. Schiller does pay attention to the plight of the "everyman," although his emphasis is traditional: Wallenstein, the leader. Mother Courage is completely outside the military establishment, because of both her gender and her social position. It is this combination that helps promote the "alienation effect." Yet even Brecht admitted that this play, for all its cynicism, evokes audience sympathy by its conclusion. Though put off by Mother Courage's greed and apparent indifference to those around her, we admire her struggle against the overwhelming odds of a system she once erroneously believed she could beat.

The pervasive grimness of *Mother Courage* can be seen in the situation as well as in the protagonist. Experience has removed her once-fervent optimism. In "The Song of the Great Capitulation," Eric Bentley contends, the audience is "invited to imagine her as a young woman who thought she could storm the heavens, whose faith seemed able to move mountains."[47] Even the title of this song is an oblique reference to Joan of Arc, though an ironic one; unlike Joan, Mother Courage does not regain her own sense of purpose. Instead, she quickly learns to follow the ways of expediency. She admits: "I had learned to drink their cup of tea ... the day soon came when I was to discover/ They had me just where they wanted me."[48] Mother Courage is a survivor, relying upon her inner strength to see her through. In the middle of the play, the chaplain states his admiration for her courage. She recognizes this part of her character as collective, belonging to her class.

In Brecht's world, economic and gender issues are readily apparent, and often converge. Feminist critic Elin Diamond notes that, for this reason, the impact of gender on Brecht's audience cannot be overlooked. As Diamond explains, gender refers to "words, gestures, appearances, ideas and behavior that dominant culture understands as indices of feminine or masculine identity."[49] Mother Courage recognizes her subservience to a heartless system, but likewise values her own will to survive, and so becomes androgynous in the truest sense. Her last exit, attached to her wagon, determined to keep on going, inspires us because of her lack of self-pity. She has lost her children, victims not only of the war but also of their mother's naïve faith in "business." But she is ready to take what tomorrow brings. Alone onstage she muses: "I hope I can pull the wagon by myself. Yes, I'll manage, there's not much in it now. I must get back into business."[50]

In effect, this conclusion allows the audience to become part of the play's structure as well as its performance. Plays that successfully achieve this are really not finished until the consciousness of the spectator thinks the issues through. Such theatrical methodology allows the audience to concentrate on the essence of an iconographic figure like Joan of Arc, and its unique combination of feminine and masculine virtues. This methodology is how we can arrive at the larger meaning, not only in these Brechtian figures, but in all of us. As Lillian Hellman would say in the 1950s, Joan's story is ours. We find it in our consciences, and our individual capacities for compassion.

Epilogue: Saintly in Slacks —
The Iconographic Joan since 1945

In light of the apparent consolidation of Joan's heroic image during the canonization era, and her unmistakable inspiration for women's causes and soldiers during World War I, it appears odd, at first glance, that dichotomy regarding the uses of Joan's legend would resurface by World War II. Yet the uneasiness regarding the New Woman, the Flapper, and the independent career girls that followed in their wake had really reconfirmed the schism that never truly faded. In France, both the collaborationist Vichy government under Marshal Pétain and the French Resistance headed by Charles de Gaulle consciously revisited Joan of Arc's era as well as her legend in their iconography and ideology. For the Vichy, Joan was represented as obedient to St. Michael and God, as well as to her traditional duties as a daughter before her mission. Most importantly, her willing sacrifice for her country's sake aligned her with right-wing and even Fascist principles. For the Resistance, her heroism and belief in her people dominated, and de Gaulle decided to use the Cross of Lorraine as its emblem.[1] Eric Jennings argues that the Vichy recast Joan in a virtually misogynistic fashion, even going so far as eliminating her transvestism, in its efforts to discourage any feminist tendencies in French girls. The two symbols for French womanhood, Joan and Marianne, had come to be modern incarnations of the Mary/Eve medieval dichotomy, as Vichy schools replaced the busts of Marianne with Pétain himself. Not only was the republican spirit removed, but also the feminine icon.[2]

The economic depression that enveloped the United States as well as Europe through the 1930s had re-ignited the supremacy of domestic virtues for women, whose job opportunities diminished. The urgent need for workers during World War II then shifted the momentum, thereby enlarging women's sphere. American women found themselves in men's factory jobs, as typists in offices, as nurses at the front. Especially for European women, the World War II experience duplicated their efforts in World War I, but by this later era, however, women demanded more credit for what they were able to do, as well as for their independent decision-making. Particularly noteworthy was the breakthrough in journalism for women. For the first time, they could be war correspondents, due to the "robustness of the American press." The abundance of daily newspapers, news periodicals and wire services "left room" for women to join the ranks in reporting the war. Although they attended press briefings only late in the war, and wrote about the daily heroism rather than the details of combat, theirs was a "special opportunity which they themselves viewed as an honor, and their country was honored by the way they fulfilled that task."[3] While many employment opportunities evaporated as returning veterans reclaimed their places in the workforce, many women would continue to work, even if only part time. More than economic factors were behind the ideological stance against the women's increasing public lives. Just as their nineteenth-century counterparts had done, post–World War II society reacted to overwhelming outside world events, especially fear of nuclear war and the Communist threat, by turning to "home" for comfort.

Even women themselves were part of the ideology that favored their dependence. Many welcomed the chance to return to lives of less pressure. Others were too unsure of themselves to venture forth. As Brett Harvey encapsulates: "What constrained them was not always the blatant sexism of barred doors and low expectations. It was their own profound belief, internalized from a lifetime of messages, that achievement and autonomy were simply incompatible with love and family ... independence equaled loneliness."[4] Harvey's perspective reflects the gradual diminishment of the feminist cause since the Votes for Women campaign had triumphed in 1920 in the U.S.[5] Forces in the popular culture similar to those discussed in connection with Brecht were at play here. The later generation of New Women wanted to have it all, including marriage and family. Gradually, the desire for careers began to ebb in the 1920s, plummet in the Great Depression, and return after the wartime need vanished. In 1924, Lorine Pruette wrote that middle-class American teenage girls seemed uninterested in careers; "their heroines were Joan of Arc and Cleopatra, romantic figures of the past rather than realistic modern role models."[6] Pruette's remark is puzzling on the one hand, and insightful on the other. Joan of Arc and Cleopatra were leaders and changed history; is that what made them "romantic figures?" Did Pruette possibly refer to the *tableaux vivants* of the suffrage days or was she inferring here that only a handful of women could really have the opportunity to change their worlds? And, those who "succeeded" risked martyrdom or suicide. The modern role models were found in men rather than women. Because the younger women saw feminist principles as irrelevant, their concern was on eradicating the sexual prudery associated with that older generation. The freer sexuality of their era turned the tables on independent lives for women and the support of a sisterhood in favor of what they believed to be the fuller life of marriage and a return to staying at home.

Even educated women after World War II were encouraged by magazine articles and movies to make a good marriage, donate their energies to good causes, and be the moral consciences of their families; in other words, their nineteenth-century "spheres" were reinstated. A key player was the new medium of television, which sought to preserve traditional "family values," especially regarding women's roles. In "Provider," an article in the "Hers" column of the *New York Times Magazine*, Alice Hoffman describes the relationship between the television image and the audience. She contends that a child growing up in the '50s believed that the only family that counted was the one on

J. Howard Miller, *We Can Do It!* American World War II poster. Rosie the Riveter, strong and still feminine, was the rallying cry to bring women into non–traditional work, for the sake of their "boys" overseas. The emphasis on cosmetics reinforced the double message for women during World War II: be capable, be strong in all ways, but don't forget to be feminine (*produced by Westinghouse for the War Production Board, National Archives/NARA Still Pictures Branch*).

156

the television screen. Hoffman claims that her mother believed in that image, expecting it to be "real and in color" in her own life. In exchange for the perfection, peace, and tranquility offered, there was only one "small bargain ... we were never to ask questions, never to think about people who ... were different in any way ... we were never, ever, to wonder what might be hidden from view, behind the unlocked doors."[7] As the studies and revisionist views of this era emerge, one theme seems recurrent: protecting the personal sphere from change and questioning served as a buffer from the inexplicable horror of atomic bombs and the Communist "domino" effect.

Literary artists after World War II in Europe and the United States reflected the increasing despair and cynicism around them, but they also tried to salvage the dignity and meaning underneath the veneer of alienation. In France, the division of the country between pro–Fascist (Vichy) and Resistance foreshadowed these attitudes during World War II. The playwright Jean Anouilh wrote an updated version of Sophocles' *Antigone* during the war, which is remarkable not only for its pointed attack on authority then and now, but because the Vichy government allowed it to be produced. He would go on to write a play about Joan, prompted by requests from French clergy. Albert Camus and Jean-Paul Sartre, as leaders in the emerging existentialist movement in France, chronicled the absurdity of life and our individual responsibility to create an order within the chaos. In his 1944 play, *No Exit*, Sartre defined hell as "other people"; in his 1942 novel *The Stranger*, Camus traced the consciousness of his anti-hero, Mersault, emphasizing his increased detachment from ordinary human ties. The American writer William Faulkner expressed the opposite viewpoint in his acceptance speech for the Nobel Prize in 1950. Faulkner called upon his audience to believe in the integrity of the human spirit, claiming: "I believe that man will not merely endure: he will prevail. He is immortal, not because he alone among creatures has an inexhaustible voice, but because he has a soul, a spirit capable of compassion and sacrifice and endurance."[8] Although Faulkner did not write about Joan of Arc, his statement could very easily apply to her words, actions, and iconographic role in post–World War II times.

One of the most representative struggles waged within individuals in dramas revolved around the issue of compromise. How much integrity was at stake to adapt to the circumstances of the status quo business world? Moral purists paid dearly; perhaps this fact explains the renewed fascination with Joan of Arc's unflinching loyalty to her Voices and her mission. Most people preferred to compromise and survive. Not surprisingly, this era would see new representations of Joan of Arc in the theater. These plays examine her plight from the inside out, probing her character for its essential attributes, more as explanation for her ability to confront authority unabashedly than for any singular achievement. Despite the distinct vantage points of the individual texts, these images urge us to think of the spirit of Joan of Arc as archetypal, thereby furnishing us with the kind of personal inspiration that was clearly lacking and greatly needed in the post–World War II era. Shaw's *St. Joan* is incorporated and/or extended in these later texts. In particular, Shaw's contention that the social structures of the fifteenth century are the real villains in Joan's story, and their omnipresence in twentieth-century life as well, are "givens" in the works of the 1940s and 1950s. Like Shaw, Maxwell Anderson, Jean Anouilh, and Lillian Hellman all admire Joan as an outstanding individual. But even more than Shaw, these later playwrights marvel at Joan's ability to transcend the oppressive spirit of her times.

Shaw's play saw several revivals during this time period, in France, Great Britain and the United States. During the 1940s several revivals of *St. Joan* were staged in Britain and more productions were staged in the 1950s on Broadway. Within a ten-year period, revivals of *St. Joan* and première productions of Maxwell Anderson's *Joan of Lorraine*, Jean Anouilh's *L'Alouette* and Lillian Hellman's English adaptation, *The Lark*, were an almost constant presence on the New York stage. This renewed fascination with Joan's story links to specific parallels to post-war social issues, especially the touting of conformity by the United States government and popular culture.

Other American plays remarkable for their analyses of political identity and loyalty also coincided with these productions: broadening and consolidating the interests in historical figures' struggles to gain acceptance and influence their own times. Arthur Miller's *The Crucible* examined the Salem witch trials, but also implicated McCarthyism in 1953. Simultaneously, in Paris, Samuel Beckett launched a new level of absurdity, with *Waiting for Godot*. Two years later, Frances Goodrich and Albert Hackett adapted *The Diary of Anne Frank* for the stage, removing any illusion of historical distance the audience might have maintained for Miller's play. American theater's devotion to examining American history continued with Jerome Lawrence's and Robert E. Lee's *Inherit the Wind* in 1955, the reenactment of the 1925 Scopes Trial.

The theme of compromise was the major concern of Maxwell Anderson's *Joan of Lorraine*. Begun in 1944, it was composed during a war which necessitated the banding together of democratic and Communist nations to eradicate the greater evil of fascism. Anderson was deeply troubled by this unlikely alliance. Throughout his life and work Anderson had been a champion of individual freedom as the highest possible good anyone could attain. In turning to the story of Joan of Arc at such a pivotal time, he hoped to discover a palatable reason for Joan's, and for her adversaries,' acceptance of the ways of expediency. The conflict in this play is between the need to compromise and the need to maintain one's faith. Both positions play a part in an individual's desire to survive bleak circumstances.

In her study of Anderson, Mabel Driscoll Bailey argues persuasively that Anderson wrote at a time when the main question was whether or not to fight, either in wars or on moral battlefields. She depicts Anderson's attitudes towards war and the corruption of authority as representative of the average American's. Although she never says so directly, Anderson's reputation as a "popular" playwright informs this position. One of the controversies over this play is its conservative position regarding rebellion. Earlier in his career, Anderson was an outspoken pacifist and critic of the corruption that plagued even the best forms of government. His collaborative anti-war play written with Laurence Stallings, a colleague of Anderson's in journalism and a World War I veteran, caused a sensation in 1923. *What Price Glory?* stripped away the grandeur of honor, glory and patriotism, even using obscene language to represent the soldier's life and plight.[9] Yet World War II was completely different in Anderson's eyes; freedom was a bigger issue than ever, which condoned even war as a means of securing it. *Joan of Lorraine* expands the boundaries of freedom, settling at last for freedom of convictions; Joan cannot reverse her destiny, but she can understand it as *hers*. Because the play uses the play-within-a-play frame, Anderson tells two stories at once: Joan's story is the subject of a play in rehearsal. The drama revolves around the conflict between the actress portraying Joan and her director. The actress, Mary Gray, is troubled by changes in the script that show Joan's willingness to work with less-than-honorable people in order to accomplish her mission. The play-within-the-play director (Masters) shrugs this off, saying: "I don't think I'd call them the forces of evil — but you have to get some of the people who are running things on your side — and they're pretty doubtful characters mostly."[10] Mary feels this is a "desecration" of Joan's story. Another concern is the choice of using real, albeit offstage, voices; the actress worries that this will give the impression of outer rather than inner sources of conviction. This time Masters does not disagree with her concept, but counters that he knows of no other way to "play" this effectively, citing specific details like phonograph needles scratching if sound effects were used instead.[11]

Self-consciously theatrical, *Joan of Lorraine* is reminiscent of Pirandello's *Six Characters in Search of an Author* (1921), a play Anderson admired. If Pirandello questions the role of actors and the autonomy of the story and its characters, Anderson treats the problem of applying the past to present-day concerns. One point of distinction between the two texts illuminates a salient point. Rather than presenting the story of Joan as a static "given," the way the characters do in Pirandello's play, Anderson presents the struggle to interpret Joan's story as ongoing and individual. To make his point, Masters describes the unethical practices in theater, such as box-office graft, that goes on in Mary's working environment. She is oblivious to these matters, and asks when dishonesty ends. Masters' cynical reply reinforces Anderson's theme: "It doesn't end. The world's like that.... And the theater's in the world, like everything else. And I still think it's worth while to put on a play about Joan of Arc — in the middle of all this. The human race is a mass of corruption tempered with high ideals."[12]

It is this point that raises the play to a serious level, and places it as part of the evolution of Joan of Arc as a cultural icon. Indirectly at least, Anderson nods to Joan's importance beyond canonization, as Joan has become representative of human potential rather than official public recognition. The concerns of Mary Gray do have another dimension — one overlooked by the critics of 1946, namely Joan's representation in this play as a dependent "good girl."[13] Deciding to emphasize portions of the historical materials that show her reluctance to tackle so immense a mission, her powerlessness as a daughter and an unworldly country girl runs counter to Shaw's Joan but, more importantly, betrays Anderson's compliance with yet another prominent trend of the late 1940s: anti-feminism. Once again, Mary does not say this directly, nor does the play undermine the actress' status as a career woman. Yet the text does highlight the power of the director, implying his superior function. The character's name doubles the meaning here. Moreover, Masters describes Joan in less than heroic terms. In a key speech he explains to the actors:

> She's always been shown on the stage as a sort of Tom Paine in petticoats, a rough, mannish hoyden, but it doesn't seem to be historically accurate. As far as the evidence goes she was a modest and unassuming village girl who never would have raised her voice anywhere if she hadn't been convinced she was carrying out God's orders. And if she was this kind of girl, and completely feminine, then her problem was how to make herself heard, how to get her message out to the world.... Well, she could have picked up an idea from her brothers as well as not.[14]

Anderson's diligent research comes through here. Describing Joan as a "Tom Paine in petticoats" was Samuel Taylor Coleridge's marginal comment in Robert Southey's poem *Joan of Arc* (1796). Southey's attitude towards Joan was far more liberal-minded. That Anderson wishes to raise the same objections to the political and social savvy of a representation of Joan as Coleridge had revealed his marginalized view of Joan's abilities. Coleridge remained indignant in his commentary, questioning Southey as to how (why?) he wished to "transmogrify the fanatic votary of the Virgin."[15] As for the comment about Joan's representation onstage, the predominance of Schiller's feminized portrait ca. 1801–1920 certainly contradicts this play's perspective.

In Anderson's text it is Mary who wishes to foreground the spirituality of Joan's mission and Masters who emphasizes her practical traits, much like General Dunois' attitude towards Joan of Arc. Nonetheless, the rest of the speech shows the recognition of her limitations rather than her solutions. Masters assumes that as a young woman Joan needed the advice, support, and role-modeling that only men could provide, aligning him with Schiller's mindset once again. Masters' reference to earlier portrayals, very likely of *St. Joan*, as showing a "mannish hoyden" reveals both his condescension and his disregard of other portions of the historical evidence that clearly support the conception of Joan of Arc as high-spirited and boisterous. Although the United States was a major world power after World War II, the world seemed more dangerous and precarious than ever. Mary Gray portrays this uncertainty, but in the face of questioning and curiosity. Harvey posits that, as a result of the fearful political climate, women made rash decisions or, worse still, "just drifted."[16] This drifting is what Anderson's protagonist is trying to avoid, as she struggles to find a viable interpretation of her role and of her position as an actress in the commercial theater.

Ironically, more women than ever before entered the workforce in the 1950s and more attended college. The magazines of the period belie these facts. Harvey cites a 1946 *Newsweek* article that claimed: "For the American girl books and babies don't mix."[17] Even college curricula began to reflect a bias towards family life; in 1953

Cornell University began a Home Economics major.[18] Ultimately, many women gave up ideas of breaking into the masculine domains and turned to marriage as an "answer" to their own insecurities as well as in compliance with social expectations.

When Mary Gray returns to rehearsal after threatening to quit she says it is because she understands the parameters of Joan's compromise. While this interpretation underscores Anderson's premise and Joan's spirituality, the play also shows clearly that the actress bows to the superior wisdom of her male director, a man who was once her "admirer." Yet it is Anderson's handling of the trial scene that crystallizes the feminized stance of *Joan of Lorraine*. It certainly is clear from the trial transcripts that Joan was physically and emotionally exhausted, but it is equally apparent that she was witty and determined. Anderson's scene contains none of the latter; instead, she despairs. By the end of the Trial of Condemnation in 1431, Joan was shown the instruments of torture. Tired and frightened, she told her judges that if they tore her limb from limb she would not and could not tell them anything else, and that anything she would say would only be due to her fear of the fire.[19] Weeks later, Joan of Arc abjured, believing that she would then be freed. Once she understood that her reward would be life imprisonment, she became infuriated. In Anderson's play, Joan claims not to know good from bad, truth from falsehood. She also volunteers to resume woman's dress rather than agreeing to do so as part of the bargain.[20] Most significant, she understands that life imprisonment is imminent even before she abjures.

Despite these serious flaws, the play's closing scenes redeem it. The last interlude (rehearsal scene) shows Mary Gray's understanding of Joan's motivation and decisions. The last scene shows Joan herself arriving at these decisions: the doubling effect is not merely clever here, but serves as an invitation for every person in the audience to examine his/her conscience for similar understanding. Mary comes to see that Joan may have compromised on little issues, but did not sacrifice her integrity; this is why she chose to die rather than remain alive after having betrayed her Voices and her principles. She also has a clear message for the post-war audience: "It doesn't matter what we try to say about her. Nobody can use her for an alien purpose. Her own meaning will always come through, and all the rest will be forgotten."[21] This remark can also be an updating of Warwick's recognition that Joan would be considered a martyr, superseding all of the actions of the authorities on both sides. In the closing scene, Joan is at prayer in her cell, preparing for death. Once she accepts her Voices' counsel that she had done all she was commanded to do she feels free to examine her own choices. Joan's final statement affirms that she would do the same all over again: "I would follow my faith, even to the fire."[22] Faith allows people to transcend circumstances, or to accept them; it is the other dominating force in the play. Not only do leaders like Joan have to have faith in something beyond themselves, but everyone does.

During the McCarthy era, artists and writers were among the first to be subpoenaed. Anderson's testimony corresponded to the angst that characterized the post–World War II era. He, like his plays, took the middle ground. He neither informed on his colleagues during the HUAC hearings, nor did he defend them. His loathing of Communism, and belief in individual freedom, seemed to leave him no other choice. But he didn't abandon his suspicion of government or authority. When the American press attacked the Greek regime in 1948, Anderson wrote to the editor of the *Atlantic Monthly* that he wondered what U.S. policy would be regarding protection of individual rights against state tyranny if a Communist threat were present. He concludes as follows: "The procedures of the Un-American Activities Committee lead me to believe that if the Communist danger were as real here as in Greece our House of Representatives would be inclined to shoot first and investigate afterward."[23]

Victor Fleming's adaptation of *Joan of Lorraine*, entitled *Joan of Arc*, starring Ingrid Bergman (1948), was written by Maxwell Anderson and Andrew Solt.[24] By the time the film was produced, however, much of Anderson's material had been removed. No longer was this a double story; it had become a spectacle for its star, Ingrid Bergman. Anderson was mortified by what Hollywood, especially Bergman, had done to his play. Not only was the rehearsal frame removed, but the filmed script was the work of Andrew Solt. In a letter to John Mason Brown dated May 18, 1949, Anderson expresses his disappointment and frustration with the film, bemoaning the lack of control of the writer in Hollywood. More disturbing to him was that Ingrid Bergman: "insisted on taking out all human touches and making Joan a plaster saint." He condemns her for "wrecking" the project, removing its "quality" and using the power she had as star to do so.[25] Brown's review of the film in the *Saturday Review of Literature* felt the dialogue to be so "flat, jarring, colloquial, or undistinguished that the movie might have been better ... silent."[26] Visually, Fleming's film is stunning and Bergman has rapturous moments. But the emphasis is on spectacle at the expense of depth, and the feminizing of Joan that was present in the original play is far greater in the film, with the exception of the battle scene at Orléans. The latter part of this scene, however, probably gave Anderson the "plaster saint" idea.

Nine years later, Otto Preminger adapted Bernard Shaw's *St. Joan*, starring the seventeen-year-old, unknown, Jean Seberg. English writer Graham Greene wrote the screenplay, and French playwright, Jean Anouilh, did the subtitles for the French version.[27] Otto Preminger's film is extremely faithful to Shaw's text in terms of dialogue in particular scenes, but Joan appears as a perky, exaggerated *ingénue* while the authority figures likewise appear more buffoon-like than obstreperous. Three major departures also mark the film as its own version: the use of the Epilogue as a frame, deletion of Scene IV (the "tent scene" which decides Joan's fate), and the visualization of the Coronation and burning, both of which are diegetic in Shaw's text. The most serious problem is using the Epilogue as a run-of-the-mill flashback technique. Shaw's Epilogue astonishes, breaks the mood of the trial and condemnation, and pulls the audience in as part of the story. Preminger's choice reduces it to its most fundamental use and makes it a way for the Dauphin and Joan to share the memories and understand them, yet another parallel to Anouilh's "memory" structure in his play.

Conceiving of authority figures as people who have had little from life is at best an embedded allusion in the texts of Shaw and Anderson. Despite their disparate views on other subjects, these two playwrights' focus consistently remains on the superiority of "other" while Anouilh highlights the contrast by exposing the extent of the mediocrity that acts as foil to the hero/ine's clear vision and superior intellectual grasp. This technique is closer to Brechtian *gestus/alienation effect* than the more traditional metaphor of theater as the world, or even life as theater. What is so characteristic of Anouilh, his conscious use of theatrical convention to underscore theme and characterization, permeates plays both comic and tragic. The forced audience awareness that it is witnessing a performance, through dialogue as well as acting style, maintains the distance necessary to judge rather than empathize. Parallels between Antigone and Joan show up in Anouilh's characterizations of each, as well as in the structures of both plays. Because he conceived of Joan as a "phenomenon," Anouilh views her as an idealized creature, like the other protagonists in the group of *pièces costumées*. Therefore, her actions transcend her own times because she represents heroic potential. At the same time, these plays consciously superimpose the superficial, appearance-oriented reality other characters accept as normal and the protagonists/heroes need to confront.

It cannot be ignored that Anouilh's *Antigone* appeared the same year the Vichy government was defeated, and women's suffrage would be granted within two years.[28] His text shows considerable sensitivity to the constraints on women as well as their differing positions on equality. The struggle between Ismene and Antigone is true to Sophocles' original concept of illustrating the angst of the decision from the dual viewpoints of the two sisters. But Anouilh's version, with its emphasis on Ismene's femininity and beauty and Antigone's more androgynous appearance, comments as well on the French debate regarding the nature of women and femininity that had waged since the time of Voltaire.[29] Their clash signals the audience to conclude that neither of them is a complete woman: Ismene is too circumspect and dependent, whereas Antigone relies too much on Romantic notions of nobility. Conversely, Creon's depiction as a jaded "businessman" kind of ruler removes the traditional possibility of seeing him as the tragic center of the story. The confrontation scene between him and Antigone has added context also: elaboration of the unworthiness of the two brothers. Creon's lack of passionate commitment to his work, but devoted attachment to what it symbolizes, is a clear comment on the collaborationist perspective.[30]

The essential features of this group of plays are the dichotomies. The heroes have a clear sense of honor and are true to themselves, but they play their roles in *commedia dell'arte* style, thereby underscoring the burlesque tone and underlying cynicism of Anouilh's vision. By reducing characters and their actions to old-fashioned, "stock" figures, events are also simplified down to their basic elements. In the Preface to her study of Anouilh, Alba Della Fazia notes that this group of plays represents an older Anouilh and "for the mature man, historical figures may be noble, but history is an eternal farce." Because Anouilh believes so few people have the courage and insight to contradict surface reality, how could history be otherwise?

The underlying premise of history as farce finds a structural correlative in the organization of the plot of *The Lark*. While the English Warwick wants to get the nasty business of Joan's burning behind him as quickly as possible, the French clergy insist that Joan's pivotal moments be played before them, ostensibly to present the evidence in a thoroughgoing, fair manner. In effect, Warwick has summarized the plot and intention of the play as neatly as the Chorus does in *Antigone*. The selection and ordering of these incidents in *The Lark* is a role granted to Joan herself, a subtle inversion of dramatic and legal conventions, as well as an undermining of who supposedly determines historic significance. Rather than commentary by a Chorus, the character herself answers practical questions, provides the exposition, and adds the analysis:

> A hand seems to have touched my shoulder, though I know no one has touched me, and the voice says—
> SOMEONE IN THE CROWD: Who is going to be the voice?
> JOAN: I am, of course. I turned to look. A great light was filling the shadows behind me. The voice was gentle and grave.... I showed I was sensible by running away to safety. That was all that happened the first time. And I didn't say anything about it when I got home...."[31]

More subtle still is Cauchon's insistence on interpreting, cautioning, and, in Brechtian fashion, reminding the actors (and the audience) that the meaning of events and Joan's choices fluctuates with circumstances and time. This vantage point, and Joan's initial reactions to the coming of her Voices, illustrate the position that the fearful atmosphere of World War II was far from over in 1950s France.

Ned Chailet's interpretation of Anouilh's view of history is apt here: we learn to understand the world we live in now by reshaping the past.[32] Yet it is Joan whose role eventually has become self-chosen; she alone symbolizes individual will because she consciously follows the directions of the Voices, despite the consequences. Anouilh's Joan never thinks of herself as an ordinary girl; such a vantage point would eradicate the possibility of her heroic nature in this world.

The impetus for Jean Anouilh to retell the story of Joan of Arc evolved from a conversation between the playwright and a prominent French priest. The priest was puzzled by Anouilh's neglect of this prominent figure from French history; Anouilh's feeling was that he had already written *Antigone*, implying a similarity of character and situation. But Joan was the "Christian Antigone" after all, claimed the priest, and so Anouilh's desire to represent Joan's struggle was born.[33]

Just as the notion of this play came in the shape of an improvisation, so, too, does its staging. According to Ned Chaillet it begins with an empty stage, gradually filled by actors in plain costumes. They are there to "enact the trial, but also ... her life. There is no ultimate distinction between history and legend; all life is theatrical. By the end of the play the stage is full: 'a beautiful illustration from a school prize.'"[34] The "school prize" probably would have been Bouten de Montvel's romanticized children's book about Joan of Arc and the Middle Ages; the illustrations from this book had caused a sensation internationally since the book's publication in the 1890s.[35] The quest for meaning in Anouilh's staging is closely connected to how the play begins and ends. The opening consists of "a simple neutral setting" while the closing is a cornucopia of visual experience; its enactment of the coronation of Charles with all characters kneeling except Joan and a pantomime of the crowning, a flash of the stained glass of the cathedral across the scene, a cannon salute and a flight of doves evokes the splendor of a moment.[36] The fact that this presentation is a pantomime emphasizes the gestures of the ritual at the expense of the language; the implication is that much of the meaning of such a moment is carried by ceremony itself.

If Anouilh believes that "all life is theatrical," then this playwright's conception of history can be linked to world events as a repetitive cycle. Alba Della Fazia contends that, to Anouilh, history is "a continuous and confused play; reigns are intermissions."[37] Because Joan had been used so blatantly as a political tool by the various French governments from the time Napoleon declared her a national symbol in 1803, she is a natural choice for Anouilh's perspective. More pessimistic than Shaw's concern that human nature does not change, Anouilh's cynicism encompasses both human nature and human institutions. His conclusion that Joan was an inexplicable phenomenon gains deeper meaning in this context. On one hand, her coming was merely accidental; on the other hand, it was a natural occurrence that was part of a scheme that most people can understand only partially. Such a position resembles the historical Joan's insistence on answering only those questions that she feels will not compromise the privileged perspective her Voices have given her. Anouilh subtly suggests that by her very act of interpreting the questions and projecting their ramifications Joan transcends the ordinary person's willingness to take a moral stand.

Early on in the text, the Promoter tries to censure Joan's reactions to the Voices, focusing attention on her hearing them in the "fairy tree": "Note the superstition. The beginning of witchcraft already. The Fairy Tree! I ask you to note that!" Cauchon is untroubled by this, reminding him that such trees exist all over France, and that children believe in their powers. When the Promoter insists that "saints ... should be sufficient," Cauchon replies: "It will be another matter when we come to the trial; I shan't spare her Voices then. But a little girl shall keep her fairies. [*Firmly*]. And these discussions are under my charge."[38] In sharp contrast to Cauchon's sympathetic portrait of Joan at Domrémy is her father's conviction that Joan has been transfixed by a lover. Her mother's interceding does no good; the father replies: "girls as innocent as babies can come to you one evening and hold up their faces to be kissed, and the next morning, though you've kept them locked in their room all night ... they're avoiding you, and lying to you. They're the devil, all at once."[39]

The apparent meaning that one must overlook possible error by the young points to Anouilh's allusion to the tendency of the peasant classes of medieval times to cling to pagan notions and customs. Attachment of Joan's "witchcraft" to this tradition stymies the more popular trend toward identification of these powers as the basis for her "unnatural" social behavior. Her father's pedestrian concerns serve as an ironic foil for Anouilh's point here, for if Joan's presence at the fairy tree can be viewed by the Church in the context of acceptable mores, then the mystique that shrouds her can be partially peeled away. Part of the ingenuity of this play is this very combination of farce and serious argument. The common people are at once part of a tradition and a group to be mocked. Beynon John encapsulates the result eloquently: "The voice that soars over the agents of political power, theological fanatics, time-serving collaborators, and the lonely victim of *L'Alouette* is a voice appalled by the cruelties of modern ideological extremism and appealing for tolerance and forgiveness."[40]

More important than these thematic issues in terms of theatrical representation is the choice to allow Joan to wear men's clothing throughout the play, rather than showing her first in her red wool dress. This gesture of Joan's, perhaps more than any other, is connected to her steadfast commitment to her Voices and her mission. The meaning is doubled because costume coding is a staple of *commedia dell'arte*. Anouilh thereby is showing how the complexities of society, represented by a gradually more cluttered stage, stand in the way of the purity of the individual spirit. But this costume is important for expressing Anouilh's purpose in two other ways, namely, fixing Joan's character as she was at the height of her success and reminding the audience that the mission that caused her rise and fall transcends societal convention.

A salient feature of the re-enactment in this play is realism of an entirely different sort: the theatrical space mirrors the world of the courtroom. The constant interruptions, continual presence of all actors, and the shift in chronology fosters a dialogic relationship between the audience and the text. From the outset, Warwick insists that he not have to endure a repeat performance of that "monstrous farce of a Coronation" when Cauchon informs him that before they can burn Joan they have "the whole story to play."[41] Warwick wants only to make sure that the proceedings damage Joan's reputation for all posterity, regardless of his own personal attraction to her. When Cauchon says they're "only" trying her for heresy, Warwick retorts that he has to have something more down-to-earth for his troops, who will find the trial's results too "rarefied." He continues: "The main thing is to say something pretty staggering, and repeat it often enough until you turn it into a truth. It's a new idea, but believe me, it will make its way."[42]

Thinking of the stage space as "neutral" early in the play causes the spectator to evaluate Joan's memories and the dominant events presented without the aid of place. Conversely, filling the space with people and only minimal furnishings foregrounds the behavior rather than the environment. Moreover, the lack of any change in outward appearance reinforces the issue of time, or, rather, timelessness, in the world of the play. The goal becomes, as Beynon John explains it, for Anouilh to "depart from the theological spirit of the fifteenth century, to ignore questions about false prophecy or excessive devotional zeal, and greatly to diminish the medieval fear of demons and dread of witchcraft."[43] This determination to avoid the reasons underlying her devotion heightens its presence as a "pure" spirit, one which befits a "phenomenon."

John elaborates this perspective by contending that the play is "not concerned with the context of her beliefs, only with their force and sincerity."[44] This directs not only the interpretation of Joan's character onstage, but the selection of details and emphases for the plot as well. The visual imagery of the stage presentation is likewise stripped of its usual context of furniture and buildings; the actors are directed by the text to specified places on the stage to signal audience attention. There are no notes in the early part of the play to denote settings and the actors move in and out of the playing area in full view of the audience. Only the bare essentials, like a table or Charles' throne, are named — almost as if the play were performed in rehearsal. Thus *mise-en-scène* reinforces theme.

Despite all of these efforts toward timelessness, both Joan's story and Anouilh's text are grounded in complex political times. In the early 1950s France was in the throes of post-war political purges, focusing on the conspirators who helped the German holocaust to send 65,000 French citizens to their fates. Although the playwright insisted on his apolitical stance, the experience of the French occupation/ Resistance seems to have "haunted him."[45] Although he kept a low political profile after the War, Anouilh reflected continuously on the nature of public experience, deciding that it was "relative" at best. Della Fazia also notes that Anouilh believes that those people who perform public duties will either be honored or dishonored — it's a matter of chance. Moreover, "The individual's position is both tragic and ludicrous, yet the vision of supreme fidelity to one's cause is not easily effaced."[46] As a result, idealism is not out of the question; it just turns inward for inspiration and nurturing. That is why Anouilh's Antigone and Joan retain their honor: it's an abstraction. In Part Two of the text, the actions of the actors reflect their position on the issues. Warwick's opening monologue summarizes his view on the events that led to these proceedings, giving one the feeling of court resuming after a recess, when the other side is given the chance to speak. As Warwick assesses the French motivations, Joan's supporters begin to withdraw; Anouilh's stage directions to them are quite clear: "Charles, La Tremouille, and the Archbishop have slyly got up and edged away from Joan, who is on her knees, praying. She starts up astonished to be alone, and sees Charles deserting her. The guards begin to drag her away."[47]

The slyness of the betrayers and the subsequent astonishment on Joan's face are gestures equally suited to melodrama and *commedia dell'arte* exaggeration. Both genres focus on the absoluteness of actions to determine qualities in characters and encourage audiences to escape reality and to deny its importance for the course of the performance. Thematically, Joan's perseverance in prayer highlights the sense of personal honor noted by Fazia; visually, this clearing of space around her is a powerful semiotic message: Joan as the lonely, alienated prisoner. Yet Joan's acknowledgement of the directive of the Voices regarding her costume, in the ironic contrast so customary in Anouilh's plays, clarifies the evolution of her role as iconoclast. Its concepts evolve when Joan recognizes that she cannot live in "their" world. She is like all the heroes in the *pièces costumées,* in that "she will be faithful to the concept of honor she has conceived for herself."[48]Warwick's cynical commentary contains many of the most telling lines to foster Anouilh's message that history is a farce, specifically regarding the expediency Joan represented to those in power; it is important to note that the speech precedes the desertion of Joan: "they agreed to use Joan as a sort of flagpole to nail their colours to: an attractive little mascot, well qualified to charm the general public into letting themselves be killed."[49]

Amazingly, in this same speech, Warwick explains the title of the play in very lofty terms:

> It was Joan: singing like a lark in the sky over the heads of your French armies on the march. I am very fond of France, my Lord: which is why I should be most unhappy if we lost her. This lark singing in the sky, while we all take aim to shoot her down: that seems very like France to me. Or at least like the best of her. In her time she has had plenty of fools, rogues and blunderers; but every now and then a lark sings in her sky, and the fools and rogues can be forgotten.[50]

Warwick's awed depiction of Joan's power also foreshadows the "school prize" picture onstage at the end of the play. And just as the appearance of a bird at any given moment is out of human control, so, too, it is impossible to explain how and why individuals like Joan appear. The connection of Joan to a soaring bird symbolizes her transcendence of time and situation, and invites the audience to see her as "phenomenon." In particular, the skylark has been traditionally depicted as a creature that is beyond the reach of earth and all the senses, except hearing. The lark was also emblematic for the French popular representation of Joan's piety, particularly in Maurice Boutet de Monvel's nineteenth century paintings, often used in children's books about Joan.

Such instantaneous recognition (at least in French audiences) was pivotal to the play's stance. With the emphasis on the higher authority of God and universal moral codes, the heroes of the *pièces costumées,* according to B. A. Lenski, oppose "an established truth that takes itself all too seriously." In the key scene of Anouilh's text, Joan looks down, rather than up as so many artists portray her. Such a critical inversion of symbol is a link to Camus' idea of the absurd; when the backdrops of life collapse, truth becomes relative. Lenski posits that this idea becomes a "powerful instrument of social critique, ridiculing through his heroes the blind, pretentious reason that claims everything is clear."[51]

From there, the impasse regarding the fate of Joan is reached via re-enactment, the stage becomes somewhat busier; more characters move out of the playing space, lighting changes, scenes shorten. Once Joan has been brought back to her cell, the other characters assemble in small groups and talk among themselves. Dramatically, this is standard; but in Anouilh's plays, characters are grouped according to their life views. Joan represents the "heroes"; the crowd and Joan's parents, the "mediocre race";

and Warwick "the compromisers." Therefore, when they interact, the semiotic meaning is doubled; the interplay of the philosophies, as characters move in and out of the playing space, underscores their differences, as well as their impact on one another. Only the Inquisitor/Promoter stands apart in his role as clear antagonist. He recognizes Joan's humanism before anyone else and this spurs him on.

Once it is clear that Joan is abandoned by all, and the exhaustion prompts her confession, the characters echo the perspectives they represent. Lenski describes the "mediocre race" as those people of "extreme opportunism, short memory, and an acute need to turn in the direction in which the wind is blowing." The "compromisers," in turn, are those who "regard ideals as children's diseases which must be overcome early in life.... Life's veterans [who] watch the awkward heroes with amusement, tenderness, and chagrin"[52] because they believe that experience has taught them that life is not what the heroes think it is. The dialogue and movement of this pivotal point in the text reveal these factors clearly.

Joan has her moment of recognition in a conversation with Warwick. When she doubts her confession's merits, Warwick assures her that she has made the right choice. It is now that her "self-chosen role" is understood:

> Unprofitable suffering. An ugly business. No, really, it wouldn't have been better. It would have been, as I told you just now, slightly plebeian, and ill-bred, and more than slightly stupid, to insist on dying just to embarrass everybody and make a demonstration.... Life isn't going to be very gay for you, I agree, not at first anyway. But things will adjust themselves in time, I don't think you need have any doubt of that.[53]

Joan's response illustrates her rejection of Warwick's compromise position as a viable option; she recognizes that the average life can never belong to her:

> Do you see Joan after living through it ["in time"], when things have adjusted themselves: Joan set free, perhaps, and vegetating at the French Court on her small pension? ... Joan accepting everything, Joan fat and complacent, Joan doing nothing but eat. Can you see me painted and powdered, trying to look fashionable, getting entangled in her skirts, fussing over her little dog, or trailing a man at her heels: who knows, perhaps with a husband?[54]

The picture of the feminized ideal life is sufficiently alien to Joan that she recants and says, "I take back my promises: they can pile their faggots, and set up their stake: they can have their holiday after all." The crowd ("mediocre race") responds quickly with cries to burn the witch, etc. Once again, Anouilh's stage directions manipulate the playing space as well as the characters' motivation: "All the actors return quickly, grasping faggots ... the movement is rapid and brutal.... The Executioner with some help makes a stake with the benches from the trial scene."[55]

Such a graphic depiction of the ease with which decisions of life and death can be reached is chilling to think about, let alone to see "constructed" before one's eyes. And just as soon as the audience has time to bemoan Joan's fate, de Beaudricourt interrupts, orders the dismantling of the stake, and reminds the actors that the coronation has not been played. Cauchon thanks him, but Charles' comment re-introduces the burlesque, coarse element to the scene: "You see! I knew they would forget my coronation. No one here remembers my coronation. And look what it cost me."[56]

The cost, at least in terms of money, should be an oblique point, but the full meaning of this outrageous interruption has many layers: tragedy becomes comedy, the whims of those in authority re-emerge, and the visual image, "this beautiful illustration from a school prize," returns to the pre-conceived image of the French audience: a rapturous saint fully absorbed in her mission.[57] The question is likewise returned to the audience: what was the cost?

The closing speech of the play precedes this sudden and full visualization of the coronation; in it Cauchon credits de Beaudricourt's insight:

> This man is quite right the real end of Joan's story, the end which will never come to an end, which they will always tell, long after they have forgotten our names or confused them all together: it isn't the painful and miserable end of the cornered animal caught at Rouen: but the lark singing in the open sky. Joan at Rheims in all her glory. The true end of the story is a kind of joy. Joan of Arc: a story which ends happily.[58]

For all the speech's apparent double-talk, the ultimate message for the audience is to remember the "phenomenon" and revel in Joan's coming; although she died for her cause, what should live on are her accomplishments and the glory which transcends the small-mindedness of the "mediocre race" or the "compromisers." The rapid transformation of the stage fulfills the conventions of melodrama with its "last minute" rescue. On a deeper level, however, it allows the promise of the Voices for her redemption to be possible, and truly envisioned.

Paul Hernadi takes a similar position in his essay on Shaw, Anouilh, and Joan, "Re-Presenting the Past: *St. Joan* and *L'Alouette*." Focusing on the nature of history and historiography, Hernadi points out that history tends to be presented narratively rather than dramatically: events are interpreted, not reflected. This is true for Shaw and Anouilh. However, their purposes are distinct. Shaw is interested in deconstructing the social structures of both fifteenth- and twentieth-century western society to reveal corruption and weakness, whereby Joan was trapped. Anouilh's emphasis is psychological, archetypal. His Joan responds to the aggressive social institution (the Inquisition) individually. Hernadi explains it as "an existential impulse to be what she is."[59] Shaw gives us more details of the story, especially regarding the trial; Anouilh, in classic Greek style, begins by telling the audience the ending and underscoring the motives and interactions of the key players. Hernadi remarks that Anouilh's text is not structured to evoke a sequence of events but "their imagined presence in *memory*—be it the playwright's memory and the spectator's or the memory of each and every stage figure."[60] What is unmistakable is that Anouilh, like Brecht, responds to Shaw's text, in terms of characterization for Joan and regarding historical vision. *St. Joan* ran in Paris from 1925 to 1935, produced by the renowned theatrical couple, the Pitoeffs; this couple launched Anouilh's popularity with their production of *Traveller without Luggage* in 1937.[61] Anouilh, like Brecht, openly acknowledged Shaw's influence on modern drama.

By the 1950s, Anouilh's plays had reached New York audiences and achieved recognition if not success. *Antigone* played in 1946, with the legendary Katherine Cornell. But a younger actress, Julie Harris, was cast in *The Rehearsal* (1951) and *Mademoiselle Colombe* (1953), in an adaptation by Louis Kronenberger. Miss Harris' vitality, childlike unabashedness, and inner conviction made her the natural choice for another Anouilh adaptation, when Kronenberger's friend Kermit Bloomgarten bought *The Lark* and helped convince Lillian Hellman to do a version of it. Julie Harris, rather than playing Shaw's Joan as she earlier had hoped to do, brought to life a Joan that Hellman called "the first modern career girl."

Unlike the other playwrights in this study, Lillian Hellman had no plans for writing a play about Joan of Arc; in fact, she was not easily persuaded to do the Anouilh adaptation, largely because she felt Shaw had done it best. When Anouilh's agent broached the subject, Hellman, with characteristic candor, said they didn't need her: "You need George Bernard Shaw, but he's dead." The agent was equally skeptical, saying that the play needed to be adapted by a poet. Despite this inauspicious beginning, Hellman redid the play, with clearly American rather than French attitudes, giving Mr. Anouilh "the first success [he had] in America."[62] Although she stripped away much of the poetic/mystical qualities of the Anouilh text, Hellman did not tamper with Joan as an archetypal representation of courage, fervor, and conscience. By the time she began to write, Hellman had concluded: "The wonderful story lay, as Shaw had seen it, in the miraculous self-confidence that carried defeated men into battle against all sense and reason, forced a pious girl into a refusal of her church, caused the terrible death that still has to do with the rest of us, forever, wherever her name is heard."[63]

Hellman, like Shaw, enjoyed the savvy of Joan far more than her orthodox spirituality. She really did not like Anouilh's play because of what she called his "bubble glory stuff." When Hellman met with Anouilh's agent, they clearly had opposite conceptions of the play, and the figure of Joan. Lillian Hellman believed that Joan was "history's first modern career girl, wise, unattractive in what she knew about the handling of men, straight out of a woman's magazine." The most outstanding feature of Joan's, in Hellman's mind, was her miraculous self-confidence. No wonder this playwright couldn't reconcile herself to closing the play with what she called "fake doves" flying over the audience's heads, symbolizing the spirit of Joan, the French, idealism.[64]

Although her comments regarding adapting *The Lark* focus more on obvious revisions, like limiting the allusions to the French experience in World War II, Hellman's version of the play offers a woman's insight into a young woman's situation; even subtle changes in dialogue reveal this wholly different viewpoint. While Anouilh is scrupulously careful to show the impact of Joan's gender as a factor in her fate, Hellman goes further and foregrounds the power she had been able to wield. One example is the admonition that she was too proud. In both texts, Joan admits this, crediting God with choosing to make her unique. Hellman's version, however, makes more of her accomplishments. In the Anouilh text, Joan says:

I know I am proud. But if God didn't mean me to be proud, why did He send an Archangel to see me, and saints with the light of heaven on them to speak to me? Why did He promise I should persuade all the people I have persuaded — men as learned and as wise as you — and say I should ride in white armour, with a bright sword given me by the King, to lead France into battle: and it has been so. He had only to leave me looking after the sheep, and I don't think pride would ever have entered my head.[65]

Hellman's adaptation highlights her self-confidence as well as her faith in God's will:

(*softly*) I know that I am proud. But I am a daughter of God. If He didn't want me to be proud, why did He send me His shining Archangel and His Saints all dressed in light? Why did He promise me that I should conquer all the men I have conquered? Why did He promise me a suit of beautiful white armor, the gift of my king? And a sword? And that I should lead brave soldiers into battle while riding a fine white horse? If he had left me alone, I would never have become proud.[66]

Anouilh's dialogue relies upon audience familiarity with the story and is sketchier than Hellman's; it is also less interested in delineating character. Hellman's technique is closer to Shaw's than Anouilh's: she is a realist and more directly a moralist than her French counterpart; therefore, her approach centers on characters in conflict with a situation and relies as much on dialogue as dramatic action for impact. As she had several times before, Hellman confronts controversy head-on, heedless of offending her audience. Her main accomplishment in *The Lark* is to show us the meaning of an exemplary young girl's experience. Her admiration for Joan is nowhere more apparent than in her representation of Joan's determination to retain her Voices' authority in the face of her accusers. At the crisis point in the trial she, like the historical Joan, asserts her autonomy and takes responsibility for it. Tragically, it was Joan of Arc's fatal error. Five hundred years later, audiences perceive the words and action as noble and worthy of emulation.

During the Trial of Condemnation, on May 24, 1431, Joan was asked if she would submit to the higher wisdom of the Church concerning her "words and deeds"; in other words, would she disavow her Voices or not? Joan's answer was shrewd: "Let all that I have said and done be sent to Rome to our Holy Father the Pope to whom after God I refer myself. As for my words and deeds, they were done at God's command."[67] The trial notes indicate that Joan of Arc took full human responsibility. Yet her truly religious nature emerged moments later when, in light of the judges' reaction, and her own fear, she recants, as she also does in these plays.

In Shaw's *St. Joan*, Joan's answer is closely aligned to the original, despite its verbosity, although she never mentions the pope. Instead, Shaw turns the attention to the dichotomy between Joan's perception of her relationship with and responsibility to God and her judges.' She begins by saying that it is "impossible" for her to say that what she has done and said did not come from God: "I will not declare it for anything in the world. What God made me do I will never go back on; and what He has commanded or shall command I will not fail to do in spite of any man alive." They perceive her answer as "flat heresy."[68] Shaw's interpretation of the trial notes underplays the religious fervor underneath the historical Joan's answer, choosing instead to foreground her resolute determination to live according to her beliefs. Shaw's Joan never allows the kind of intimidation that *had* to be part of Joan of Arc's reaction to her grueling ordeal. This speech could be the source of critical complaints that Bernard Shaw created a "Protestant" Joan: her stance here is, essentially, antinomianism.

Anouilh's treatment is succinct, yet far vaguer than Shaw's or the original trial transcript. Joan says, "after a pause," that: "In what concerns the Faith, I trust myself to the Church. But what I have done I shall never wish to undo." The Promoter is given the larger say here, so that Anouilh can convey the extent of his obsession with the danger of man acting outside of God's authority, as simultaneous with Joan's rise to the level of "hero." He asks the priests and Cauchon: "Do you see Man raising up his head, like a serpent ready to strike us dead? Do you understand now what it is you have to judge?"[69]

In Hellman's version of *The Lark*, Joan's position on her own actions is more sharply defined; the Inquisitor's speech is given a sociological rather than a theological context. Joan tells Cauchon: "For that which is of the Faith, I turn to the Church, as I have always done. But what I am, I will not denounce. What I have done, I will not deny."[70] In her expansion of both parts of the speech, Hellman has shown both the contrast of the two halves and their common thread: Joan's obedience to what she believes to be her authority. Note also the difference between "undo" and "deny." Undoing implies acknowledgement of an action that one wants to eradicate or, in another sense, destroy. To deny is refusal to acknowledge or to withhold. Thus Hellman's Joan is the most dangerous to the mindset of people who trust in dogma. Hellman's Inquisitor refers to her as the enemy known as "natural man," a link to the thinking of the Enlightenment and Romanticism: the beginnings of secularization. Hellman's Joan goes further than Anouilh's in her depiction of the schism between individuality and obedience, when she has the Inquisitor say: "I have need to remind you, Masters, that he who loves Man does not love God."[71]

Hellman's assessment of the iconographic importance of Joan of Arc explains more than a vantage point of a play; it reveals the mindset of a generation. Many American soldiers' participation in World War II was prompted by a genuine belief in the cause of anti-fascism, and an idealistic hope in the possibility of reversing the loss of confidence in our institutions by a return of their credibility. Hellman herself had been coaxed into anti–Fascist activity by her girlhood friend, Julia, an aristocrat and a free spirit. Julia was a physician turned activist; she wrote to Lillian in the 1930s, urging her to come to Europe to help smuggle much-needed funds from Germany to Moscow. Hellman's Jewish heritage and name put her in considerable danger. With her characteristic blend of hesitation, cowardice, and spunk, along with encouragement from her lover, Dashiell Hammett, Lillian did it. She transported thousands of dollars by wearing a "loaded" hat on the train.[72]

173

Joan's story, especially her motives, dovetail perfectly with this point of view. Her adherence to her mission from her Voices, despite the consequences she knows she will face, paralleled the soldiers' endurance of hellish conditions and overwhelming losses. Ann Casson confirms these connections in her recollection of playing *St. Joan* during World War II:

> What completely staggered me was that after the fury of the recantation and saying, "Your counsel is of the *devil* and mine is of *God*," the whole audience rose and clapped. It was just extraordinary to see how the spirit really can break through all things, because it was all these people who had been away from home for a long time and had been doing things that they knew were hateful. It was a wonderful sort of recognition, linking Joan with all people who hate imprisonment or being forced to lead a regimented life that they know is absolutely against the spirit.[73]

Lillian Hellman's text of *The Lark* gives the last word to Joan; it is a very self-effacing speech: "I wasn't paying any attention to Charlie. I knew what Charlie was like. I wanted him crowned because I wanted my country back. And God gave it to us on this Coronation Day. Let's end with it, please, if nobody would mind."[74] In light of Hellman's reputation as a difficult and headstrong playwright and woman, the last phrase is puzzling. To use her own words, it seems to be "right out of a women's magazine" of the 1950s. The question is, does the qualification of these last words belie the assertiveness of the rest of the speech? Turning to the original, Anouilh's *L'Alouette* provides illumination, but in an unexpected way; his text ends with Cauchon's remark that Joan's real story is the coronation, and that it ends happily. The tone and message of Hellman's ending couldn't be more different. In one brief speech, Hellman conveys the double intention of granting Joan autonomy and acknowledging the participation of the audience in her story. Rather than seeking their approval, Hellman's Joan invites them in; her version more than any other sees the story as ongoing. Conversely, there is a no-nonsense understanding that what happened must be accepted. The essence of the speech combines Franklin and Eleanor Roosevelt–style pragmatism and an acceptance of imperfection. The implication is that what matters is not the details, but the outcome. One reviewer who caught the uniqueness of Hellman's character and Harris' portrayal in this play was William Hawkins. His commentary in the *New York World-Telegram and* the *Sun* emphasizes her "inner conviction," claiming: "This Joan in Miss Harris' hands is frightening because she so often seems a child playing at real army. The great difference is, of course, that she means it all."[75] Hawkins' remarks can be applied to the playwright as well as to the actress. Hellman's personal experience with anti–Fascist activities had jolted her out of the protected view of world events that she, like many other Americans, hid behind, whether consciously or not.

Three years before *The Lark* premiered, Lillian Hellman had been subpoenaed to testify before the HUAC. Her companion of twenty-five years, Dashiell Hammett, had been jailed; other friends had "taken the Fifth," or had disappointed Hellman greatly by becoming "friendly witnesses." Her memoir about this era, *Scoundrel Time*, characterizes their moral angst. Lillian Hellman wanted no part of informing on any-one else. Her own participation in Communist activities was minimal at most. She opted to send a letter offering to tell the committee anything they wanted to know about her, but nothing about anyone else. In her often-quoted resolution, she declares: "I will not cut my conscience to fit this year's fashions." She claims that she is largely apolitical, having "no comfortable place in any political group," an attitude very like Jean Anouilh's. Hellman's upbringing was "old-fashioned" and "American." She cred-its certain "homey things" which became the foundation of her personal values: "to tell the truth, not to bear false witness, not to harm my neighbor, to be loyal to my country ... I respected these ideals of Christian honor."[76] Here Hellman herself becomes a Joan-figure, due to her unflinching and resolutely individualistic moral positions. Curiously, no such parallels were drawn at the time between Lillian Hellman and her Joan. Carl Rollyson, Hellman's authorized biographer, claims: "There is no play in which Hellman put more of herself. It is a cry of conscience."[77] How telling it is that no one pointed this out in the original reviews of *The Lark*. Hellman understood her audience and its fears, as well as her subject, when she said that Joan of Arc appealed to what was best in us: our collective conscience.

Multiple revivals of Bernard Shaw's *Saint Joan* and Bertolt Brecht's *St. Joan of the Stockyards* in New York in the 1990s both continue and extend the messages of these plays. As benefactors of Joan's story, we know that both the status quo and its oppo-sition must encompass a broader understanding of the rights and moral responsibili-ties of individuals and communities, whether they be world leaders or ordinary citizens. An individual's right to act responsibly and independently is Joan's legacy to us ... and to those who follow.

Concentrated interest in revivals of Shaw's and Brecht's plays about Joan in the 1990s could be explained in unremarkable terms: the centennial of Shaw's first play, *Widower's Houses* (1892), and Brecht's place as the godfather of unconventional, polit-ical drama. Conversely, the ideological crises of the times parallel those of the texts, lending a more urgent and more fundamental cause for producing them now. The Royston Theater Company produced *St. Joan* in 1992 and the National Actors Theater included it in its New York season in 1993. *St. Joan of the Stockyards* was produced by students at New York University in the midst of the first Gulf War in 1991 and by Iron-dale Productions in 1993. New biographies, films, novels, and television shows about Joan of Arc emerged around the millennium and into the first decade of the twenty-first century, and these continue to illustrate the divergent uses of Joan in the popu-lar imagination.

What has continued to puzzle writers throughout the twentieth century about Joan's character — her apparent contradictions of martial glory and ready tears — can be seen as balanced portions of a normal psyche when judged by contemporary psy-chological thinking that privileges the notion that individuals carry both masculine and feminine traits and tendencies. Therefore, Joan's difficulty with her judges no

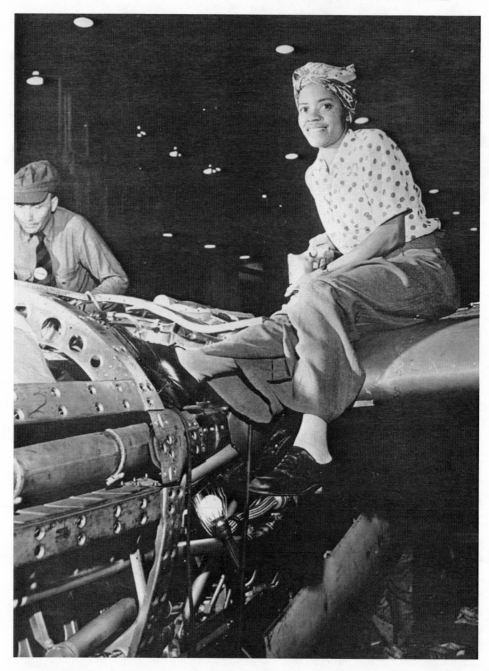

Riveter at Lockheed Aircraft Corp., Burbank, California. Here she is in action: a riveter atop an aircraft, hair wrapped up for safety's sake, trousers wide and man-tailored, socks and shoes to fit her task, and the pride of a job well done clearly expressed by the smile on her face. She represents the wartime opportunity — and evidence that the have-nots were then part of the action, although true inclusion was still elusive (*National Archives/NARA Still Pictures Branch*).

longer startles. We admire her audacious remarks. When Joan claims that she can tell them no more because there is nothing more *they would understand* we realize that she had the audacity to tell a truth that was inconceivable to authority figures who believed — to the point of *hubris* — that they should be *her* judges and interpreters.[78] The foregoing "enlightened" view represents one side of the more contemporary ideology; the other viewpoint is the resurgence of 1950s "family values," and the idealized mother-figures that bind that backlash system together.

While it is true that political and economic factors since the 1990s have caused a longing for an idealized past, contemporary scholars of that past caution us to see that the problems were largely there already, but the style of the 1950s was to ignore them. Moreover, the intervening decades have brought changes that make repeating that past not only unlikely but impossible. If a contemporary figure like Hillary Clinton can undergo drastic image shifts in a short time span, Joan's treatment by authority figures as well as the mass public can be viewed as more plausible. Perhaps this is yet another clue as to the permanence of the questions surrounding Joan of Arc. Of all the post-canonization literary works about her, Shaw's *St. Joan* seems to encompass the most scope. The Epilogue of this play remains provocative, in particular the closing line, which asks when the world will be ready to receive its saints. In 1923, the sting of this question would have been more acute, in light of Joan's recent canonization, and the connection of the final echoed question, "How long, O lord, how long?" to a World War I poem as well as Psalm 6 of David. In today's context, however, Shaw's scene also provides the possibility for an individual rather than a cultural significance for Joan. Despite their unwillingness to have Joan return to them in life, the characters all find a private meaning from their connection to her story. In his review of the 1992 production of *St. Joan*, Wilborn Hampton focuses on this precise point when he characterizes Shaw's play as "basically a sermon on the nature of faith and a caution to prophets of any age against overstaying their welcome."[79] Now that the change in Joan's official status is more than eighty years behind us, perhaps it seems the individuation of the spiritual quest is now firmly ensconced in the popular imagination. This was the kind of spiritual nourishment that Joan of Arc herself both understood and cherished. At the same time, our treatment of iconoclasts continues to highlight society's need to flex its muscle. No, we no longer use the stake; we just keep them static.

Chapter Notes

Prologue

1. In Stanley Weintraub, ed., *Saint Joan Fifty Years After: 1923/24–1973/74* (Baton Rouge: Louisiana State University Press, 1973), 29.

2. *Oxford English Dictionary, Compact Ed.*, Vol. I (A-0) (1971; Oxford: Oxford University Press, 1982), 1342.

3. Weintraub, 8.

4. A legend was already known before Joan of Arc even approached military authorities in 1429: the Prophecy of Merlin. Two things had been predicted; one, that a woman would ruin France, and two, that a virgin from Lorraine would emerge to save it. The first prediction came true in 1420 when the Dauphin Charles VII's mother declared her son illegitimate, thereby ceding the French throne to the English king, Henry V. The second was embodied by Joan of Arc.

5. See the chapter on visual images for a more detailed discussion of this trend.

6. Virginia Woolf. *A Room of One's Own* (1929; reprint, New York: Harcourt Brace Jovanovich/ Harvest, 1989), 99.

Introduction

1. Nadia Margolis' exhaustive annotative bibliography, *Joan of Arc in History, Literature, and Film* (Garland Pub., 1990), lists more than 1500 sources for "Johannic Studies." She breaks these into subject categories, and then organizes them chronologically.

2. Deborah Fraioli, "The Literary Image of Joan of Arc: Prior Influences," *Speculum*, Vol. 56, No. 4 (Oct. 1981), 811.

3. Merlin had prophesied that France would be destroyed by the action of a woman and then saved by a Virgin from the Lorraine region. When Joan seemed to "fit the bill," as it were, dichotomous response was as likely a story as the prophecy itself. The Eve/Mary implications of the prediction would be played out later, after Joan's rise, and as part of her fall.

4. Fraioli, 811–12.

5. Christine de Pizan, "Song of Joan of Arc."

6. In the online version of the *Catholic Encyclo-pedia*, New Advent.org, the article on St. Joan of Arc refers to the chief charges of the Trial of Condemnation (1431) as heresy and monstrous attire. See also the letter from Henry VI included in the Epilogue of *The First Biography of Joan of Arc*, trans./annotated by Daniel Rankin and Claire Quintal (1964). In the letter Henry VI refers to Joan's cross-dressing multiple times as the most flagrant of her various crimes and presumptions.

7. Warner provides a very thorough explication of the coding and its social significance in *Joan of Arc: The Image of Female Heroism* (New York: Alfred A. Knopf, 1981), 143–5.

8. Warner, *Joan of Arc*, 24.

9. Daniel Rankin and Claire Quintal, *The First Biography of Joan of Arc—With the Chronicle Record of a Contemporary Author.* (Pittsburgh: University of Pittsburgh Press, 1964), Epilogue, 54.

10. Anatole France describes this phenomenon in great detail in the first volume of his 1909 biography of Joan, *The Life of Joan of Arc*—see my discussion in chapter 3.

11. In her post-canonization biography of Joan, *St. Joan of Arc* (1936), Vita Sackville-West comments that Joan's mother, Isabel, remains one of history's unsung heroes, and urges her readers to think of her in this way. After all, the perseverance and courage Mme. Darc demonstrated was certainly well beyond the scope of a person of her gender and social class.

12. Chapter 2 cites evidence from witnesses at the Rehabilitation Trial which illustrates these points in detail.

13. The scholar was Jacques L'Averdy, but the wide dissemination of the transcripts and their import would not occur until Jules Quicherat brought forth a multi-volume treatise about the transcripts in the 1840s, which was translated later into languages other than French.

14. See Toni Bentley's review of Lyndall Gordon's new biography of Mary Wollstonecraft in the May 29, 2005, edition of the *New York Times Book Review*, 1, 5–6.

15. See R. M. Janes, "On the Reception of Mary Wollstonecraft's: A Vindication of the Rights of Woman," *Journal of the History of Ideas*, Vol. 39, No. 2 (Apr.-Jun. 1978), 293–302.

16. S. T. Coleridge, "Table Talk" (as recorded by his nephew H. N. Coleridge), 1 September 1832. Online, *www.etextlib.virginia.edu/stc/Coleridge/table_talk.html*.

17. By the *Belle Époque* this trend would reverse, as actresses gained power as well as acclaim in the public eye. Sarah Bernhardt in particular would become a living cultural icon, in the theater, on film, in portraits and advertisements, and as a designer of clothing and jewelry in her own right. See chapter 2 for more detailed discussion of Bernhardt and her multiple connections to Joan and the thesis of this study.

18. See my analysis of this in the chapter on the historical Joan.

19. Dror Wohrman, "Percy's Prologue: From Gender Play to Gender Panic in Eighteenth-Century England," *Past and Present*, No. 159 (1998), 114.

20. Garrick, qtd. in Wohrman, 114.

21. Vern and Bonnie Bullough, *Cross Dressing, Sex and Gender* (Philadelphia: University of Pennsylvania Press, 1993), 116.

22. Thomas Paine, "from *The American Crisis Number 1*," in Paul Lauter et al., eds., *The Heath Anthology of American Literature*, 5th ed. (Boston: Houghton-Mifflin, 2005), Vol. A, 965.

23. Lauter, Vol. A, 966.

24. Abigail Adams, "Letter to John Adams, March 31, 1776," in Lauter, Vol. B, 979.

25. John Adams, "Letter to Abigail Adams, July 3, 1776," Ibid., 979–80.

26. Elizabeth Fox-Genovese, "Culture and Consciousness in the Intellectual History of Europe," *Signs*, Vol. 12, No. 3 (Spring 1987), 538.

27. John Adams, "Letter to Mercy Otis Warren, April 16, 1776," in Lauter, Vol. B, 980.

28. Regine Pernoud and Veronique Clin (trans. Jeremy Duquesnay Adams), *Joan of Arc: Her Story* (New York: St. Martin's/Griffin, 1998).

29. See chapter 3 for the centrality of Bernhardt's role in social and political causes as well as theater and film. I draw my analysis from her own memoirs, as well as an essential cultural study, Susan Glenn's *Female Spectacle: The Theatrical Roots of Modern Feminism* (Cambridge: Harvard University Press, 2000).

30. More detailed discussion of this portrait can be found in chapter 5.

31. See chapter 3 for the detailed treatment of these phenomena.

32. See the illustrations by Charles Dana Gibson, and World War I posters from the Library of Congress.

33. Anne Hollander, *Sex and Suits: The Evolution of Modern Dress* (New York: Kodansha, 1995), 53.

34. Bullough and Bullough, 118.

35. "The Cult of Domesticity and True Womanhood." Online, www.library.csi.cuny.edu/dept/history/lavender/386/truewoman.html. Retrieved 6/2/2006., p 1 of 6.

36. Frohlich's work can be found at the following website: *www.stjoan-center.com/novelapp/joan04.html*

37. Judith Butler, *Gender Trouble* (London: Routledge, 1990), viii.

38. Butler, x–xi.

39. See the more detailed explication of the canonization documents in chapter 3.

40. Vita Sackville-West, *St. Joan of Arc* (1936; reprint, New York/London: Image Books, 1991), 142–3.

Chapter 1

1. One of the controversies which surrounded Shaw's *St. Joan* upon its appearance in 1923 was Shaw's implication that Joan's attitudes towards the Church Militant (the Church dogma) paralleled those of Protestantism. His Preface to the play explains the point clearly. Scene IV of the play, commonly referred to as the "tent scene," shows the politics of expediency which sealed Joan's fate. See the explication of this scene in chapter 4.

2. Warner, *Joan of Arc*, 101.

3. Susan Schibanoff, "True Lies: Transvestism and Idolatry in the Trial of Joan of Arc," in Bonnie Wheeler and Charles T. Wood, eds., *Fresh Verdicts on Joan of Arc* (New York: Garland Press, 1996), 37, 31.

4. See the Epilogue.

5. Warner, *Joan of Arc*, 132-5.

6. Schibanoff, 41.

7. Schibanoff, 53.

8. The Church Militant was distinct from the Church Triumphant, which was belief in God, the Holy Trinity, and the Word.

9. Joan jumped from the tower as a prison escape attempt. No one could explain how she survived the fall and how it was that no broken bones resulted. Vita Sackville-West's discussion in *St. Joan of Arc* (1936) is particularly lively and informative. See discussion of this work later in this chapter.

10. The theologians examined Joan at Poitiers at the request of the Dauphin, so that he would be sure of her before approving her role at Orléans.

11. Karen Sullivan, "'I Do Not Name to You the Voice of St. Michael': The Identification of Joan of Arc's Voices," in Wheeler and Wood, 88.

12. W. T. Jewkes and J. B. Landfield, eds., *Joan of Arc: Fact, Legend, and Literature* (New York: Harcourt, Brace & World, 1964), 12.

13. Joan, qtd. in Jewkes and Landfield, 12.

14. R. Howard Bloch, "Medieval Misogyny," in

R.H. Bloch and Frances Ferguson, eds., *Misogyny, Misandry, and Misanthropy* (Berkeley: University of California Press, 1989), 12.

15. Bloch and Ferguson, 13. Bloch's explanation provides a rich context for Charge V against Joan, which specifically claims that her male dress betrays her self-worship — see above.

16. Warner, *Joan of Arc*, 197.

17. Karen Sullivan, *The Interrogation of Joan of Arc* (Minneapolis: University of Minnesota Press, 1999), xv–xvii.

18. In Jewkes and Landfield, 91.

19. Jewkes and Landfield, 91–2.

20. Warner, *Joan of Arc*, 9.

21. Warner, *Joan of Arc*, 159–61.

22. Vita Sackville-West, *St. Joan of Arc* (1936; reprint, New York: Image Books, 1991), 150.

23. D. Rankin and C. Quintal, trans. and annot., *The First Biography of Joan of Arc — With the Chronicle Record of a Contemporary Author* (Pittsburgh: University of Pittsburgh Press, 1964), 125.

24. Rankin and Quintal, 124–5.

25. Andrew Lang, *The Maid of France: Being the Story of the Life and Death of Jeanne d'Arc* (1908; New York: Crown ed., 1913), 262–3.

26. Anatole France, *The Life of Joan of Arc*, 2 vols., trans. Winifred Stephens (New York: John Lane, 1909), II: 268.

27. Warner, *Joan of Arc*, 18–19.

28. Elizabeth Petroff, *Consolation of the Blessed* (New York: Alta Gaia Society, 1979), 2–3.

29. Petroff, *Consolation*, 8, 13.

30. Elizabeth Petroff, *Body and Soul: Essays on Medieval Women and Mysticism* (New York: Oxford University Press, 1994), 106.

31. France, II: 223.

32. France, II: 307.

33. Sackville-West, 135.

34. Sackville-West, 165. This line of thinking was also apparent in Virginia Woolf's *A Room of One's Own* (1929). In particular, I refer to the depiction of women's absence from history books, and Woolf's recognition of men's rage towards women that is part of this episode.

35. Sackville-West, 165, 168.

36. Sackville-West, 44.

37. France, II: 325, 339.

38. Lang, 254–5.

39. France, II: 391–2.

40. Regine Pernoud, *Joan of Arc by Herself and by Her Witnesses*, trans. Edward Hyams (New York: Stein & Day, 1966), 169.

41. Pernoud, 218.

42. Qtd. in Pernoud, 171.

43. Sackville-West, 261.

44. Sackville-West, 266.

45. Jewkes and Landfield, 44.

46. Jewkes and Landfield, 44–7.

47. This attribute of Joan's was picked up in many literary interpretations, some of which use the answer as dialogue.

48. Qtd. in Jewkes and Landfield, 53.

49. Henry Ansgar Kelly, "Joan's Last Trial: The Attack of the Devil's Advocates," in Wheeler and Wood, 207–8.

50. Kelly, 219–228.

51. Sackville-West, 9–10.

52. Virginia Woolf, *Orlando* (1928; reprint, New York: Harvest/Harcourt Brace 1956), 138–9.

53. Joan as cited by Sackville-West, 7.

54. Sackville-West, 8–9.

55. Sackville-West, 3–4.

56. Marjorie Garber, *Vested Interests: Cross-Dressing & Cultural Anxiety* (New York: Routledge, 1992), 131–2.

57. Sackville-West, 25.

58. Sackville-West, 11.

59. Sackville-West, 149.

60. Sackville-West, 149.

61. Woolf, *Orlando*, 227–9.

62. Sackville-West, 231.

63. Sackville-West, 231–2.

64. Warner, 125.

65. Warner, 106.

Chapter 2

1. Woolf, *Room*, 65.

2. Stephane Michaud, "Artistic and Literary Idolatries." In *A History of Women*, Vol. IV — *Emerging Feminism from Revolution to World War*, G. Fraisse and M. Perrot, eds. (Cambridge: Belknap Press of Harvard University Press, 1993), 121.

3. Michaud, 121–2.

4. Joan of Arc was already an established symbol in the popular imagination by the time of the French Revolution, but the revelation of the historical documentation coincided with dramatic shifts in the power structure of France and other European countries. In this way, the material came to the fore at a fortuitous moment.

5. Warner, *Joan of Arc*, 256.

6. Henri Guillemin, *Joan, Maid of Orléans*, trans. Harold J. Salemson (New York: Saturday Review Press, 1973), 250.

7. Pernoud and Clin, 243.

8. R. R. Palmer and Joel Colton, *A History of the Modern World*, 6th ed. (1950; New York: Alfred A. Knopf, 1986), 482–3.

9. Palmer and Colton, 573.

10. Palmer and Colton, 482–3.

11. See chapter discussions on visual images of Joan of Arc and women for examples.

12. Carol Mattingly, *Appropriate/ing Dress: Women's Rhetorical Style in Nineteenth-Century America* (Carbondale: Southern Illinois University Press, 2002), 14–5.

13. Jean Jacques Rousseau, "Of Primitive Societies." The Social Contract. In *Social Contract*, ed. Ernest Barker (New York: Oxford University Press, 1962), 170.

14. Rousseau, *Emile* (from Book Five). Online, *www.ilt.columbia.edu/pedagogies/rousseau/em_eng_bk5.html.*

15. It would take nearly a century for Wollstonecraft's model to be enacted. See discussions of bicycles, dress reform, and emancipated women in this chapter and in chapter 4.

16. Mary Wollstonecraft, *A Vindication of the Rights of Woman*, ed. Miriam Kramnick (New York: W. W. Norton, 1993), 257–8.

17. "Letter, March 22, 1429," in Willard Trask, ed. and trans., *Joan of Arc: In Her Own Words* (New York: Books & Co., 1996), 28.

18. Gary Kelly, "Gender, Class and Cultural Revolution," in *Revolutionary Feminism: The Mind and Career of Mary Wollstonecraft* (New York: St. Martin's Press, 1996), 1–22.

19. Trask, 7.

20. Trask, 11–12.

21. Jules Michelet, *Joan of Arc*, trans. and intro. by Albert Guerard. (1847; Ann Arbor: University of Michigan Press, 1967), 101–2.

22. This is a quote from the Trial of Condemnation, 1431, used by Michelet in his *Joan of Arc*, 114–17.

23. Bernard Shaw, in his Preface to *St. Joan* (1923), finds it necessary to devote a section to the issues surrounding Joan's sanity. In the section on Joan's voices and visions, Shaw concludes that she must be judged sane in spite of her voices because "they never gave her any advice that might not have come to her from her mother wit exactly as gravitation came to Newton" (New York: Penguin, 1951), 14.

24. Michelet, 100.

25. Michelet, 53.

26. Michelet, 104.

27. James Darmesteter, "Joan of Arc in England," in *English Studies*, trans. Mary Darmesteter (London: T. Fisher Unwin, 1896), 572.

28. Intriguingly, Michelet chose not to discuss Napoleon's self-serving use of Joan; Mark Twain would do so in his 1896 fictionalized biography. See chapter 3.

29. Jacques Barzun, "Jules Michelet and Romantic Historiography," in *European Writers: The Romantic Century*, Vol. 5, ed. Jacques Barzun (New York: Scribner's, 1985), 571–2.

30. Mill, in Abrams, Christ, and Greenblatt, eds., *Norton Anthology of English Literature: The Victorian Age*, Vol. 2B. 7th ed. (New York: W. W. Norton, 2000), 1159–60.

31. Barzun, 573.

32. Michelet, 8.

33. Michelet, 11.

34. See particularly Book 12 of Rousseau's *Emile*.

35. Michelet, 10.

36. Barzun, 575.

37. Michelet, 3–6.

38. Joan as cited by Michelet, 16.

39. See the Epilogue. Maxwell Anderson's 1946 *Joan of Lorraine* embraces the spirit and the "data" of Michelet.

40. Michelet, 17.

41. Michelet, 107–8.

42. Michelet, 22.

43. Barzun, 576–7.

44. Barzun, 578.

45. Michelet, 52.

46. Michelet, 51.

47. See further reference to Schiller's play in chapter 4.

48. Thomas DeQuincey, *Joan of Arc and the English Mail Coach*, ed. C. M. Stebbins (Boston: D. C. Heath, 1910), 5.

49. DeQuincey, 6.

50. Herein lies the difference: DeQuincey was knowledgeable about the Rehabilitation portrait of Joan, as well as the original one.

51. DeQuincey, 19.

52. DeQuincey, 15.

53. DeQuincey, 30.

54. Allison Sulloway, *Jane Austen and the Province of Womanhood* (Philadelphia: University of Pennsylvania Press, 1989), 7.

55. Sian Miles, introduction to George Sand's *Marianne* (New York: Carroll & Graf, 1988), 12–13.

56. Sand, George. "To Members of the Central Committee, April, 1848," in Miles' introduction to *Marianne*, 53.

57. Sand, 57.

58. See the foreword to *Marianne* by Marilyn French for further critical overview. Chapter 4 will elaborate on the Marianne figure, and its evolution ca. 1792–1945.

59. Elizabeth Barrett Browning, "To George Sand A Desire" and "To George Sand A Recognition," in Abrams et al., Vol. 2B, 1178–9.

60. Barrett Browning, 1184–5.

61. Abrams, Christ, and Greenblatt, eds., "Queen Victoria and the Victorian Temper," in *The Norton Anthology of English Literature: The Victorian Age*, 7th ed., Vol. 2B (New York: W. W. Norton, 2000), 1045.

62. During the first half of the nineteenth century, Elizabeth Barrett (Browning) was the most popular poet, and the obvious choice for Poet Laureate. Tennyson was beloved as well, but more so later on. The queen's choice shows as much about her own frame of reference as it does about the two poets.

63. Alfred, Lord Tennyson, "The Lady of Shalott," in Abrams et al., Vol. 2B, 1204–8.

64. Alfred, Lord Tennyson, "The Princess," http:

//whitewolf.newcastle.edu.au/words/authors/T/
TennysonAlfred/verse/princess. Retrieved 19 July
2006.

65. Tennyson was a member of the same social
circle as the man who wanted to marry Florence
Nightingale, and whom she refused after a six-year
period when all expected them to wed. See Gillian
Gill, *Nightingales: The Extraordinary Upbringing
and Curious Life of Miss Florence Nightingale* (New
York: Random House, 2005), 223.

66. Alfred, Lord Tennyson, "The Woman's
Cause Is Man's," from *The Princess,* in Abrams et
al., Vol. 2B, 1229 n.1.

67. Gill, 8–9.

68. Lytton Strachey, "Florence Nightingale," in
Eminent Victorians (1918; reprint, New York:
HBJ/Harvest, 1969), 140–1.

69. Strachey, 156–7.

70. Strachey, 159–62.

71. Strachey, 166.

72. Sarah Stickney, *The Women of England: Their
Social Duties and Domestic Habits* (1839), in Abrams
et al., Vol. 2B, 1722.

73. John Stuart Mill, *The Subjection of Women,*
ed. Sue Mansfield (Arlington Heights, Illinois: Harlan Davidson, 1980), 14.

74. Harriet Taylor, "The Enfranchisement of
Women" [1851], in Andrew Roberts, *John Stuart
Mill and Harriet Taylor on Freedom as Self Development.* Online, *www.mdx.ac.uk.www/study/ymill-
fre.htm.*

75. Such criteria would describe medieval standards for the qualities of the "lady" as well.

76. John Ruskin, "Sesame and Lilies," in *Sesame
and Lilies: The Two Paths; The King of the Golden
River,* intro. Sir Oliver Lodge (Everyman's Library
No. 219; London: Dent, 1937), 62–3.

77. Mill, 15.

78. Sally Mitchell, "The Forgotten Women of
the Period: Penny Weekly Family Magazines of the
1840s and 1850s," in Martha Vicinus, ed., *A Widening Sphere: Changing Roles of Victorian Women*
(Bloomington: Indiana University Press, 1977),
29–31.

79. Mitchell, 40.

80. Olympe de Gouges, "The Rights of Women,
1791." Online, *www.pinn.net/%8Esunshine/book-
sum/gouges.html.*

81. "Declaration of Sentiments and Resolutions,
Seneca Falls," in Miriam Schneir, ed., *Feminism:
The Essential Historical Writings* (New York: Vin-
tage, 1994), 81–2.

82. "Letter from Prison of St. Lazare, Paris," in
Schneir, 91.

83. Claire G. Moses, "The Legacy of the Eighteenth Century: A Look at the Future," in Samia
Spencer, ed., *French Women and the Age of Enlightenment* (Bloomington: Indiana University Press,
1984), 412–14.

84. "The Women's International Congress, Paris,
1900," Online, www.hca.heacademylac.uk/resources
/TDG/reports/tumblety-Feminist_Congress.role_
play.doc. Retrieved 7/8/06.

85. Frances Power Cobbe, "Duties of Women:
A Course of Lectures: excerpt from No. 6," in *Vic-
torian Prose: An Anthology,* ed. R. J. Mundhenk and
L. M. Fletcher (New York: Columbia University
Press, 1999), 326.

86. See the next chapter for the explanation and
analysis of the international connection between
Joan of Arc and woman suffrage.

87. The origin and pervasiveness of this concept is described in chapter 4.

88. Anatole France, *The Life of Joan of Arc,*
trans. Winifred Stephens (New York/London: John
Lane, 1909), Vol. I, v–vi.

89. France, xxii.

90. France, xxvii.

91. France, xxxvii.

92. Andrew Lang, *The Maid of France: Being
the Story of the Life and Death of Jeanne d'Arc* (New
York: Crown ed., 1913), 4–5.

93. Lang, 2.

94. Lang, 1.

95. France, I: 45

96. France, I: 169.

97. France, I: 169–70.

98. France, I: 190.

99. Here Lang contradicts many others, who
report Joan as sturdy but rather short. However,
nineteenth-century English fiction, beginning with
Jane Austen, tends to emphasize height as a means
of power.

100. Lang, 83.

101. Lang, 106.

102. See the discussion in chapter 4 about theatrical types; the context is transvestism in Victorian theater.

103. "Dangerous Beauty: Funny, She Didn't
Look Jewish, But It Was Sarah Bernhardt's Cross
to Bear. Leslie Camhi on Celebrity and the J Word,"
New York Times Style Magazine, 26 Feb. 2006, 140.

104. Qtd. by curators for the Jewish Museum of
New York, "Sarah Bernhardt and the Art of High
Drama" [exhibit], 2 December 2005–2 April 2006.

105. Sarah Bernhardt, *My Double Life,* trans.
Victoria Tietze Larson (Albany: State University of
New York Press, 1999), 59.

Chapter 3

1. Walter Besant, from "The Queen's Reign,"
in Abrams et al., Vol. 2B, 1738–9.

2. Dr. Henry J. Garrigus, in the January
Forum, from *Public Opinion,* 30 January 1896. Online, *www.vassar.edu/projects/1896/bicycle.html.*

3. Harper's Magazine, from *Public Opinion,*

16 January 1896. Online, *www.vassar.edu/projects/1896/bicycle.html*.

4. Susan Ware, *Modern American Women: A Documentary History* (Belmont, Calif.: Wadworth, 1989), 5.

5. A columnist named Alexis offered an explanation in *The Ladies World*, May 1894 issue, p. 11: "A man can breathe from below the waist line, while the majority of women breathe from the upper part of the chest only, thus failing to oxidize their blood." On the back page of the same issue, a corset company ad shows four women in varying positions, bent over and frozen; the picture has a lot more meaning when paired with Alexis' quote about women's breathing.

6. Helene E. Roberts, "The Exquisite Slave: The Role of Clothes in the Making of the Victorian Woman," *Signs: Journal of Women in Culture and Society*, Vol. 2, No. 3 (1977), 568.

7. Oscar Wilde, *An Ideal Husband*, Act 2. Online, *www.online-literature.com/wilde/ideal_husband/2/*.

8. Elaine Showalter, *Sexual Anarchy: Gender and Culture at the Fin de Siècle* (New York: Viking, 1990), 7.

9. Showalter, 3.

10. Oscar Wilde, *The Importance of Being Earnest*, Act II (1899; reprint, New York: Dover Publications, 1990), 34–5.

11. See Virginia Frohlich, "The Process of Saint Joan's Canonization," from her (unpublished) novel *The Lost Chronicles, The Story of Joan of Arc*. Online, www.stjoan-center.org/novelapp/joaap04.html. Retrieved 7/26/04.

12. I am referring here to the definite distinctions drawn around cross-dressing in the Middle Ages, and St. Thomas Aquinas' criteria for acceptance or rejection of individuals based upon these. See the discussion in chapter 2 for more detailed explanation.

13. According to Marina Warner's essay "Personification and the Idealization of the Feminine," this attitude influenced art, architectural decoration, and literature. Specifically, the palinodes about Joan of Arc during this period conclude that, in addition to her "derring-do and daring, she was nothing but a charming little thing, whom God had called to display incongruously virile virtues." In Rosenthal and Szarmach, eds., *Medievalism in American Culture*, (1989), 101.

14. Mark Twain, *Personal Recollections of Joan of Arc* (New York: Harper & Row, 1896), xiii-xiv.

15. This is a clear allusion to the opening of Jean-Jacques Rousseau's *The Social Contract*: "Men are born free, but everywhere are in chains." Rousseau's influence on the American founding fathers, particularly Jefferson's rhetoric in the Declaration of Independence, clearly aligns Twain's as-

sessment with casting Joan as a spunky rebel with a just cause.

16. Twain, xiv–xv.

17. Twain, 96.

18. Twain, 113.

19. Twain, 139–41.

20. Twain, 142–3.

21. Twain, 255.

22. Twain, 355

23. Twain, 353.

24. Anne Hollander, *Sex and Suits: The Evolution of Modern Dress* (New York: Kodansha Intl., 1994), 53, 41.

25. Amy Kesselman, "'The Freedom Suit': Feminism and Dress Reform in the United States, 1848–1875," *Gender and Society*, Vol. 5, No. 4 (Dec. 1991), 500.

26. Kesselman, 502.

27. Charlotte Perkins Gilman, "Why Women Do Not Reform Their Dress," in *Charlotte Perkins Gilman: A Nonfiction Reader*, ed. Larry Ceplair (New York: Columbia University Press, 1991), 23–4.

28. Charlotte Perkins Gilman, *The Dress of Woman: A Critical Introduction to the Symbolism and Sociology of Clothing* (Westport, CT: Greenwood Press, 2002), 10–12. Originally in her journal *The Forerunner* in 1915.

29. Lenard R. Berlanstein, "Breeches and Breaches: Cross-Dress Theater and the Culture of Gender Ambiguity in Modern France," *Comparative Studies in Society and History*, Vol. 38, No. 2 (Apr. 1996), 339–40.

30. Christopher Kent, "Image and Reality: The Actress and Society," in Vicinus, *A Widening Sphere*, 94.

31. Elaine Hadley, "The Old Price Wars: Melodramatizing the Public Sphere in Early-Nineteenth-Century England," *PMLA*, Vol. 107, No. 3 (May 1992): 524–36, 532–3.

32. Rachel Brownstein, *Tragic Muse: Rachel of the Comédie-Francaise* (Durham: Duke University Press, 1995), x.

33. Brownstein, ix.

34. Brownstein, xii.

35. Hollander, 45.

36. Brownstein, 223–4.

37. Nadia Margolis' brief commentary on the play speaks of its inspiration from Schiller's play; Margolis calls it one of the best French dramas of the nineteenth century, but notes the dominance of the "pathetic-romantic interests over historical ones." See *Joan of Arc in History, Literature, and Film* (New York: Garland Press, 1990), 323–4.

38. Brownstein, 174. Two years later, when France became a republic, more would come of this visual association; see chapter 5.

39. Isadore Singer and Edgar Mels, "Felix, Elisa-Rachel," *Jewish Encyclopedia* online. Bibliography: Janin, *Rachel et la Tragédie*, Paris, 1858; Mrs. Arthur

Kennard, *Rachel*, Boston, 1885; *Harper's Magazine*, Nov. 1855. Online, *www.jewishencyclopedia.com/ view.jsp?artid=94&letter=F* E

40. Brownstein, 41.

41. See Brownstein, 174.

42. Sally Mitchell, "The Forgotten Women of the Period: Penny Weekly Family Magazines of the 1840s & 1850s," in Vicinus, *A Widening Sphere*, 29–34, 40.

43. Fanny Fern, "The Working-Girls of New York," in Perkins and Perkins, eds., *The American Tradition in Literature*, 11th ed. (Boston: McGraw-Hill, 2007), 463–4.

44. Joel H. Kaplan and Sheila Stowell, *Theatre & Fashion: Oscar Wilde to the Suffragettes* (London: Cambridge University Press, 1994), 84–5.

Chapter 4

1. Hugh Nisbet, qtd. in Roberts, 554.

2. Mattingly, 113.

3. Ware, 16.

4. Frances Willard, "Frances Willard Learns to Ride a Bicycle," in Ware, 16–17.

5. Willard, in Ware, 18.

6. Roberts, 569.

7. Mattingly, 114–15.

8. Chapter 2 will show how and when these developments took place. Also see chapters 3 and 4 on mass-produced images of women and their connection to canonization-era representations of Joan of Arc.

9. Monika Elbert, "Striking A Historical Pose: Antebellum Tableaux Vivants, Godey's Illustrations, and Margaret Fuller's Heroines," *New England Quarterly*, Vol. 75, No. 2 (June 2002), 236, 266.

10. Edith Wharton, *The House of Mirth*, ed. Shari Benstock (Boston: Bedford Books of St. Martin's Press, 1994), 137–9.

11. Christina Rossetti, "In An Artist's Studio," in Abrams et al., Vol. 2B, 1586.

12. Stephen F. Eisenman, *Nineteenth Century Art: A Critical History* (London: Thames & Hudson, 1994, 2002), 81.

13. Eisenman, 81.

14. Carol Duncan, *The Aesthetics of Power: Essays In Critical Art History* (Cambridge/New York: Cambridge University Press, 1993), 157–8.

15. Pernoud and Clin, 242.

16. See the museum's website, www.metmuseum.org, for further details.

17. Roberts, 567.

18. Duncan, 83–4.

19. Curator's notes, "Sarah Bernhardt: The Art of High Drama" [exhibit], Jewish Museum of New York, 2 Dec. 2005–2 Apr. 2006.

20. Sarah Bernhardt, *My Double Life: The Memoirs of Sarah Bernhardt*, trans. Victoria Tietze Larson (Albany: State University Press of New York, 1999), 231–2.

21. Curator's notes, "Sarah Bernhardt: The Art of High Drama."

22. Bernhardt (Larson), 59.

23. Glenn, 12.

24. Glenn, 134.

25. Arvia MacKaye Ege, *The Power of the Impossible: The Life Story of Percy & Marion MacKaye* (Falmouth, Maine: Kennebec River Press, 1992), 142–7.

26. Percy MacKaye, *Jeanne D'Arc* (New York: Macmillan, 1907), 93–5.

27. Glenn, 133.

28. Martha Vicinus, "Male Space and Women's Bodies: The English Suffrage Movement," in *Women in Culture and Politics: Century of Change*, ed. Judith Friedlander, et. al. (Bloomington: Indiana University Press, 1986), 212.

29. Griselda Pollack's review of Lisa Tickner's work, *The Spectacle of Women: Imagery of the Suffrage Campaign 1907–1914*, points to Tickner's interpretation of the use of Joan by the British suffragettes. Pollack contends that Joan was used as an answer to the degrading images of radical women as deviant women. Pollack calls figures like Joan "pure fantastic heroines."

30. Glenn, 135–6.

31. The articles in the *New York Times* traced the citations by the Fire Dept. regarding the unsafe practice of collecting fabric scraps over a nine-month period, but it was not until after the tragedy that the legal proceedings went forward. Many people at the time, as well as contemporary scholars, feel that it was the immigrant population of young girls of Jewish and other "undesirable" ethnicities that encouraged the blind eye to the working conditions in the factory.

32. Rose Schneiderman, "We Have Found You Wanting," in Leon Stein, ed., *Out of the Sweatshop: The Struggle for Industrial Democracy* (New York: Quadrangle/New Times Book, 1977), 196–197 (first published in *The Survey*, 8 April 1911; Online, *www.ilr.cornell.edu/trianglefire/texts/stein*).

33. Glenn, 12–13.

34. Glenn, 127.

35. Glenn, 128.

36. J. C. Furnas, *Great Times: An Informal Social History of the U.S. 1914–1929* (New York: Putnam, 1974), 192.

37. Furnas, 215–16.

38. Inez Hayes Irwin, *The Story of Alice Paul and the National Woman's Party* (Fairfax, VA: Delinger's Publishers, 1977 [1964]), 292

39. Irwin, 294.

40. Maurine Weiner Greenwald, *Women, War and Work: The Impact of World War I on Women Workers in the United States* (Westport, CT: Greenwood Press, 1980), 5.

41. Greenwald, 34–5.

42. Ernest Dupuy, *Five Days to War: April 2–6, 1917* (Harrisburg, PA: Stackpole Books, 1967), epilogue.

43. Dupuy, 180.

44. Special thanks to Lauren Beigel, who brought me a postcard reproduction of this poster, thereby engaging my curiosity about how the visual image affected public attitudes.

45. Biographer Vita Sackville-West notes that not much is really known about Joan of Arc's appearance, other than the fact that she was dark-haired, stocky, and had a somewhat swarthy complexion. See Sackville-West's *St. Joan of Arc*, 1–5.

46. Furnas, 232.

47. Furnas, 228.

48. Ann Bleigh Powers, "The Joan of Arc Vogue in America, 1894–1929," *The American Society Legion of Honor Magazine* (1978): 187.

49. Powers, 184.

50. Alfred Bryan and Willie Weston (words) and Jack Wells (music), "Joan of Arc They Are Calling You" (New York: Waterson, Berlin, & Snyder, 1917)—popular song from 1917.

51. Visual images in World War I posters make this very clear; see the discussion in chapter 4 and the illustrations that pertain to that analysis.

52. The vast and varied ways in which Joan of Arc was an emotional as well as religious and patriotic symbol during World War I is part of chapter 4.

53. *New York Times*, 16 May 1920, Sec. 7: 6

54. Qtd. in Guillemin, 251.

55. Palmer and Colton , 575.

56. Frohlich, "The Process of Saint Joan's Canonization."

57. Warner, *Joan of Arc*, 264. See also chapter 2 for discussion of these two trials.

58. Greenwald, 5.

59. Claire Tylee, *The Great War and Women's Consciousness: Images of Militarism and Womanhood in Women's Writings, 1914–1964* (Iowa City: Iowa University Press, 1990), 53.

60. Jewkes and Landfield, 165–6.

Chapter 5

1. Bernard Shaw, *Saint Joan* (1923; reprint, New York: Penguin, 1950), 149, 159.

2. Stanley Weintraub, *Saint Joan Fifty Years After: 1923/4–1973/4* (Baton Rouge: Louisiana State University Press, 1973), 3.

3. Obraztsova in Weintraub, 226, 229.

4. Hearts burning or drowning were considered evidence of diabolical inspiration during Joan's time.

5. Shaw, *Saint Joan*, 154.

6. Shaw, *Saint Joan*, 102.

7. "Primary Documents," Online, *www.WORLDWARI.COM*.

8. Shaw, *Saint Joan*, 51.

9. Shaw, *Saint Joan*, 52–3.

10. Shaw, *Saint Joan*, 18, 27. See also the discussion of Florence Nightingale in chapter 3 and the Pankhursts and suffragettes in chapter 4.

11. Shaw, *Saint Joan*, 70.

12. Shaw, *Saint Joan*, 80, 82.

13. A drab referred to a dirty, sluttish woman, and came into the language around the sixteenth century. It was still popular in the 1920s.

14. Shaw, *Saint Joan*, 90–1.

15. Shaw, *Saint Joan*, 92.

16. There was a real penchant among the 1920s critics in England, France, and the United States to hold Shaw's play accountable to historical "accuracy" because so much of the facts had been unavailable for previous writers in English and because Shaw himself boasted about the accuracy of the characterization. He even called *Saint Joan* a "chronicle" play. The really important objections of the critics centered around two issues. One was the implication that Joan was almost "Protestant," an anachronistic as well as an insulting impression from their viewpoint. The other issue was their belief that Shaw had cast Joan of Arc into the mold of "flapper." See Jeanne Foster, "Super Flapper," and T. S. Eliot, "Shaw, Robertson and 'The Maid,'" in Stanley Weintraub's collection *Saint Joan Fifty Years After*, 29, 93.

17. Shaw, *Saint Joan*, 89.

18. Shaw, *Saint Joan*, 101–2.

19. Shaw, *Saint Joan*, 113.

20. Shaw, *Saint Joan*, 127.

21. Shaw, *Saint Joan*, 137.

22. Sophocles, *Antigone*, trans. E. F. Watling, in *The Theban Plays* (New York: Penguin, 1947), 150.

23. Shaw, *Saint Joan*, 158.

24. Psalm 6, King David, in *New Catholic Edition of the Holy Bible* (New York: Catholic Book Publishing, 1953), 619–20.

25. First published in London, 1917; reprinted in 1918 in *The Muse in Arms*. The editor of this publication, E. B. Osborne, called the book "a collection of war poems, for the most part written in the field of action, by seamen, soldiers, and flying men who are serving, or have served, in the Great War." Online, *www.WORLDWARI.COM*.

26. Shaw, *Saint Joan*, 155–8.

27. Shaw, *Saint Joan*, 143.

28. J. L. Wiesenthal, *Shaw's Sense of History* (Oxford: Clarendon Press, 1988), 127.

29. Margery Morgan, *The Shavian Playground: An Exploration of the Art of G. B. Shaw* (London: Methuen, 1972), 245.

30. Morgan, 240.

31. Shaw, *Saint Joan*, 10.

32. Barbara Bellow Watson, *A Shavian Guide to*

the Intelligent Woman (London: Chatto & Windus, 1964), 14.

33. Shaw, *Saint Joan*, 24.

34. Jane W. Stedman, "From Dame to Woman: W. S. Gilbert and Theatrical Transvestism," in Martha Vicinus, ed., *Suffer and Be Still: Women in the Victorian Age* (Bloomington: Indiana University Press, 1972), 22.

35. Stedman, 36.

36. Bernard Shaw, *Major Barbara* (New York: Penguin, 1951), 56. This scene "answers" Ruskin on two levels: his positions on the education of males as well as females. Ruskin had delivered two lectures on the subject, known together as *Sesame and Lilies*. The one directed toward males, "Of King's Treasuries," despaired over people's view of education as merely a means to an end. Ruskin criticized the need to be "conspicuous … obtaining a position which shall be acknowledged by others to be respectable or honourable." Ruskin, *Sesame and Lilies; The Two Paths; The King of the Golden River*. Intro. Sir Oliver Lodge. (Everyman's Library No. 219. London: Dent, 1937), 2.

37. Michael Holroyd, *Bernard Shaw*. Vol. 2: *The Pursuit of Power* (New York: Vintage, 1991), 147–8.

38. Shaw, *Major Barbara*, 26.

39. Holroyd, Vol. 2, 104.

40. Sonia Lorichs, "'The Unwomanly Woman' in Shaw's Drama," in Rochelle Weintraub, ed., *Fabian Feminist: Bernard Shaw & Woman* (University Park: Penn. State University Press, 1977), 104.

41. Shaw, *Major Barbara*, 51.

42. Holroyd, Vol. 2, 101.

43. Shaw, *Major Barbara*, 71.

44. Shaw, *Saint Joan*, 77.

45. Podmore, cited in Holroyd, Vol. 2, 132.

46. Michael Holroyd, *Bernard Shaw*. Vol. 1: *The Search for Love* (New York: Vintage, 1990), 133.

47. Holroyd, Vol. 1, 179.

48. Shaw, *Pygmalion*, 245.

49. Error Durbach, in *Shaw's Plays*, ed. Sandie Byrne (New York: W. W. Norton, 2000), 528–9

50. Shaw, *Pygmalion*, 168–9.

51. Shaw, *Pygmalion*, 192–3.

52. Fraser Harrison, *The Dark Angel: Aspects of Victorian Sexuality* (New York: Universe Books, 1978), 168.

53. Shaw, *Pygmalion*, 223.

54. Shaw, *Pygmalion*, 247.

55. Shaw, *Pygmalion*, 244–5.

56. Shaw, *Pygmalion*, 178.

57. Vicinus, "Male Space and Women's Bodies," 217.

58. See the discussion of the radical suffrage campaigns in chapters 4 and 5.

Chapter 6

1. Martin Esslin , *Brecht: The Man and His Work* (New York: Anchor Books, 1961), 257.

2. See Kevin J. Harty, "Jeanne Au Cinéma," in Wheeler and Wood, 237–64.

3. Harty, 243.

4. Harty discusses several important films, from France and Italy, that are either political or religious in their intention. Several of these had international viewings.

5. See John Fuegi, *Brecht & Company*, for a contextual treatment of these factors.

6. Bertolt Brecht, *The Trial of Joan of Arc at Rouen 1431* (adaptation of Anna Seghers' radio play of 1935), trans. R. Manheim and ed. R. Manheim and J. Willett, in *Collected Plays*, Vol. 9 (New York: Vintage, 1973), 167.

7. Brecht, *The Trial*, 169.

8. Brecht, *Collected Plays*, Vol. 9, 401–02.

9. Shaw, *St. Joan*, 112.

10. Bertolt Brecht, *The Visions of Simone Machard*, trans. W. Rowlinson and H. and E. Rank, in *Collected Plays*, Vol. 7, Part One (London: Methuen, 1985), 36–7.

11. Some fifteenth-century chronicles say Joan also worked in a hostelry. Voltaire used this in his 18th-century mock-epic.

12. Brecht, *Visions of Simone Machard*, 5, 9.

13. During World War II, both Vichy supporters and the Resistance used posters for disseminating political messages. Joan of Arc was used by both sides. The Vichy poster scene was in Rouen, in flames, and said that criminals always return to the scene of their crimes. See Warner, *Joan of Arc*, for reproductions of the posters and Warner's fascinating explanation of their significance.

15. Brecht, *Visions of Simone Machard*, 268–9.

16. See the discussion in chapter 5 about the rise in the number of impoverished people from 1870 (founding of Salvation Army) to 1905 (date of the premiere of Shaw's *Major Barbara*).

17. Detlev Peukert, *The Weimar Republic: The Crisis of Classic Modernity* , trans. R Deveson (New York: Hill & Wang, 1989), 85–88.

18. Brecht, *St. Joan of the Stockyards*, trans. F. Jones (Bloomington: Indiana University Press, 1969), 92.

19. Peukert, 81–3.

20. Peukert, 38. The suffrage would be removed by the Nazi regime.

21. John Fuegi, *Brecht & Company: Sex, Politics, and the Making of Modern Drama* (New York: Grove Press, 1994), 152.

22. Fuegi, 171–2.

23. Peukert, 99.

24. Peter Jelavich, *Berlin Cabaret* (Cambridge: Harvard University Press, 1993), 150–1.

25. Upton Sinclair, *The Jungle* (1906; reprint, New York: New American Library, 1960), 200.

26. Brecht, *St. Joan of the Stockyards,* intro. by Grab, 10.

27. Asa Briggs, "Hats, Caps, and Bonnets," in *Victorian Things* (Chicago: University of Chicago Press, 1988), 263.

28. Briggs, 272.

29. Dale Fetherling, *Mother Jones, the Miner's Angel: A Portrait* (Carbondale: Southern Illinois University Press, 1974), 108.

30. Eve Merriam, "Mother Jones," in *Growing Up Female in America: Ten Lives* (New York: Doubleday, 1971), 183.

31. Edward M. Steel, *The Correspondence of Mother Jones* (Pittsburgh: University of Pittsburgh Press, 1985), xxv.

32. Brecht, *St. Joan of the Stockyards*, Act III, 44–5.

33. Ibid., 44.

34. The allusion to Sinclair's *The Jungle* here is two-fold: plot element and socialist point of view.

35. Brecht, *St. Joan of the Stockyards,* Act IV, 51.

36. See Dale Fetherling's biography of the same title for an in-depth look at Mother Jones' work at organizing the miners, her interaction with the wives as active support systems, and her determination to force the power structure to see these people as individuals, not just numbers of people.

37. Brecht, *St. Joan of the Stockyards,* Act V, 59.

38. In one of her legal battles, Mother Jones went up against John D. Rockefeller, Jr. Like Joan says of Pierpont Mauler, Jones believed Rockefeller to be a product of his industrialist environment. The two exchanged letters, even New Year's telegrams, for years following this episode. See Mary Field Parton, *The Autobiography of Mother Jones* (Chicago: Charles H. Kerr, 1925); Fetherling, *The Miner's Angel*; and Steel, *The Correspondence of Mother Jones.*

39. Brecht, *St. Joan of the Stockyards*, Act VIII, 82–3. As successful as Mother Jones' 1903 "March of the Mill Children" was, President Theodore Roosevelt would not come out of his summer home to see or speak to them. See Parton, Fetherling, Merriam (citations above).

40. Ibid., Scene IX, 95.

41. Ibid., Scene X, 115.

42. Ibid., Scene X, 120.

43. Altering the cause of Joan's death links this play, at least obliquely, to Schiller's *Maid of Orléans* (1801). Schiller has her die in battle — see chapter 1.

44. Ibid., Scene XI, 122.

45. Ibid., Scene XI, 125.

46. Ibid.

47. E. Bentley, intro. to Bertolt Brecht, *Mother Courage* (New York: Grove Press, 1966), 15.

48. Brecht, *Mother Courage*, Scene Four, 68.

49. Elin Diamond, "Brechtian Theory/Feminist Theory toward a Gestic Feminist Criticism," *Drama Review* 32 (1988), 84.

50. Brecht, *Mother Courage*, Scene Twelve, 111.

Epilogue

1. Warner, *Joan of Arc*, caption for photographs following page 100.

2. Eric Jennings, "'Reinventing Jeanne': The Iconology of Joan of Arc in Vichy Schoolbooks, 1940–1944," *Journal of Contemporary History*, Vol. 29, No. 4 (Oct. 1994): 711–34.

3. Nancy Caldwell Sorel, *The Women Who Wrote the War* (NY: Arcade, 1999), prologue.

4. Brett Harvey, *The Fifties: A Women's Oral History* (NY: HarperCollins, 1993), xviii.

5. British women over 30 were enfranchised in 1918, but women under 30 did not win the privilege until 1928. German women had the franchise in 1919, lost it under the Nazi regime, and regained it. French women did not have it until after World War II.

6. Elaine Showalter, ed., *These Modern Women: Autobiographical Essays from the Twenties* (NY: The Feminist Press at CUNY, 1989), 13.

7. Alice Hoffman, "Provider," *New York Times Magazine*, 1 Nov. 1992, sec. 6: 22.

8. William Faulkner, "Acceptance Speech ... Nobel Prize, 1950," in *The Faulkner Reader* (NY: Modern Library, 1966), 4.

9. Mabel Driscoll Bailey, *Maxwell Anderson: The Playwright as Prophet* (London/New York: Abelard-Schuman, 1957), 98–9.

10. Maxwell Anderson, *Joan of Lorraine*. Acting ed. (NY: Dramatists Play Service, 1947), 20–1.

11. Anderson, *Joan of Lorraine*, 29.

12. Anderson, *Joan of Lorraine*, 47.

13. The opening night reviews, largely positive, concentrated more on praising Ingrid Bergman's magnetic, mystical portrayal of Joan. See *New York Theater Critics' Reviews*, Vol. VII, No. 22.

14. Anderson, *Joan of Lorraine*, 18–9.

15. That Anderson knew of this commentary shows how much background research he had done in the two years that he worked on this play. Of course it is also possible to read the political put-down in contemporary terms: another way to support the conservative stance of this text.

16. Harvey, xiii.

17. Qtd. in Harvey, 70.

18. Reviewing a *Life* magazine issue of 1953 will show you a group of these women; yes, they're wearing twin sweater sets and pearls to cooking classes....

19. See chapter 2 for trial transcripts discussion. This statement is from the proceedings of

Wednesday, May 9. Also see Shaw's *St. Joan*, Scene VI, for an almost verbatim speech (my chapter 5). Anderson's condensing of trial materials is weighted in favor of her desperation rather than her ire. Interestingly, Marina Warner (in her *Joan of Arc: The Image of Female Heroism*) also believes that Joan was more frightened than hostile during this trial.

20. Anderson, *Joan of Lorraine*, 74.

21. Anderson, *Joan of Lorraine*, 79. Both the French Resistance and the pro-Nazi Vichy government used Joan of Arc as their symbol during World War II. Marina Warner's *Joan of Arc: The Image of Female Heroism* contains illustrations of these propaganda posters.

22. Anderson, *Joan of Lorraine*, 81.

23. Qtd. in Lawrence Avery, *Dramatist in America: Letters of Maxwell Anderson* (Chapel Hill: University of North Carolina Press, 1977), 223–4.

24. Nadia Margolis, *Joan of Arc in History, Literature and Film: A Select, Annotated Bibliography* (NY: Garland Publishing, 1990), 396.

25. Qtd. in Avery, 231.

26. Qtd. in Avery, 232, fn. 2.

27. Qtd. in Margolis, 400. Anyone familiar with the closing scene of Anouilh's *L'Alouette*, and in particular his stage directions calling for flying doves as part of the coronation scene, will be sure to notice this as part of Preminger's filming of the coronation in *St. Joan*. Since Anouilh contributed to the film it is an interesting twist, particularly because Bernard Shaw would never have approved of this choice. Shaw was trying to get away from the stained-glass saintly image, although it is interesting to speculate about his reaction to Anouilh's ironic use of the icon.

28. See Claire G. Moses, "The Legacy of the Eighteenth Century: A Look at the Future," in Samia Spencer, ed., *French Women and the Age of Enlightenment* (Bloomington: Indiana University Press, 1984.) Moses chronicles the movement towards realization of the feminist goals that began in the 18th century from the time of the Franco–Prussian War until 1944. The Chamber of Deputies passed a universal suffrage bill in 1919, the same year as Germany, but the Senate did not act upon it until the dissolution of the Vichy regime in 1944.

29. In her analysis of women in his poems, "Voltaire and Women," Gloria M. Russo posits that his ideal woman was a combination of strength and tenderness: "la gloire, l'honneur, la vertu, le devoir" [pride, reputation, virtue, and duty], in Spencer, 294.

30. See chapter 6 for a brief discussion of the Brecht/Feuchtwanger/Berlau play, *The Visions of Simone Machard*, set in World War II France. This text shows the mind-set of the collaborationist character.

31. Anouilh, *The Lark*, in *Five Plays*, trans.

Christopher Fry, intro. Ned Chaillet (London: Methuen, 1987), One, 229.

32. Chaillet, intro. to *Five Plays*, xiii.

33. B. A. Lenski , *Jean Anouilh: Stages in Rebellion* (Atlantic Highlands, N.J.: Humanities Press, 1975), 94.

34. Chaillet, xxi.

35. My late friend and colleague Professor Ernie Simon, of Ramapo College of New Jersey, grew up in France and caught the significance of Anouilh's stage directions and explained to me how strong the cult of Joan was for French children during World War II. As an expert in French literature, Professor Simon understood the totality of Anouilh's ironic acknowledgment of popular culture implicit in such a closing moment. He told me that another key source for the iconographic story would be Lavisse, *Histoire de France*. The schoolbook story would include: Domrémy (the Voices), meeting de Beaudricourt, Chinon (recognition of the Dauphin), Orléans, the crowning in Reims, the story of the soldier who swore and fell into a well (happens before Orléans), the trial and burning with Cauchon as the villain. (There is a play on words here: Cauchon's name is pronounced like "cochon"— French for "pig.")

36. Anouilh, *The Lark*, 329.

37. Alba Della Fazia, *Jean Anouilh* (NY: Twayne Authors Series, 1969), 105.

38. Anouilh, *The Lark*, 231.

39. Anouilh, *The Lark*, 231.

40. Beynon S. John, *L'Alouette and Pauvre Bitos* (London: Grant & Cutler, 1984), 26.

41. Anouilh, *The Lark*, 227–8.

42. Anouilh, *The Lark*, 237.

43. John, 18.

44. John, 19.

45. Della Fazia, 22.

46. Della Fazia, 26.

47. Anouilh, *The Lark*, 283.

48. John, 113.

49. Anouilh, *The Lark*, 282. This view of Joan as a mascot is a nod to Voltaire's 18th-century mock epic, *La Pucelle*. See also Anatole France's 1909 biography, *The Life of Joan of Arc*.

50. Anouilh, *The Lark*, 282–3.

51. Lenski, 40.

52. Lenski, 36–7.

53. Anouilh, *The Lark*, 322.

54. Anouilh, *The Lark*, 323. This speech alludes to Strindberg's *Miss Julie*; Julie's broken engagement was to a man she tried to train as a dog. Further, Julie's mother had assumed male responsibilities. Gender blurring had damaged Julie, in Strindberg's view.

55. Anouilh, *The Lark*, 324.

56. Anouilh, *The Lark*, 328.

57. Eric Jennings' article about Vichy France and its schoolbooks, epilogue note 2 above, reiterates

the extreme emphasis on the obedience of Joan to king and country, and would thereby exclude any traces of the political factors that destroyed her. For the Vichy, Joan's sacrifice was worth emulating because it was for nationalistic fervor.

58. Anouilh, *The Lark*, 329.

59. Paul Hernadi, "Re-Presenting the Past: *St. Joan* and *L'Alouette*," in Harold Bloom, ed. and intro., *Major Literary Characters: Joan of Arc* (NY: Chelsea House, 1992), 151.

60. Hernadi, 157.

61. Chaillet, xii.

62. Lillian Hellman, *Pentimento* (New York: Signet, 1973), 166–7.

63. Hellman, *Pentimento*, 166.

64. Hellman, *Pentimento*, 166–7.

65. Anouilh, *The Lark*, 235.

66. Lillian Hellman, *The Lark*, in *Collected Plays* (Boston: Little, Brown, 1971), 555.

67. In Jewkes & Landfield, *Joan of Arc: Fact, Legend, and Literature* (New York: Harcourt, Brace & World, 1964), 37.

68. Shaw, *St. Joan*, 129.

69. Anouilh, *The Lark*, 302.

70. Hellman, *The Lark*, 589–90.

71. Hellman, *The Lark*, 590.

72. A large section of Hellman's memoir, *Pentimento* (1973), is devoted to the relationship between Lily and Julia, and these events. It was also filmed as *Julia* in 1977, with Jane Fonda as Lily, Jason Robards as Hammett, and Vanessa Redgrave as Julia.

73. Casson in Holly Hill, *Playing Joan: Actresses on the Challenge of Shaw's St. Joan* (New York: Theatre Communications Group, 1987), 35.

74. Hellman, *The Lark*, 602.

75. William Hawkins, "Review of *The Lark* by Lillian Hellman," *New York World-Telegram and the Sun,* 18 Nov. 1955; *New York Theater Critics' Reviews*, Vol. XVI (1955).

76. Lillian Hellman, *Scoundrel Time* (New York: Bantam, 1977), 90.

77. Carl Rollyson, *Lillian Hellman: Her Legend and Her Legacy* (New York: St. Martin's Press, 1988), 357.

78. For an explanation of this aspect of the original Trial of Condemnation (1431), see chapter 1.

79. Wilborn Hampton, "The Story of St. Joan with a Shavian Touch," *New York Times*, 23 Feb. 1992, sec. 2:51.

Bibliography

Abrams, Christ, and Greenblatt, eds. "Queen Victoria and the Victorian Temper." In *The Norton Anthology of English Literature: The Victorian Age*. 7th ed. Vol. 2B. New York: W. W. Norton, 2000.

Adams, Abigail. "Letter to John Adams, March 31, 1776." In Lauter, Paul, et al., eds. *The Heath Anthology of American Literature*. 5th ed. Boston: Houghton-Mifflin, 2005.

Adams, John. "Letter to Abigail Adams, July 3, 1776" and "Letter to Mercy Otis Warren, April 16, 1776." In Lauter et al., eds., *Heath Anthology of American Literature* 5th ed.

Anderson, Maxwell. *Joan of Lorraine*. Acting edition. New York: Dramatists Play Service, 1947.

_____. "Looking Backward." *New York Times*, 1 December 1946, sec. 2: 3.

Anouilh, Jean. *L'Alouette/The Lark*. Trans. Christopher Fry. In *Five Plays*. Intro. Ned Chaillet. London: Methuen, 1987.

_____. *Antigone*. Trans. Lewis Galantière. 1946. In *Five Plays*. Vol. I. New York: Hill & Wang, 1984.

Avery, Lawrence, ed. *Dramatist in America: Letters of Maxwell Anderson*. Chapel Hill: University of North Carolina Press, 1977.

Bailey, Mabel Driscoll. *Maxwell Anderson: The Playwright as Prophet*. London/New York: Abelard-Schuman, 1957.

Barzun, Jacques. "Jules Michelet and Romantic Historiography." In *European Writers: The Romantic Century*. Vol. 5. Ed. Jacques Barzun. New York: Scribner's, 1985.

Bentley, Toni. "Sense and Sensibility." Review of Lyndall Gordon, *Vindication: A Life of Mary Wollstonecraft*. *New York Times Book Review*, 29 May 2005: 1, 5–6.

Berlanstein, Lenard R. "Breeches and Breaches: Cross-Dress Theater and the Culture of Gender Ambiguity in Modern France." *Comparative Studies in Society and History*, Vol. 38, No. 2 (April 1996): 338–69.

Bernhardt, Sarah. *My Double Life: The Memoirs of Sarah Bernhardt*. Trans. Victoria Tietze Lar-son. Albany: State University of New York Press, 1999.

Besant, Walter. From "The Queen's Reign." In Abrams, Christ, and Greenblatt, eds. *The Norton Anthology of English Literature: The Victorian Age*. 7th ed. Vol. 2B. New York: W. W. Norton, 2000.

Bible. Psalm 6. In *New Catholic Edition of the Holy Bible*. New York: Catholic Book Publishing, 1953.

Bloch, R. Howard. "Medieval Misogyny." In *Misogyny, Misandry, and Misanthropy*. Ed. R. Howard Bloch and Frances Ferguson. Berkeley: University of California Press, 1989.

Bloom, Harold, ed. *Major Literary Characters: Joan of Arc*. New York: Chelsea House, 1992.

Brecht, Bertolt. *Mother Courage and Her Children*. 1955. Trans. E. Bentley. New York: Grove Press, 1966.

_____. *St. Joan of the Stockyards*. Trans. F. Jones, Intro. F. Grab. Bloomington: Indiana University Press, 1969.

_____. *The Trial of Joan of Arc at Rouen 1431*. (Adaptation of Anna Seghers' play). Trans. R. Manheim. Ed. R. Manheim and J. Willett. In *Collected Plays*, Vol. 9. New York: Vintage, 1973.

_____. *The Visions of Simone Machard*. Trans. W. Rowlinson and H. and E. Rank. In *Collected Plays*, Vol. 7 Part One. London: Methuen, 1985.

Briggs, Asa. "Hats, Caps, and Bonnets." In *Victorian Things*. Chicago: University of Chicago Press, 1988.

Browning, Elizabeth Barrett. "Aurora Leigh"; "To George Sand A Desire"; "To George Sand A Recognition." In Abrams et al., eds. *The Norton Anthology of English Literature: The Victorian Age*.

Brownstein, Rachel. *Tragic Muse: Rachel of the Comédie Française*. Durham: Duke University Press, 1995.

Bryan, Alfred and Willie Weston (words) and Jack Wells (music). "Joan of Arc They Are

Calling You." New York: Waterson, Berlin, & Snyder, 1917.

Bullough, Vern, and Bonnie Bullough. *Cross Dressing, Sex and Gender*. Philadelphia: University of Pennsylvania Press, 1993.

Butler, Judith. *Gender Trouble*. London: Routledge, 1990.

Cobbe, Frances Power. "Duties of Women: A Course of Lectures: excerpt from No. 6." In *Victorian Prose: An Anthology*, ed. Rosemary J. Mundhenk and LuAnn M. Fletcher. New York: Columbia University Press, 1999.

Coleridge, Samuel T. *Samuel Taylor Coleridge: The Oxford Authors*. Ed. H. J. Jackson. Oxford/New York: Oxford University Press, 1985.

"Cult of Domesticity and True Womanhood." Online. www.library.csi.cuny.edu/dept/history/lavender/386/truewoman.html.

"Dangerous Beauty: Funny, She Didn't Look Jewish, But It Was Sarah Bernhardt's Cross to Bear. Leslie Camhi on Celebrity and the J Word," *New York Times Style Magazine*, 26 Feb. 2006, 140.

Darmesteter, James. "Joan of Arc in England." In *English Studies*. Trans. Mary Darmesteter. London: T. Fisher Unwin, 1896.

Della Fazia, Alba. *Jean Anouilh*. New York: Twayne Authors Series, 1969.

DeQuincey, Thomas. *Joan of Arc and the English Mail Coach*. Ed. C. M. Stebbins. Boston: D. C. Heath, 1910.

Diamond, Elin. "Brechtian Theory/Feminist Theory toward a Gestic Feminist Criticism." *Drama Review* 32 (1988): 82–92.

Duncan, Carol. *The Aesthetics of Power: Essays in Critical Art History*. Cambridge/New York: Cambridge University Press, 1993.

Dupuy, Ernest R. *Five Days to War: April 2–6, 1917*. Harrisburg, PA: Stackpole Books, 1967.

Ege, Arvia MacKaye. *The Power of the Impossible: The Life Story of Percy & Marion MacKaye*. Falmouth, ME: Kennebec River Press, 1992.

Eisenman, Stephen. *Nineteenth-Century Art: A Critical History*. London: Thames & Hudson, 1994, 2002.

Elbert, Monika. "Striking a Historical Pose: Antebellum Tableaux Vivants, Godey's Illustrations, and Margaret Fuller's Heroines." *New England Quarterly*, Vol. 75, No. 2 (June 2002): 235–75.

Esslin, Martin. *Brecht: The Man and His Work*. New York: Anchor, Books, 1961.

Faulkner, William. "Acceptance Speech ... Nobel Prize, 1950." In *The Faulkner Reader*. New York: Modern Library, 1966.

Fazia, Alba Della. *Jean Anouilh*. New York: Twayne World Authors Series, 1969.

Fern, Fanny. "The Working-Girls of New York." In George Perkins and Barbara Perkins, eds. *The American Tradition in Literature*. 11th ed. Boston: McGraw-Hill, 2007.

Fetherling, Dale. *Mother Jones, the Miner's Angel: A Portrait*. Carbondale: Southern Illinois University Press, 1974.

Fleming, Victor. *Joan of Arc*. With Ingrid Bergman. RKO, 1948.

Fox-Genovese, Elizabeth. "Culture and Consciousness in the Intellectual History of Europe." *Signs*, Vol. 12, No. 3 (Spring 1987): 529–47.

France, Anatole. *The Life of Joan of Arc*. 2 vols. Trans. Winifred Stephens. 1908; New York/London: John Lane, 1909.

Fraoili, Deborah. "The Literary Image of Joan of Arc: Prior Influences." *Speculum*, Vol. 56, No. 4 (October 1981): 811–30.

Frohlich, Virginia. "The Process of Saint Joan's Canonization." From (unpublished) novel *The Lost Chronicles, The Story of Joan of Arc*. Online. www.st.joan-center.org/novelapp/joaap04.html.

Fuegi, John. *Brecht & Company: Sex, Politics, and the Making of the Modern Drama*. New York: Grove Press, 1994.

Furnas, J. C. *Great Times: An Informal Social History of the U.S. 1914–1929*. New York: Putnam, 1974.

Garber, Marjorie. *Vested Interests: Cross-Dressing & Cultural Anxiety*. New York: Routledge, 1992.

Garrigus, Dr. Henry J. In the "January Forum, from Public Opinion, 30 January 1896." Online. *www.vassar.edu/projects/1896/bicycle.html*.

Gill, Gillian. *Nightingales: The Extraordinary Upbringing and Curious Life of Miss Florence Nightingale*. New York: Random House, 2005.

Gilman, Charlotte Perkins. *Charlotte Perkins Gilman: A Non-Fiction Reader*. Ed. Larry Ceplair. New York: Columbia University Press, 1991.

_____. *The Dress of Woman: A Critical Introduction to the Symbolism and Sociology of Clothing* (orig. in her journal, *The Forerunner*, in 1915). Westport, CT: Greenwood Press, 2002.

Glenn, Susan. *Female Spectacle: The Theatrical Roots of Modern Feminism*. Cambridge: Harvard University Press, 2000.

Gould, Jean. "Maxwell Anderson." In *Modern American Playwrights*. New York: Dodd & Mead, 1966.

Greenwald, Maurine Weiner. *Women, War and Work: The Impact of World War I on Women Workers in the United States.* Westport, CT: Greenwood Press, 1980.

Guillemin, Henri. *Joan, Maid of Orléans.* Trans. Harold J. Salemson. New York: Saturday Review Press, 1973.

Hadley, Elaine. "The Old Price Wars: Melodramatizing the Public Sphere in Early-Nineteenth-Century England." *PMLA*, Vol. 107, No. 3 (May 1992): 524–37.

Hampton, Wilborn. "The Story of St. Joan with a Shavian Touch." *New York Times*, 23 Feb. 1992, sec. 2: 51.

"*Harper's Magazine*, from Public Opinion, 16 January, 1896." Online. *www.vassar.edu/projects/1896/bicycle.html.*

Harrison, Fraser. *The Dark Angel: Aspects of Victorian Sexuality.* New York: Universe Books, 1978.

Harty, Kevin J. "Jeanne au Cinéma." In Wheeler, Bonnie, & Charles T. Wood, eds. *Fresh Verdicts on Joan of Arc.* New York: Garland Press, 1996, 237–264.

Harvey, Brett. *The Fifties: A Women's Oral History.* New York: HarperCollins, 1993.

Hawkins, William. Review of *The Lark* by Lillian Hellman. *New York World-Telegram and The Sun*, 18 Nov 1955. In *New York Theater Critics' Reviews.* Vol. XVI (1955).

Hayman, Ronald. *Brecht: A Biography.* New York: Oxford University Press, 1993.

Hellman, Lillian. *The Lark.* In *Collected Plays.* Boston: Little, Brown, 1971.

_____. *Pentimento.* New York: Signet, 1973.

_____. *Scoundrel Time.* New York: Bantam, 1977.

Hernadi, Paul. "Re-Presenting the Past: *St. Joan* and *L'Alouette.*" In *Major Literary Characters: Joan of Arc.* Ed. and intro. Harold Bloom. New York/Phila.: Chelsea House, 1992.

Hill, Holly. *Playing Joan: Actresses on the Challenge of Shaw's St. Joan.* New York: Theatre Communications Group, 1987.

Hoffman, Alice. "Provider." *New York Times Magazine*, 1 Nov. 1992, sec. 6: 22.

Hollander, Anne. *Sex and Suits: The Evolution of Modern Dress.* New York: Kodansha Intl., 1995.

Holroyd, Michael. *Bernard Shaw. Volume 1: The Search for Love.* New York: Vintage, 1990.

_____. *Volume 2: The Pursuit of Power.* New York: Vintage, 1991.

Irwin, Inez Hayes. *The Story of Alice Paul and the National Woman's Party.* Fairfax, VA: Delinger's Publishers, 1977.

Janes, R. M. "On the Reception of Mary Wollstonecraft's: A Vindication of the Rights of Woman." *Journal of the History of Ideas*, Vol. 39, No.2 (Apr.-Jun. 1978): 293–302.

Jelavich, Peter. *Berlin Cabaret.* Cambridge: Harvard University Press, 1993.

Jennings, Eric. "'Reinventing Jeanne': The Iconology of Joan of Arc in Vichy Schoolbooks, 1940–44." *Journal of Contemporary History*, Vol. 29, No. 4 (October 1994): 711–34.

Jewkes, Wilfred T. and Jerome B. Landfield, eds. *Joan of Arc: Fact, Legend, and Literature.* New York: Harcourt, Brace & World, 1964.

"*Joan of Lorraine.*" Reviews of the play by Maxwell Anderson. In *New York Theater Critics' Reviews*, Vol. VII (1946).

John, Beynon S. *L'Alouette and Pauvre Bitos.* London: Grant & Cutler, 1984.

Kaplan, Joel and Sheila Stowell. *Theatre & Fashion: Oscar Wilde to the Suffragettes.* London: Cambridge University Press, 1994.

Kelly, Gary. *Revolutionary Feminism: The Mind and Career of Mary Wollstonecraft.* New York: St. Martin's Press, 1996.

Kelly, Henry Ansgar. "Joan's Last Trial: The Attack of the Devil's Advocates." In Wheeler and Wood, *Fresh Verdicts on Joan of Arc*, 207–208.

Kent, Christopher. "Image and Reality: The Actress and Society." In Martha Vicinus, ed. *A Widening Sphere: Changing Roles of Victorian Women.* Bloomington: Indiana University Press, 1977.

Kesselman, Amy. "'The Freedom Suit': Feminism and Dress Reform in the United States, 1848–1875." *Gender and Society*, Vol. 5, no. 4 (Dec. 1991): 495–510.

Lamb, Charles. *The Complete Works and Letters.* N.Y.: Modern Library, 1935.

Lang, Andrew. *The Maid of France: Being the Story of the Life and Death of Jeanne d'Arc.* 1908. New York: Crown ed. 1913.

Lauter, Paul, et al., eds. *The Heath Anthology of American Literature.* 5th ed. Boston: Houghton-Mifflin, 2005.

Lenski, B. A. *Jean Anouilh: Stages in Rebellion.* Atlantic Highlands, N. J.: Humanities Press, 1975.

Lorichs, Sonja. "The 'Unwomanly Woman' in Shaw's Drama." In *Fabian Feminist: Bernard Shaw & Woman.* Ed. Rochelle Weintraub. University Park: Penn State University Press, 1977.

MacKaye, Percy. *Jeanne D'Arc.* New York: Macmillan, 1907.

Margolis, Nadia. *Joan of Arc in History, Literature and Film: A Select, Annotated Bibliography.* New York: Garland Publishing, 1990.

Mattingly, Carol. *Appropriate/ing Dress: Women's Rhetorical Style in Nineteenth-Century America.* Carbondale: Southern Illinois University Press, 2002.

Merriam, Eve. "Mother Jones." In *Growing Up Female in America: Ten Lives.* New York: Doubleday, 1971.

Michaud, Stephane. "Artistic and Literary Idolatries." In *A History of Women. Vol. IV: Emerging Feminism from Revolution to World War.* Ed. Genevieve Fraisse and Michelle Perrot. Cambridge: Belknap Press of Harvard University Press, 1993.

Michelet, Jules. *Joan of Arc.* Trans. and intro. Albert Guerard. 1847. Reprint, Ann Arbor: University of Michigan/Ann Arbor Paperbacks, 1967.

Mill, John Stuart. *The Subjection of Women.* Ed. Sue Mansfield. Arlington Heights, Illinois: Harlan Davidson, 1980.

Miller, Douglas T. and Marion Nowak. *The Fifties: The Way We Really Were.* Garden City, N.Y.: Doubleday, 1977.

Mitchell, Sally. "The Forgotten Women of the Period: Penny Weekly Family Magazines of the 1840s and 1850s." In Vicinus, ed., *A Widening Sphere,* 29–34.

Morgan, Margery. *The Shavian Playground: An Exploration of the Art of G. B. Shaw.* London: Methuen, 1972.

Moses, Claire. "The Legacy of the Eighteenth Century: A Look at the Future." In Spencer, Samia, ed. *French Women and the Age of Enlightenment.* Bloomington: Indiana University Press, 1984.

Mundhenk, Rosemary J., and LuAnn M. Fletcher, eds. *Victorian Prose: An Anthology.* New York: Columbia University Press, 1999.

New York Times. [Articles regarding the canonization of St. Joan.] 16 May 1920, sec. 2: 6; sec. 7: 6; 19 May 1920, sec.1: 8.

Obraztsova, A. "A People's Heroine." In *Saint Joan: Fifty Years After, 1923/4–1973/4.* Ed. Stanley Weintraub. Baton Rouge: Louisiana State University Press, 1973.

Oxford English Dictionary. Compact Edition. Oxford: Oxford University Press, 1971.

Paine, Thomas. "From *The American Crisis* Number 1." In Lauter et al., eds., *The Heath Anthology of American Literature.*

Palmer, Robert. "How Long, O Lord, How Long?" "Primary Documents." Online. *www.WORLDWARI.COM.*

Palmer, R. R. and Joel Colton. *A History of the Modern World.* 6th ed. New York: Alfred A. Knopf, 1984.

Parton, Mary Field. *The Autobiography of Mother Jones.* Intro. Clarence Darrow. Chicago: Charles H. Kerr, 1925.

Perkins, George, and Barbara Perkins, eds. *American Tradition in Literature.* 11th ed. Boston: McGraw-Hill, 2007.

Pernoud, Regine. *Joan of Arc by Herself and by Her Witnesses.* Trans. Edward Hyams. New York: Stein & Day, 1966.

_____ and Veronique Clin. *Joan of Arc: Her Story.* Rev. and trans. Jeremy Duquesnay Adams. Ed. Bonnie Wheeler. New York: St. Martin's-Griffin, 1998.

Petroff, Elizabeth. *Body and Soul: Essays on Medieval Women and Mysticism.* New York: Oxford University Press, 1994.

_____. *Consolation of the Blessed.* New York: Alta Gaia Society, 1979.

Peukert, Detlev. *The Weimar Republic: The Crisis of Classic Modernity.* Trans. R. Deveson. N.Y.: Hill & Wang, 1989.

Pollock, Griselda. "The Spectacle of Women: Imagery of the Suffrage Campaign 1907–1914." *Journal of Design History,* Vol. 3, No. 1 (1990): 69–72.

Powers, Ann Bleigh. "The Joan of Arc Vogue in America, 1894–1929." *The American Society Legion of Honor Magazine* (1978): 177–91.

Preminger, Otto. *St. Joan.* With Jean Seberg. United Artists, 1957.

Rankin, Daniel, and Claire Quintal, trans. and annot. *The First Biography of Joan of Arc— With the Chronicle Record of a Contemporary Author.* Pittsburgh: University of Pittsburgh Press, 1964.

Roberts, Helene. "The Exquisite Slave: The Role of Clothes in the Making of the Victorian Woman." *Signs: Journal of Women in Culture and Society,* Vol. 2, No. 3 (1977), 554–69.

Rollyson, Carl. *Lillian Hellman: Her Legend and Her Legacy.* New York: St. Martin's Press, 1988.

Rousseau, Jean Jacques. From *Emile*-Book 5. Online. www.ilt.columbia.edu/pedagogies/rousseau/em_engl_bk5.html.

_____. *The Social Contract.* Ed. Ernest Barker. New York: Oxford University Press, 1962.

Ruskin, John. *Sesame and Lilies; The Two Paths; The King of the Golden River.* Intro. Sir Oliver

Lodge. Everyman's Library No. 219. London: Dent, 1937.

Russo, Gloria. "Voltaire and Women." In Samia Spencer, ed. *French Women and the Age of Enlightenment.*

Schibanoff, Susan. "True Lies: Transvestism and Idolatry in the Trial of Joan of Arc." In Wheeler and Wood, eds., *Fresh Verdicts on Joan of Arc.*

Sackville-West, Vita. *St. Joan of Arc.* 1936. New York/London: Image Books, 1991.

Sand, George. *Marianne.* Trans. and intro. Sian Miles; foreword Marilyn French. New York: Carroll & Graf, 1988.

"Sarah Bernhardt: The Art of High Drama." Curator's Notes [exhibit]. Jewish Museum of New York, 2 December 2005–2 April 2006.

Schiller, Friedrich. *The Maid of Orléans.* In *Joan of Arc: Fact, Legend, and Literature.* Ed. Jewkes and Landfield. New York: Harcourt, Brace & World, 1964.

Schneir, Miriam, ed. *Feminism: The Essential Historical Writings.* New York: Vintage, 1994.

Shaw, George Bernard. *Major Barbara.* New York: Penguin, 1951.

_____. *Pygmalion and Major Barbara.* New York: Bantam, 1992.

_____. *St. Joan.* New York: Penguin, 1951.

_____. *Shaw's Plays.* Ed. Sandie Byrne. New York: W.W. Norton, 2000.

Showalter, Elaine. *Sexual Anarchy: Gender and Culture at the Fin de Siècle.* New York: Viking, 1990.

_____, ed. *These Modern Women: Autobiographical Essays from the Twenties.* New York: The Feminist Press at CUNY, 1989.

_____ and English Showalter. "Victorian Women and Menstruation." In *Suffer and Be Still: Women in the Victorian Age.* Ed. Martha Vicinus. Bloomington: Indiana University Press, 1972.

Sinclair, Upton. *The Jungle.* 1906. Reprint, New York: New American Library, 1960.

Singer, Isidore, and Edgar Mels. "Felix, Elisa Rachel." In *Jewish Encyclopedia.* Online. Bibliography: Janin, Rachel et la Tragédie, Paris, 1858; Mrs. Arthur Kennard, Rachel, Boston, 1885: Harper's Magazine, Nov., 1855. Online. *www.jewishencyclopedia.com/view/jsp.*

Sophocles. *Antigone.* Trans. E. F. Watling. In *The Theban Plays.* New York: Penguin, 1947.

Sorel, Nancy Caldwell. *The Women Who Wrote the War.* New York: Arcade, 1999.

Southey, Robert. *Joan of Arc: An Epic Poem.* Bristol: Cottle, 1796.

Spencer, Samia, ed. *French Women and the Age of Enlightenment.* Bloomington: Indiana University Press, 1984.

Stedman, Jane W. "From Dame to Woman: W. S. Gilbert and Theatrical Transvestism." In *Suffer and Be Still: Women in the Victorian Age.* Ed. Martha Vicinus. Bloomington: Indiana University Press, 1972.

Stickney, Sarah. *The Women of England: Their Social Duties and Domestic Habits.* In Abrams et al., eds., *The Norton Anthology of English Literature: The Victorian Age.*

Steel, Edward M. *The Correspondence of Mother Jones.* Pittsburgh: University of Pittsburgh Press, 1985.

Stein, Leon, ed. *Out of the Sweatshop: The Struggle for Industrial Democracy.* New York: Quadrangle/New Times Book, 1977.

Strachey, Lytton. *Eminent Victorians.* New York: HBJ/Harvest, 1969.

Sullivan, Karen. "I Do Not Name to You the Voice of St. Michael: The Identification of Joan of Arc's Voices." In Wheeler and Wood, *Fresh Verdicts on Joan of Arc,* 85–111.

_____. *The Interrogation of Joan of Arc.* Minneapolis: University of Minnesota Press, 1999.

Sulloway, Allison. *Jane Austen and the Province of Womanhood.* Philadelphia, University of Pennsylvania Press, 1989.

Taylor, Harriet. "The Enfranchisement of Women" [1851]. In Roberts, Andrew. *John Stuart Mill and Harriet Taylor on Freedom as Self Development.* Online. *www.mdx.ac.uk. www/study/ymillfre.htm.*

Tennyson, Alfred Lord. "The Lady of Shalott," from "The Princess." In Abrams et al., eds., *The Norton Anthology of English Literature: The Victorian Age.*

_____. "The Princess." *http://whitewolf.new castle.edu.au/words/authors/T/TennysonAlfred /verse/princess.*

Thomas, Charles. *The Life and Works of Friedrich Schiller.* New York: Henry Holt, 1901.

Trask, Willard. *Joan of Arc: In Her Own Words.* New York: Books & Co., 1996.

Twain, Mark. *Personal Recollections of Joan of Arc.* N.Y: Harper & Row, 1896.

Tylee, Claire. *The Great War and Women's Consciousness: Images of Militarism and Womanhood in Women's Writings, 1914–1964.* Iowa City: Iowa University Press, 1990.

Valency, Maurice. *The Cart and The Trumpet.* New York: Oxford University Press, 1973.

Vicinus, Martha. "Male Space & Women's Bodies: The English Suffrage Movement." In *Women in Culture and Politics: A Century of Change.* Ed. Judith Friedlander et al. Bloomington: Indiana University Press, 1986.

_____, ed. *Suffer and Be Still: Women in the Victorian Age.* Bloomington: Indiana University Press, 1972.

_____, ed. *A Widening Sphere: Changing Roles of Victorian Women.* Bloomington: Indiana University Press, 1977.

Voltaire. *The Works of Voltaire: A Contemporary Version.* Vol. XL, XLI. Ed. John Morley. London: E. R. DuMont, 1901.

Ware, Susan. *Modern American Women: A Documentary History.* Belmont, Calif.: Wadsworth, 1989.

Warner, Marina. *Joan of Arc: The Image of Female Heroism.* New York: Alfred A. Knopf, 1981.

_____."Personification and the Idealization of the Feminine." In Bernard Rosenthal and Paul Szarmach, eds. *Medievalism in American Culture: Papers of the Eighteenth Annual Conference for Medieval and Early Renaissance Studies.* Binghamton: Medieval and Renaissance Texts & Studies, Vol. 55, 1989.

Watson, Barbara Bellow. *The Shavian Guide to the Intelligent Woman.* London: Chatto and Windus, 1964.

Weintraub, Rochelle, ed. *Fabian Feminist: Bernard Shaw & Woman.* University Park: Penn. State University Press, 1977.

Weintraub, Stanley, ed. *Saint Joan Fifty Years After: 1923/4–1973/4.* Baton Rouge: Louisiana State University Press, 1973.

Wharton, Edith. *The House of Mirth.* Ed. Shari Benstock. Boston: Bedford Books of St. Martin's Press, 1994.

Wheeler, Bonnie, & Charles T. Wood, eds. *Fresh Verdicts on Joan of Arc.* New York: Garland Press, 1996.

Wiesenthal, J. L. *Shaw's Sense of History.* Oxford: Clarendon Press, 1988.

Wilde, Oscar. *An Ideal Husband*, Act 2. Online. *www.online-literature.com/wilde/ideal_husband /2.*

_____. *The Importance of Being Earnest.* New York: Dover Publications, 1990.

Willett, John., ed. and trans. *Brecht on Theatre: The Development of an Aesthetic.* 1964. Reprint, New York: Hill & Wang, 1989.

_____. *The Theatre of Bertolt Brecht: A Study from Eight Aspects.* 3d ed., rev. New York: New Directions, 1968.

Wohrman, Dror. "Percy's Prologue: From Gender Play to Gender Panic in Eighteenth-Century England." *Past and Present,* No. 159 (1998): 114–59.

Wollstonecraft, Mary. *A Vindication of The Rights of Woman.* Ed. Miriam Kramnick. New York: W. W. Norton, 1993.

"Women's International Congress, Paris, 1900." Online. www.hca.heacademylac.uk.resources/ TDG/reports/temblety-Feminist.*Congress. role_play.doc.*

Woolf, Virginia. *A Room of One's Own.* 1929. Reprint, New York: Harcourt Brace Jovanovich, 1981.

_____. *Orlando.* 1928. Reprint, New York: Harvest/Harcourt Brace 1956.

Index

197